Group Processes and
Personal Change

Group Processes and Personal Change

Peter B. Smith
Reader in Social Psychology
University of Sussex

Harper & Row, Publishers
London

Cambridge San Francisco
Hagerstown Mexico City
Philadelphia Sao Paulo
New York Sydney

First published 1980
Harper & Row Ltd
28 Tavistock Street
London WC2E 7PN

British Library Cataloguing in Publication Data

Smith, Peter Bevington
  Group processes and personal change.
  1. Social groups
  2. Social interaction
  I. Title
  301.18'5   HM131

  ISBN 0–06–318146–0
  ISBN 0–06–318151–7 Pbk

Typeset by Inforum Ltd, Portsmouth
Printed and bound by A. Wheaton and Co Ltd, Exeter

Contents

Section 1

Basic Issues

CHAPTER 1
INTRODUCTION

This book is concerned with the way in which small groups may be used to create various kinds of personal change. It presents an overview of the broad range of experiential small group methods which have developed during the past thirty years, and seeks to understand them through recourse to theories and empirical findings which derive most directly from social psychology. This chapter will commence by considering in a preliminary way the prospects for a fruitful mingling of these two areas.

The small group occupied a central position in the early development of social psychology. Some researchers were concerned with the manner in which group members' presence aided or hindered work on a task, while others focussed on the leader's behaviour, group conformity pressures, and the use of groups to facilitate changes in behaviour. The study of group dynamics was seen as complex but central to social psychology. In the subsequent history of the subject the group has been seen as steadily less central. Researchers have reasoned that they may more adequately understand social influence processes if they focus on the *individual's* experience of social influence. Thus, studies of leadership processes and conformity become secondary to studies of attitude change and social facilitation; studies of group cohesiveness give way to analyses of interpersonal attraction and of person perception. The voices which have been most persuasive have been those which argue that to understand a phenomenon one must analyse it into separate basic components.

There is of course a good deal to be said in favour of such arguments. Early analyses of group behaviour were often vague and diffuse, whereas more recent theory in social psychology has sometimes achieved a much more sharply delineated focus. To some this sharp clarity is the prime goal of social psychology. To others, social psychology will only have come of age when it is able to take on the analysis of social behaviour in the complexity with which it occurs outside of the laboratory. As Golembiewski (1962) argued, laboratory experimentation has rarely been concerned with small group behaviour as such, but rather with 'ad hoc collectivities' of strangers assembled for short periods of time. Behaviour occurring within such collectivities can certainly be thought of as representative of small group behaviour, but it is small group behaviour which is likely to be highly atypical. As Weick (1967) puts it:

> A person who is in an experiment is like the newcomer on the job, often has low confidence in his judgments, is easily influenced, misunderstands instructions, is uninformed, finds the job novel and interesting, is cautious, and tolerates many demands that would anger him in more familiar settings.

Small groups are interesting precisely because of the ways in which they differ from this. They provide the routine, long-term context within which many people spend their work and leisure hours. The manner in which individual and group act and react on one another over time has been vividly portrayed by Homans (1950) in his classic analysis of a series of case studies of groups. Perhaps the most interesting aspect of Homans' analysis was the manner in which the groups are shown not as agents of change in individual behaviour, but as sources of stability and resistance to change. For example, workers in an industrial plant were shown as maintaining an absolutely steady productivity record, and status within a gang of unemployed men remained stable despite some pressure for change. Case studies of families, which provide the longest-lasting group experience for most people, have a similar flavour. Admittedly, many of the published case studies of families portray those families who seek out some kind of clinical assistance (e.g., Laing and Esterson, 1964; Henry, 1972), but many of them focus on the long-term continuance of behaviour patterns which have ceased to have adaptive value to some or all of the members of the family. Everyday experience suggests that many normal families have similar if less acute difficulties.

The contrast between short-term studies of laboratory groups and long-term case studies of real-life groups provides the starting point for this book. If we wish to understand the processes whereby groups and individuals influence one another, neither procedure appears ideal. Laboratory social psychology has focussed on influences which may well turn out to be ephemeral; in contrast, case studies have often highlighted settings where major influence processes have occurred, but in which the system's energy is by now primarily engaged in maintaining the status quo rather than in inducing change. The search for settings in which what has so far been called 'major' influence occurs may not prove easy, as the incidence of major change is likely to be low in contrast to the more routine elements of living.

It may be useful initially to distinguish some different types of possible change. Figure 1 envisages four possible types. The simplest instance is where a member of Group A shows changed behaviour while Group A itself remains unchanged. This has been termed *conformity*, although as Hollander and Willis (1967) point out, there are further ways in which the individual's behaviour may be affected by the group which are not classifiable as conformity. For instance, if the individual does the *opposite* of what the group is demanding, they term this behaviour *anticonformity*. Conformity has been much studied in laboratory experiments, many of which seek to explore the manner in which the group majority influences the individual. Writers within this tradition often appear to see conformity as the only type of change, contrasting it with independence, which is equated with lack of change.

Figure 1.   *A taxonomy of types of change*

Where does the change occur?

Who changes?	Within Group A	Within Group B
The individual changes	Conformity	Personal change
The group changes	Group development	Contingent group development

A second type of change is that found where the whole of Group A undergoes some type of change or development. Tuckman (1965) has reviewed a wide variety of studies and concluded that many groups do pass through a developmental sequence of changes. The groups he surveyed included therapy groups, training groups, and groups within laboratory experimental settings. Tuckman delineated four developmental phases which he termed 'forming', 'storming', 'norming', and 'performing'. It is noteworthy that the great majority of groups which he studied were those of temporary duration. At least among short-term groupings it does, therefore, seem practicable to separate out group development from individual conformity. In a series of ingenious studies, Moscovici and Faucheux (1972) have shown how even the traditional laboratory conformity experiment can be restructured so as to illustrate group development rather than individual conformity. Moscovici showed that on a series of ambiguous judgement tasks, where a small minority of group members gave answers which were consistently repeated, the majority judgements became more similar to those of the minority. Essentially Moscovici has inverted Asch's (1956) well-known study of group effects on the individual. Asch made the majority his accomplices and showed how they could induce the individual's conformity. Moscovici made the minority his accomplices and showed how *they* could induce a development in the way that the rest of the group made judgements.

In both of the types of change so far discussed, the change occurs simply within the setting in which it first arises. A particularly interesting type of change is that which first occurs in one group but is later expressed within another group, which we may call Group B. Instances might be the student who acquires new values while at university and uses these to create a modified role within the family, or a client in therapy who acquires therein the courage to confront adversaries in other settings. Changes which are transferable from the group of origin to other groups are here referred to as *personal changes*, since the only element in common between the group of origin and other groups is likely to be the person who makes the change. The creation of such personal change is a major goal of our society, as exemplified by such institutions as education, training, psychotherapy, and some aspects of social work. By no means all attempts at the creation of personal change succeed. Indeed in some instances one might be glad that particular attempts failed, for instance where they were based on ethically offensive premises. Leaving these instances to one side for the moment, the creation of personal change provides social psychology with something of a challenge. How far can the insights so far obtained be used to construct more adequate systems for the creation of personal change? It must be conceded that social psychology does not yet match up to this challenge very adequately. Most of the existing work concerns conformity rather than personal change, and the hypothesis that similar processes underly both types of change is tenuous and implausible.

The fourth type of change envisaged in Figure 1 is that in which change within Group A induces a contingent group development in Group B. An instance of this would be in a bargaining situation, where a change in the stance of one party would be quite likely to induce changes in the stance of the other. A further instance is the use of training programmes in an attempt to induce changes in the functioning of organizations. Current knowledge concerning the creation of contingent group development is still more sketchy than that which concerns personal change.

The task of this book is to attempt an analysis of the creation of personal change. It will focus in particular on the developing technology of sensitivity training. This will be undertaken both through review of the research literature in this field, and through discussion of a series of studies undertaken by the author. The aim is to provide a book which has elements of both a research monograph and a text. To fall into the one pattern or the other would be to collude with the growing schism between academic social psychology and practical technologies such as sensitivity training. As Kurt Lewin, who was a key figure in the origins of both social psychology and sensitivity training, is often quoted as saying, 'there is nothing so practical as a good theory'. The theory advanced in this book may or may not be a good one, but its intention is *both* to contribute to a diversification of current theories of social influence *and* to encourage a more research minded approach among practitioners and participants of sensitivity training.

Sensitivity training is perhaps uniquely suitable as a basis upon which to construct a theory of personal change. While social psychological experimenters assert with some fervour that the deceptions they impose upon their subjects do not generate long-term effects, sensitivity trainers claim with equal fervour that T-groups (training groups) do generate such long-term effects. Unlike most of the other attempts to create personal change, such as psychotherapy, counselling, social work, and so forth, sensitivity training is often undertaken in a short-term intensive manner. It thus achieves some of the qualities important to experimentalists, such as standardization and lack of confounding with other life events, while at the same time lasting long enough to become highly involving and far from trivial to participants.

Sensitivity trainers and their trainees would very properly react against a portrayal of T-groups simply as a good place for researchers to test out their theories. The equalitarian ethos of the personal growth movement is distinctly suspicious of 'experts', particularly those who are not willing to share equally the personal risks involved in the creation of a successful group experience. Perhaps for this reason, the findings of research into sensitivity training are not all that widely known among sensitivity trainers. The personal growth movement often stresses the importance of learning present awareness, rather than construing situations in terms of past history, elaborate theories, or generalized principles. Within such a framework, research data may seem like mystification of the obvious, or even a denial of the values of trainers. This book will argue that there remain numerous questions as to how best to conduct sensitivity training, and that answers to these questions are best arrived at both through the awareness of research data, and through a continuance of the spontaneity, willingness to innovate, and respect for others which have characterized the growth of sensitivity training so far. In a field as contentious as this one, research studies do not provide answers which will be accepted, but they do provide data which will be argued over and interpreted this way or that. The utilization of these data is crucial if sensitivity training and various other group learning methods are not to go down in history as passing fads, tried and cast aside before they were adequately understood.

The book is divided into four sections. In the first of these the nature of sensitivity training is explored. Chapter 2 considers the origins of sensitivity training and describes some typical instances of current practice. Chapter 3 provides a companion piece to this, since it describes the state of research into the effectiveness of sensitivity training. Since there do appear to be some lasting consequences of sensitivity training, it makes sense to examine next theories seeking to explain what occurs during training and why the effects last when they do. This is done in Chapter 4, which provides the most central element to the book. The second section focusses in turn on the major elements in the construction of effective sensitivity training. Chapter 5 examines the leader's behaviour, while Chapter 6 looks at other elements in a training design by which the leader may seek to influence the outcome of the programme. These include the way the T-groups are composed, meetings in smaller or alternative groupings, intergroup activities, and large plenary sessions of various kinds. Frequently overlooked, they often occupy a substantial amount of time in a programme.

The third section of the book acknowledges that sensitivity training is but one of a potentially bewildering range of approaches to small group learning. The four chapters in this section examine four of the principal directions in which the field has diversified. The focus in each of these chapters is on description of practice, presentation of available research findings, and consideration of the approach in the light of the theory first advanced in Chapter 4. Interpretive approaches, which are discussed in Chapter 7, have a history as long as that of sensitivity training but have until recently engendered little empirical work. Chapters 8 and 9 review two of the most recent developments – the encounter movement and the self-help group movement. Chapter 10 considers organizational development, which seeks to create change not in individuals but in whole groups or organizations. Practitioners in this field draw on the technology of sensitivity training but their prime goal is the creation of contingent group development rather than personal change.

The final section explores the social context of sensitivity training. Any procedure which claims to be able to create personal change must confront a variety of further dilemmas. Critics of sensitivity training have not held back in suggesting that the method falls down in almost all the ways in which it could. Chapter 11 discusses these contentious issues.

Very many people have influenced and sustained my interest in the subject matter of this book, not least the members of the several hundred T-groups I have conducted over the past sixteen years. I should like to mention in particular Galvin Whitaker, Matthew Miles, and Warren Bennis, who eased my passage into this field; and David Moscow, Cary Cooper, Mel Berger, Rus Gandy, Michael Willson, Jenny Bell, and many others who debated the ideas herein with me on many occasions. Finally I owe a debt to the five or six hundred T-group members (not all in my groups) who filled in questionnaires for me and reported at many points in this book, when they most often felt they had more important matters to reflect upon.

CHAPTER 2
THE ELEMENTS OF
SENSITIVITY TRAINING

The origins of what have become known as T-group methods are well documented. The events which are usually taken as the beginning occurred at a training workshop in community relations in Connecticut during the summer of 1946 (Benne, 1964). The course comprised a number of workshop groups whose task was to discuss and role-play problems they faced in seeking to uphold the recently enacted Fair Employment Practices Act. Each of the three groups also had a research function. During each evening, Kurt Lewin, who was directing the research aspect of the workshop, arranged for the research observers to meet with the group leaders to compare perceptions of the day's events. After a few days one or two of the participants expressed interest in attending these evening meetings. This was agreed, and word soon got around until all participants were attending. The meetings were of course transformed. From a relaxed mulling over the groups' behaviour during the day, they became an arena for feedback to individuals and the comparison of perceptions. Statements which might previously have gone unchallenged were now open to debate. One person's perception was as valid a source of data as was another person's. The T-group had been invented – by accident.

The invention had several components which have become crucial elements in the subsequent development of the T-group. These were a focus on here-and-now behaviour, the giving and receiving of feedback, voluntary participation, and a reduction of power differentials between leaders and participants. Each of these issues will be taken up in due course. The immediate effect of the 1946 workshop was that a decision was taken to set up a further workshop the following summer in which the more traditional types of group work using discussion and role-playing would be augmented by a focus on the study of the group's own behaviour. This was to take place in basic skill training groups, each of which again had a leader and a research observer. The success of the 1947 workshop led to the establishment of National Training Laboratories (NTL) and a steady growth in the use of the evolving new method. By 1949 it was felt that the basic skill training group was being asked to carry on too many potentially conflicting activities. The term T-group (training group) was now differentiated to describe groups set up to study their own behaviour. In addition there were A-groups (action groups) whose task was to work on ways of creating change in participants' back-home settings. T-groups and A-groups had different staff members and it was found in practice that the intended differentiation of function did not work too well. The T-group sessions tended to be more emotionally involving. A-group leaders found themselves either concurring in their A-group becoming a secondary T-group, or else insisting in a somewhat authoritarian manner that the group stayed within its brief, even though that was not what most members preferred.

The A-group did not survive, but numerous further attempts were made to find an appropriate structure for the training programme or laboratory, as it came to be called. The design required was one which not only preserved the T-group as a central element, but also contained other elements intended to help participants conceptualize what they were experiencing and to apply what they had learned to their particular back-home circumstances. Contemporary approaches to such questions of training design are explored more fully in Chapter 6. As Benne (1964) points out, during the fifties almost all the innovations in training design involved sessions over and above the T-group sessions. T-groups were seen as basic, while the remaining sessions augmented or amplified their effect. More recently, numerous attempts have also been made to modify the type of T-group experience to suit particular circumstances. Some of the more extensive of these adaptations have been the development of the encounter movement and of organizational development, which are discussed in Chapters 8 and 10.

The central element around which the variations discussed above have evolved is thus the T-group. To those who have not participated in one, a clear conception of such a group is hard to come by. The boundaries of the typical T-group are relatively clear. T-groups are frequently held residentially, meet for quite long periods of time, comprise eight to twelve members and have one or two leaders. The leader is often described as 'not leading', but it will be seen in a later chapter that this description is incorrect. It is probably more correct to say that the appointed leader, who is usually known as the trainer, leads the group in a manner different from that to be expected from everyday social convention. Whereas leaders of groups are usually expected to structure activities, facilitate decision procedures and so forth, T-group trainers usually decline to undertake these activities. Instead they express interest not in *what* the group does, but in *how* it is done. If a group decision is arrived at on some issue, the leader may focus on how members feel about the decision, who they perceived as taking what roles in its achievement, or how the decision affects their own position in the group. The focus is on the processes whereby the group members are interacting with one another. Although we all have some awareness of group process in everyday living, the prospect of focussing solely upon it for a number of days usually sounds somewhat unnerving to those who are new to it. The procedure appears likely to be either embarrassing, boring, or alarming. Most participants do indeed experience each of these reactions at some time or other during training, but such feelings tend to be outweighed by interest and involvement.

Required resources

If a T-group which can effectively undertake this relatively novel task is to be established, it is likely that the trainer must not only withhold a traditional leadership role, but must also contribute the type of resources the group will need in order to achieve the task. Some of these resources will not be behaviours visible during group meetings but actions taken in advance. For instance, those active in the early development of the T-group were insistent that if T-groups were to succeed they must be conducted upon a 'cultural island'. By this it was meant that the T-group requires an uninterrupted block of time, during which the participant's ties to everyday relationships are minimized. The creation of such an 'island' is easiest where training is residential, although later experience has shown that T-groups can, under some circumstances, be effective even where they are run on a basis of one or two sessions per week. The ideal of the cultural island also implies that the members shall initially be strangers to one another. The purpose of creating such a separate 'island' is that it should make it easier for the T-group to develop a set of norms favouring the open expression of feelings and reactions within the group. In everyday living, norms frequently exist regulating the degree to which one should be open with others, both those whom one knows well and those who are relative strangers. Miles (1964) has analysed the sociological context of the cultural island. He points out that there exists within society a range of 'temporary systems', whose properties have much in common with those envisaged for the T-group. For instance, holidays, carnivals, long journeys, temporary working parties and project groups, training programmes, and certain kinds of drama all create temporary systems. According to Miles, all such systems are characterized by a more open expression of feelings, a greater willingness to take risks, and a search for novelty. These are all attributes which the T-group trainer would wish to encourage.

The second resource which the trainer has to contribute is a conception of the group's agenda. One way of bolstering the encapsulation of the developing group is to encourage the group only to attend to the here-and-now, i.e., behaviour occurring within the confines of the group, as soon as possible after it has occurred. While such an emphasis may be experienced by participants as bewilderingly restrictive, it contains also some reassuring qualities. The restriction indicates that whatever anxieties or difficulties participants face in their everyday lives, within the group they are the equal of others and will not find their difficulties are seized upon by others. The trainer's stance also provides reassurance to a participant who may be initially sceptical that there *is* (or will be) quite sufficient going on within the group to provide a basis for worthwhile learning. Just as the early emphasis on the cultural island has been somewhat tempered by experience, so has trainers' insistence that the here-and-now be the only focus of the group's attention. It is frequently found that where participants choose to share with others some of their particular background, an understanding of their stance within the group is made much easier. Lieberman et al. (1973) showed that among the sample of groups which they studied, those which did not insist on focussing exclusively on the here-and-now led to greater lasting personal change.

One simple model of the T-group's agenda is that contributed by two trainers named Joe Luft and Harry Ingham (Luft, 1963). Immortalized as the *Johari Window*, it is frequently employed to help participants conceptualize T-group process. The implicit and necessary assumption of the model is that behaviour within the T-group is differentially visible to each member. Although some behaviour is 'public' and visible to all, initially this

Figure 2.   *Classification of behaviour in the T-group*

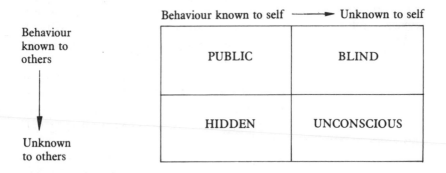

area is small. Some of my behaviour may be invisible to others, such as, for instance, anxious feelings when first making a statement to the group. Such behaviour falls within the 'hidden' area, and although much of it is not strictly overt behaviour, it is an important element in the participant's experience within the group. Other aspects of my behaviour may be visible to others but not to myself, such as if I make a friendly gesture towards another which is received as cold or demanding. Such effects of my behaviour are termed the 'blind' area. Finally the model envisages an unconscious area of the group's process, of which neither self nor others are aware. In terms of the model, the group's agenda comprises the reduction of the hidden and blind areas and the enlargement of the public areas. Reduction of the hidden area occurs through self-disclosure by the participant. Reduction of the blind area occurs through feedback from others. Thus self-disclosure and feedback are two central procedures of the group. Recently Esposito et al. (1975) investigated whether changes experienced by participants did match those envisaged. Members of student groups were asked to distribute one hundred points between the four areas in a manner which they felt represented their current position. During the course the points allocated to the public area rose from a mean of 38% to 51%. The blind area declined from 15% to 13% and the hidden area from 33% to 25%. The study lacked controls, but it does appear to show that in these particular groups, participants were most aware of learning through self-disclosure.

The third element which the trainer contributes to the group is a willingness to participate personally in its procedures. This does not necessarily mean that trainers will go along with pressures which groups may put on them to behave in this or that way. But it does mean that they will acknowledge their presence in the groups, show interest in others' reactions to them, and treat discussion of their behaviour and its effects on others as valid topics. In this way they seek to convey a number of messages to the group about effective ways to proceed. They show by their actions that learning in the group is most likely to occur if everyone's perceptions of events in the group are treated as equally valid. They show that participating in the group need not entail abdicating one's personal priorities. Finally they assert by their interest that everyone has something to learn in a group, not just a novice. If trainers are so clear about the messages they wish to convey to groups, why, one might ask, do they not spell these messages out more directly? If one approached a range of trainers with such a question their answers would most likely be diverse. Group leaders within the encounter tradition would be likely to answer that they do indeed spell out points such as these. They would add that frequently they find that the most effective way to get the points across are through the use of structured exercises and nonverbal activities. Group leaders within the Tavistock tradition, to be explored in Chapter 7, would argue that such points must not be spelled out. Learning in the group will be greatest where leaders do not make rules as to what should or should not occur, but restrict themselves to a precisely delineated interpretive role. Trainers in the T-group tradition would fall somewhat between these two positions. Most trainers do make some kind of initial statement about the goals and procedures of groups and their intended role within a particular group. But they are not surprised when such statements are not 'heard' by participants. There are process problems in the initial stages of a T-group which make it difficult for much of what is said to be heard in more than a momentary sense. Such process problems are likely to include anxiety in the face of a fairly large group of strangers and a low initial level of trust in them. Only when these initial process problems have been overcome, trainers would say, will group members be able to utilize the trainer and indeed other group members as learning resources.

Case history of a group

The account of sensitivity training so far given is necessarily abstract. An experience which is personally vivid for many group members can sound drab or even puzzling when compressed into a few descriptive phrases.

Some authors seek to overcome this difficulty through the use of transcribed excerpts (e.g., Rogers, 1970) or even relatively complete transcripts (e.g., Mann, 1970). The difficulty here is that excerpts may, for excellent reasons, be focussed on highlights or moments which illustrate particular principles, whereas complete transcripts tend to be unmanageably long.

In an attempt to at least partially overcome these difficulties, a case study of a group will be presented, based upon the method of coding group interaction devised by Bebout and Gordon (1972). An *episode* is a sequence of group interaction which is focussed on the same theme for at least four or five minutes. Episodes are punctuated by *transitions*. Interactions not classifiable as an episode are known as *interludes*. Bebout and Gordon distinguish six types of transition: shift in focus or content, shift in level of feeling, shift in specificity, silence, structured leader intervention, and unstructured leader intervention. The group to be described took place in England in the mid-seventies. It was part of a residential five-day workshop attended by people from a wide range of occupations. The group comprised two leaders and eleven members and was tape recorded with their consent. The coding system was applied to alternate sessions, commencing with the second. In the account which follows all names have been changed.

The second session contained six episodes, none of them longer than ten minutes. In the first of these, Richard expressed anger at his inability to take initiatives or get things started in the group. His discontent extended also to many aspects of the way the course had started off. The second episode was a general discussion of how much and how often one might look for emotional intensity in relations with others. Next came an episode concerning remarks made by Richard and Chris both during the session and the previous evening, which were seen by Jane and Jill as sexist. Then followed a short episode focussed on difficulties in expressing aggression. The fifth episode concerned research forms completed the previous day, which had led several members to reflect on their relations with others in their everyday lives. In the final episode Richard suggested that those who were 'in' the group were those sitting on the floor. Several of those who were thus defined as 'out' responded by saying that they felt comfortable, but that becoming involved would be a great effort. The episodes were only loosely connected and totalled 42 minutes (48% of the total session time). The remaining interludes included silences totalling about 10 minutes.

In session four, which lasted for 2½ hours, there were ten episodes. The first two of these focussed on members' feelings evoked by a series of nonverbal exercises carried out in a preceding community session of the total workshop. The first episode focussed on reactions to an exercise concerning aggression, while the second was related to an exercise on empathy and caring. There followed an episode of general discussion about the difficulty of expressing caring in back-home settings. The cotrainer Pat then expressed some irritation about not having been involved in earlier discussions of whether or not to move to another room. This episode was quickly followed by an expression of anger at Chris by Richard. An interchange developed between the two, with Richard angered by Chris's imperviousness to his criticisms of his past and present behaviour in the group, and Chris adamant that the problem was Richard's not his. In a further episode other members of the group expressed how they had felt during the confrontation between Richard and Chris. Phil, the trainer, then suggested that the group arrange themselves nonverbally in a line representing how much influence each person was currently having in the group. This was done and led to an extended discussion of how each of the members felt about where they had been positioned in the line-up. Pat then spoke about the difficulty she had had in expressing strong feelings she had been experiencing during the day, but which it now felt possible for her to share. The session closed with two brief episodes focussed on what happens in the group when aggressive feelings are expressed. The episodes totalled 108 minutes (73%). The remaining interludes included no silences of any substantial duration.

The sixth session was not clearly recorded, so the seventh was coded instead. There were six episodes, of which the first five were directly linked. In the first of these Ray, the youngest member of the group, asked whether women in the group felt maternal towards him. As this was explored by the group, the issue broadened also to include whether or not the men felt paternal. In the second episode Ray related some aspects of his relation to his father, while some other members saw parallels between what he said and his relations in the group to Chris. There followed an episode based on pooling of feelings as to what was easy or difficult about allowing oneself to acknowledge childlike feelings in oneself. This led to two short episodes in which Ray and Rachel cried, while being comforted by other members. Each of them had been prominent in the preceding episode. In the final episode, Ivor recounted how he found that during emotional times in the group he experienced anger but always choked it back. He wanted to create a setting in which it would be safe to express that anger. He and Richard then reenacted an exercise based on the expression of anger which they had first done together the previous day. On this occasion Ivor was able to express his feelings in the way he wished. The episodes totalled 75 minutes which was 71% of the session. The remaining periods included a good deal of laughter at the end, and a substantial amount of silence.

The ninth session contained seven episodes, most of which showed some linkage to one another. In the first of these, Jane expressed her reactions to each member of the group in turn. From this emerged a further episode in which Jane and Pat examined their relationship between one another. The focus was on the way in which initial competition had prevented them from seeing things they had in common. There followed a brief episode in which Donald said that he felt some pressure from the group to take a more active role. Some members encouraged him to resist such pressure, while others did wish him to be more active. The focus of attention then returned to Jane, who expressed some of the sadness she felt. This led into an exploration of her relation to Ray. Initially they had had a playful, spontaneous relationship, but each now felt constrained by awareness of a sexual element in their feelings. In the next episode, other members of the group shared with one another how far they found it possible or useful to differentiate sexual feelings from other types of feelings for a person. The final episode of the session was centred on Tim's statement that he felt sexually attracted to a member of the group, but that it would not be good for the group for him to say who it was. This episode concluded with Tim not revealing his feelings, although several other members did say that they felt attracted to others in the group. The focus of this episode was on how far it would or would not damage the trust in the group for such feelings to be expressed openly. The episodes lasted 105 minutes (73%).

During the eleventh session the group switched off the tape recorder, so the twelfth session was coded instead. This also contained seven episodes. In the first of these Ray expressed his reactions to each of the other members of the group. Donald then described how in the previous session he had wanted to express criticism of what was happening in the group, but had not done so for fear of being destructive. Next, Jill described the development of her feelings towards Phil over the previous twenty-four hours. Chris quickly responded, saying he had been identifying with Donald's attempt to explore destructive feelings and was very angry at the return to 'mawkish sentiment' exemplified by Jill's statement. This episode also terminated abruptly as Pat asked Tim how he reacted to Jill's earlier statement. It emerged that the person to whom Tim had been referring in session nine had been Jill. He expressed some regret about not having explored his feelings in a more direct manner. During this episode Ivor left the room, and the episode terminated with members expressing concern for him. Alice went in search of him and they soon returned. The group now returned to Chris's earlier attack, which had angered many members and provided the explanation for Ivor's departure. Chris was adamant that he was attacking the group's procedures rather than individuals, while others found it difficult to accept that his reactions to the events in the group were so different from their own. The session closed with a brief episode in which members discussed in a more abstract way how far the group was able to tolerate differences. The episodes lasted 98 minutes (83%). This session was at times confusing with members cutting across one another in sometimes painful ways. Issues in the group became more clearly polarized.

The fourteenth session was the final one, and it contained six episodes, the first four of which involved pairs of people in the group. In the first of these, Pat shared with Donald some regrets she had about a feeling of having blocked his learning in the group. Next there was an interchange of warmth between Ivor and Phil, reducing the fears which each had had of the other. There followed an interchange between Chris and Donald, which focussed on the constraints they sometimes experienced on expressing affection to men.

This gave way to another interchange of acceptance between two men, in this case Richard and Ivor. Pat then reviewed the manner in which she saw her behaviour during the week as selfish, while others encouraged her to relabel her perception as having done during the week those things which had been most important to her. In the closing episode the group stood as a tight circle, and jokingly reflected on some of the events of the week. The episodes in this session totalled 66 minutes (79%) and there was somewhat more silence than there had been since the early sessions.

The account presented of this group is inevitably fragmented, since not every session was coded. Thus for instance, although the group finished session twelve in some disarray, there was little direct reference to this in the final session. Many of the issues left over after session twelve were, in fact, taken up in the subsequent session thirteen. The sample of sessions presented does nonetheless illustrate a number of aspects of how a T-group functions. It is clear that the group developed various standards or norms about what were or were not appropriate behaviours in the group. These standards included the encouragement of self-disclosing statements by group members and the sharing of personal reactions or feedback between one another. There are also clear developmental trends through the history of the group. It is hard to say how typical this group is of current practice. It was certainly not atypical, but like any group it had some differentiating qualities. There was a good deal of emphasis on touching and nonverbal communication, thus showing some influence from the newer, encounter-oriented approaches (Chapter 8). The group also adhered rather firmly to looking at its here-and-now behaviour, but it tended to focus on relationships between different pairs of group members, in preference to analysing the dynamics of the group as a whole. Each of these elements in this group's history will be taken up further in the ensuing sections of this chapter.

Group norms

A number of researchers have attempted to obtain descriptions of the climate of relationships which evolves within the group. One manner in which this can be done is through the study of group norms. By cataloguing the behaviours approved and disapproved by group members, it should be possible to view the group not in terms of the trainer's intentions but in terms of what is actually achieved. Luke (1972) studied twelve ten-day residential groups for people involved in higher education. He found group norms to be relatively stable during the groups. The norms most frequently endorsed, in order of importance, were:

- sharing impressions of self and others' behaviour.
- expression and acceptance of feelings.
- awareness of the impact of self and others' behaviour.
- development of trust in self and others.
- efforts by members to change their behaviour.

Luke does not report data on whether there were any differences between the groups. Neither does he test how far these norms, which appear to have been expressed more in the form of values or goals, were in fact achieved. Lieberman et al. (1973) studied eighteen encounter groups of students at Stanford University. Members completed a 48-item checklist entitled 'Do's and Don'ts', rating how far each behaviour would or would not be seen as appropriate if it occurred in the group. A norm was said to exist where two-thirds or more of a group agreed that a particular behaviour would or would not be appropriate. It was found that virtually all groups approved of asking for feedback, talking about the here-and-now, giving feedback, challenging the leader, and probing a member who has been silent. Virtu-ally all groups disapproved of putting down a member who has just opened up with personal feelings, talking a lot without showing one's real feelings, and being frequently absent from the group. Apart from these shared norms, a wide variety was found in the other norms which the various groups endorsed. When the number and type of norms in each group were compared to measures of lasting personal change after the groups, it was found that there were no strong relationships. Thus the studies of norms show us that groups do, by and large, create a normative structure which is in line with that intended by trainers. However, the existence of that structure does not necessarily mean that the group will have lasting effects. Further elements are required before a fruitful outcome is assured.

Self-disclosure

One further obvious element required is that the norms endorsed by members do lead to actual self-disclosure and feedback within the group. Self-disclosure or the sharing of previously hidden aspects of oneself cer-tainly constitutes a major element of many groups. However, some difficul-ties stand in the way of an assessment of how much self-disclosure occurs in groups. In the sense implied by the Johari Window model, almost any expression of feelings in the group, whether it be about oneself or about others, must be considered as self-disclosure. Thus self-disclosure in a group might be highly related to the amount of talking one did. Jourard (1964) has popularized a less all-embracing concept of self-disclosure. He sees self-disclosure as having significance to the degree that it concerns something intimate. If one takes this view of self-disclosure, then counts of the frequency of disclosure might be expected to bear little relation to its significance. One group member who discloses to the group some specific thing, which has rarely if ever been discussed with others, might be consi-dered more self-disclosing than others who talk frequently and share a wide variety of rather more routine feelings. These distinctions have some impor-tance in relation to research into groups. Hurley and Hurley (1969) asked members of T-groups to complete a self-disclosure questionnaire devised by Jourard. They also obtained ratings from group members as to who had been most disclosing during group sessions. It was found that there was a significantly *negative* correlation between the two measures of self-disclosure. Goodstein et al. (1976) listened to a sample of tape recordings of groups and identified which members had made most significant disclosures about themselves. It was found that there was no positive correlation between this measure and members' ratings at the end of the groups as to who had disclosed most. On the other hand, there was a close correspondence between members' ratings of self-disclosure and members' ratings of who had participated most. These studies suggest that group members usually interpret the concept of self-disclosure rather broadly and equate it with participation. There is very little research evidence about the frequency of the more emotionally intense types of self-disclosure in groups.

Lieberman et al. (1973) asked the members of the groups they studied to record details of particularly important incidents for them during the groups. Of the descriptions received, about 20% referred to self-disclosure. References to self-disclosure were no more frequent among those who showed lasting personal change after the group than among those who did not. Thus, as with the presence of particular norms in the group, the occurrence of self-disclosure may facilitate learning but it does not by itself assure that process. In order to find relationships between self-disclosure and personal change, it is necessary to subdivide between different types of self-disclosure and also different reactions to the act of self-disclosure by others. Lieberman et al. did this and their findings will be further explored in Chapter 4.

Feedback

Feedback is seen as the central procedure of T-groups even more frequently than is self-disclosure. As with self-disclosure there is a certain amount of ambiguity as to what is or is not to be regarded as feedback. Any communication process, whether it be in pairs or larger groupings, involves a continuous flow of feedback from one party to another. Feedback on one's message to another is customarily obtained not only through verbal comment but through a variety of nonverbal cues, such as nods, facial gestures, posture, proximity, voice tone, and so forth. Within the T-group, the term feedback is usually employed to mean direct verbal statements to the other about one's reactions to recent behaviour or to the person in general. Outside of groups, such reactions are not all that frequent, and often enough the only feedback one obtains on an action is a lack of direct response from others. Although we all use such nonresponses as data relevant to our further actions, the potentialities for misinterpretation of such nonresponse are legion. The emphasis of the T-group is thus not so much that there shall be feedback where there is none in nongroup settings, but rather that learning opportunities for group members will be enhanced where feedback is more direct and more immediate.

French et al. (1966) studied the role of feedback in inducing changed self-identity in members of two T-groups. A specific feedback exercise was incorporated in the two-week training design. It was found that self-identity changed most on those scales upon which feedback was focussed. The durability of these changes after training appeared to depend not so much upon the receipt of feedback as upon whether or not the trainee reported wishing to make changes on that scale. Kolb et al. (1968) reported an experiment with student T-groups. Each student was required to set a goal for the change of some aspect of his behaviour within the group. In two of the groups students were encouraged to give one another feedback as to how far their change projects were succeeding. In the other two groups students were encouraged to tackle their change project individually. It was found that 44% of students in feedback groups did achieve changes, compared to only 5% in no-feedback groups. In a further study, the authors found that feedback was related to the achievement of change only in the later stages of the group.

Lieberman et al. (1973) found that among the key incidents reported by members of the groups they studied, 13% involved the giving or receiving of feedback. Receiving feedback was rated higher by members as a source of their learning than any other procedure within the groups. However, it was found that the receipt of feedback and its positive evaluation by members was found just as frequently among those who showed no long-term personal change after the groups, as among those who did show such change. Once more we must conclude that while feedback may provide a basis for learning in the group, the actual event of receiving feedback does not by itself assure a lasting effect. The preceding studies suggest some reasons why this might be so. The French et al. study suggests that feedback will only be effective where it is addressed to an aspect of behaviour which the participant wishes to change. The Kolb et al. study suggests that feedback may only achieve effects at certain stages in the group. Further studies to be reported in Chapter 4 indicate that feedback phrased in some ways is much more likely to lead to change than other types of feedback.

Adelson (1975) studied the incidence of feedback at different stages of two student T-groups. It was found that the amount of feedback tended to increase over time. Lundgren and Schaeffer (1976) undertook a similar but more extensive study. Samples were taken from tape recordings of four residential ten-day T-groups. Over the sessions sampled it was found that 27% of participant speech and 39% of trainer speech was classified as feedback. These means compare with an initial score of 23% in the Adelson study, rising to 38% by the end. Lundgren and Schaeffer report ratings of the quality of the feedback given early and late in the group. It was found that later in the group feedback became somewhat less focussed on the here-and-now, less directive, and more expressive of feelings. Feedback offered by trainers tended to differ from that offered by members, particularly early on in the groups. Trainer feedback was reported to be more confronting and emotionally distant than was member feedback. Although all the differences reported here were significant, Lundgren and Schaeffer also indicate that there were substantial differences between the four groups studied.

The Lundgren and Schaeffer study provides further clues as to why attempts to link the incidence of feedback directly to learning from group experience have met with only a qualified success. If the types of behaviour classifiable as feedback are different at different points in the group's history, it is unlikely that an overall measure of feedback will be a good predictor of change. Feedback at some points in the group will be more appropriate than at others. A similar point could of course be made with regard to self-disclosure.

Group development

It is very evident that the climate of relationships in T-groups develops over time. Indeed such development is central to the rationale for the T-group method. If it were possible for participants to learn about their behaviour in a short-term transient interchange with others, there would be no call for the somewhat cumbersome procedure of establishing a cultural island which then creates its own learning climate. A good deal of learning from experience does of course occur, and there are some who would argue that what is not learned from experience can most simply and directly be achieved through various types of social skill training. These approaches may well have a contribution to make, but they necessarily operate within a context which does not approximate the climate of relationships created by T-groups. Each approach may be able to facilitate learning which is congruent with the climate of relations within which it occurs.

Some controversy exists as to whether the process of group development within T-groups is unique to each group, or whether there is a common pattern which emerges with some regularity. A number of case studies have suggested that what happens within particular groups is explicable primarily in terms of their trainers. For instance, Reisel (1961(a)) showed that two T-groups developed in contrasting ways which were explicable in terms of the personality needs of their trainers. Lundgren (1971) related the different course of two groups to initial differences in trainers' styles. Such findings do not contradict the possibility that there may also be common elements in the development of different groups. Indeed Reisel (1961(b)) did show some elements in common between the groups he studied. As mentioned in Chapter 1, Tuckman's (1965) review suggested that there may be a common sequence to development not just in T-groups but in a much wider range of groups. He suggested four stages of group development and called them 'forming', 'storming', 'norming', and 'performing'. By this he implied that, after an initial period of confusion, groups next experience a phase of conflict. This is followed by a more harmonious time, which in turn gives way to a period during which the group is able to work effectively together. Tuckman drew on a number of articles describing T-group development, of which the best known is that by Bennis and Shepard (1956). These authors describe an idealized sequence of six phases, which between them span the last three of Tuckman's four. Bennis and Shepard see issues of conflict and authority as salient in the group early on, most likely as a consequence of the unusual manner in which trainers choose to exercise their leadership role. The initial phase is one of dependence on the leader. When the leader fails to provide the directive leadership which members seek, this leads to a phase of rebellion and counterdependency. The leader may be in some way symbolically deposed. In this way a third phase is reached in which the group is able to see the leader as a person rather than an omnipotent figure. Resolution of the group's difficulties with the trainer opens the way to the exploration of relationships between group members. A personal or 'honeymoon' phase is followed by one in which there is tension between those who seek a highly personal group and those who wish for a less personal group. Resolution of this tension leads to the final phase, consensual validation, in which group members are able to relate effectively to one another on the basis of accurate rather than distorted perceptions.

The Bennis and Shepard theory is widely quoted as indicating the manner in which T-groups develop. In fact, like a number of the other studies cited by Tuckman, the authors did not systematically test their theory. It was formulated as an idealized distillation of the authors' experiences as T-group trainers. One difficulty in evaluating such formulations is that particular sequences of development may indeed occur in groups led by a particular trainer or group of trainers. However, these phases may not be inevitable but instead could be a consequence of their particular trainer style. Reader and Von Mayer (1966) suggest five conditions which must hold true if the Bennis and Shepard progression is to occur. These include a relatively inactive trainer, at least some comments from the trainer addressed to group processes rather than to individuals, and no opportunity for feedback in pairs and subgroups outside of sessions. These conditions were quite frequently encountered in T-group laboratories in the fifties, but they are now much less often found.

There are some studies which have tested more systematically for the presence of developmental trends. Since many of them are based on the laborious task of coding interactions in the group, the sample size has not always been as large as one might hope. Mills (1964) presents a case study of a single student group. His coding scheme involved scores for whether each interaction referred to events within the group or outside it, whether the affective tone was positive, negative, or neutral, and whether others referred to are male or female, and superior or subordinate. Focus on events within the group increased and negative affect decreased, as one might expect. There was also a rebellion against the leader, as Bennis and Shepard could foresee. However, the major novelty about Mills' formulation is the manner in which it demonstrated the impact of the external environment upon process within the group. This was noticeable both in relation to beginnings and ends of term during the student year and in relation to the termination of the group. Thus group development must be seen not as inexorable, but as a product of a particular balance of factors acting both within and outside the group.

Mann (1966) sees group development primarily in terms of the evolution of the group's relationship with the leader. Four student groups were studied and only those contributions seen as relevant to leader-member relations were coded. Perhaps because relevance was defined to include symbolic as well as overt references to leader-member relations, the percentage of interactions found relevant was high, varying between 50% and 98% in different sessions. The phases found by Mann closely resemble those of

Tuckman, except that Mann adds a final phase entitled *separation*. Gibbard and Hartman (1973) adapted Mann's coding system to refer to all group interactions and applied it to two further student groups. They were particularly interested in how far group development could be seen in terms of oedipal relationships. They noted two principal developmental changes: (1) decreasing libidinal involvement with the leader and increasing libidinal involvement with fellow-members, and (2) a relatively low level of inter-member hostility during periods of hostile confrontation with the leader, and an increase in intermember hostility once the confrontation has passed. These findings are consistent with the Bennis and Shepard model although expressed in a more psychoanalytic framework.

Dunphy (1968) studied another two student groups. However, in this study the method employed was to ask the students to keep diaries and then submit the diaries to content analysis based on a computer programme known as the General Enquirer. Such a procedure has the advantage of impartiality of coding, but tends to produce considerable complexity. Six phases were detected. The first three of these were primarily counterpersonal and negative. In the first of these an attempt was made to impose external standards, which gave way to individualistic rivalry and aggression. Phase four was transitional and was marked by a new concern with absenteeism and communication. In the last two phases emotional concerns, particularly affection, predominated.

Farrell (1976) also studied student self-analytic groups. His sample included three groups. He too found an initial authority-centred phase, but this was followed by movement towards intimacy. Conflict then arose, which extended to renewed attacks on the leader. Final phases of cohesion and separation resembled those found in other studies. Farrell thus stresses that the conflict with authority occurs later than do other writers. He fails to specify who were the leaders of the groups which he studied.

Babad and Amir (1978(b)) studied the development of three groups of occupational therapy students in Israel. A single rater coded the behaviour of each group member during a given time period. The group leaders were described as 'generally nondirective and with a here-and-now orientation'. It was found that the groups followed the sequence specified by Bennis and Shepard.

The empirical studies of group development so far discussed have a good deal in common with one another. The authors of the studies were mostly also the group leaders. The groups were composed of students who were frequently all men, as were the leaders. The leaders were all influenced by psychoanalytic thinking, and most likely favoured the relatively inactive style utilized by leaders working within the psychoanalytic tradition (see Chapter 7). In terms of the suggestions of Reader and Von Mayer (1966), these groups appeared to favour the emergence of Bennis and Shepard-type group development, and the findings do, on the whole, favour that model.

Some studies sampling a wider range of T-groups have also been made. Lakin and Carson (1964) studied four residential two-week T-groups for mental health workers. Ratings were completed by members after every session on eleven scales. Competition was found to decrease over time, while cooperation increased. Attention to the group's atmosphere also showed significant trends but these peaked at different points for different groups. Overall, Lakin and Carson were more impressed by the divergences between the groups' development than the similarities. Levine (1971) studied twelve English student T-groups in all of which he was the trainer. Ratings were completed after each week's meeting. After factor analysis, the scores showed decreases in detachment, flight, artificiality, and looking to members for support, and increases in fight and intimacy. Lundgren (1977) made an observation study of five ten-day residential T-groups. He found significantly more concern with involvement and control issues in week one and more concern with solidarity in week two. Concerns with conflict and with interpersonal openness were equally high in either week. When Lundgren summarized the points at which scores on each of his variables reached their peak during the group, they fell in the sequence: involvement, control, openness, conflict, solidarity. None of these studies provides clear support for the Bennis and Shepard model. At the most general level they did show a progression from impersonal, distant relationships to a warm, affectionate group, as Bennis and Shepard propose. But at the more detailed level, neither Levine nor Lakin and Carson found separate phases, while Lundgren found concern with openness throughout the group and particularly at the middle. Bennis and Shepard might expect greatest openness in their final consensual validation phase, and they would also expect conflict earlier than it was found. Although these studies had more adequate samples than their predecessors, none of them yet provides a wholly satisfactory account of group development. Levine's groups all had the same leader, Lakin and Carson found a great deal of variance between groups, while Lundgren's were coded live by observers, with all the attendant biases which that entails.

Most of these problems were overcome by Lundgren and Knight (1978). They studied twenty different ten-day residential T-groups. Their sample was of NTL groups and should therefore be broadly representative of current practice at the time the data were collected (1972). Codings were made from tape recordings, yielding a total of seventeen indices. The changes found fell most readily into three phases, although the authors stress that the transitions were gradual rather than abrupt. The *initial encounter* occurred during the first day or two. During this phase trainers were inactive and focussed upon the group as a whole. Members spoke about the group rather than themselves, were positive rather than negative, were directive and made high use of the pronoun 'we'. The second phase, *interpersonal confrontation*, lasted until early in the second week. Trainers became more active and focussed less on the group. Members spoke more of themselves and of other individuals. They became more negative but less directive. Use of the pronoun 'we' fell and then rose again. The final phase, *mutual acceptance*, occupied the latter part of the second week. Trainers were at their most active and most focussed on individual behaviour. Members were markedly less negative towards one another.

The most striking aspect of these findings is that there was no evidence of confrontation with the trainer. A general progression is once more found from distant, impersonal relations to warm, affectionate relations. Conflict is found in the middle phase but it is concerned with member-member relations. That aspect of the Bennis and Shepard model, which asserts that confrontation of differences precedes cohesion, is upheld, but the substantive detail of the pattern is quite different.

The groups studied by Lundgren and Knight differ in many ways from those upon which earlier theories of group development were built. In former times, T-group participants might quite frequently not be aware of the manner in which T-group learning procedures differed from other educational approaches. More recently, group members have frequently attended other groups previously or at the least are informed about how groups proceed. The members of Lundgren and Knight's groups appear to have accepted their trainers' initial passivity. Such acceptance might be much less readily forthcoming in settings where participants are not so well informed or where authority and status issues are more salient.

Further data relevant to the middle, confrontation phase in groups are provided by a series of studies focussed on the incidence of negative affect in groups. These studies have not attempted an overall description of group development but have examined the incidence of anxiety, depression, and hostility at different points in the group. Lubin and Zuckerman (1967) studied four six-day T-groups for juvenile court judges. Anxiety, depression, and hostility were found to rise until the end of the third day and then fall back to their initial level. Long et al. (1971) found a rise followed by a fall on scales measuring fatigue and stress in two weekend encounter groups. Rohrbaugh (1975) studied seven five-day T-groups comprising civilian employees of military establishments. He found rises in anxiety, depression, and hostility between days one and two, once more followed by a decline. In contrast to the earlier findings, the decrease was much more marked than the initial increase. Smith and Lubin (1980) studied three further samples of English T-groups, of varying duration with a total sample size of thirty-two groups. It was found that among one-day experimental student groups no variation occurred over time. In three-day groups of management students, the familiar pattern of rise and fall was found for depression and hostility. In five-day groups at a business school, the rise and fall occurred on all three scales, but was followed by a second rise of depression and hostility.

The rise and fall pattern for negative affect is thus widespread but not universal. The second rise in the English five-day groups was attributed to the effect of an intergroup exercise. Like the Bennis and Shepard sequence, the peaking of negative affect at the middle of the group may be dependent on the absence of strong influences from outside the group.

In summary, almost all of the studies suggest that T-groups experience a period of tension, conflict, or negative affect in the early to middle phase. Such conflict is not necessarily focussed around the leader. This then gives way to a more harmonious group climate. The status of this generalization needs some examination. Many of the studies, including that by Lundgren and Knight (1978), emphasize that in addition to the overall trends found there was very substantial variation from one group to another. The generalized description of group development derived from research is therefore not a description of the *inevitable* path a group will follow. At best it is a description of the *average* path. Tuckman and Jensen (1978) acknowledge that the earlier Tuckman model of this average path needs amending to include a termination or ending phase, which they call 'adjoining'.

Reflecting on the variability of group development poses a question, which has so far been left to one side: which of the elements found in group development may be necessary to the creation of personal change? It is highly likely that at least some of the elements in group development are common to the experience of any group of people getting to know one another, as Tuckman suggested. Are there distinctive qualities to T-groups or other learning groups, which facilitate the creation of personal change?

Of all the studies of group development reviewed, the only one which also included a measure of personal learning from the group was Rohrbaugh (1975). He found that a high score on personal change was associated with a wide range of negative affect during the week. One could envisage two types of change which would fit this finding. One would be the familiar rise and fall of negative affect. The other would be high initial negative affect which fell during the week. Rohrbaugh's subjects appeared to fit the second pattern.

Another study which compared the outcome of groups with processes occurring at different stages was that by Marks (1972). Her study was part of a larger one (Bebout and Gordon, 1972) examining more than one hundred student-led groups at Berkeley. Marks selected three groups which proved to have particularly high scores on personal change and three which were low. The recordings of sessions were analysed into a series of episodes, a much less laborious procedure than the more microscopic types of coding undertaken by some of the other researchers. Initially there appeared few differences between the groups. Successful groups had fewer episodes per session, that is they were less likely to jump from one issue to another. By the middle sessions the successful groups showed many more episodes classified as feeling expression and as confrontation of problems or conflict. Unsuccessful groups had many interlude episodes, in which there was no clear focus. In the final sessions these differences became still more marked, with a considerable increase in feeling expression in the successful groups. These findings provide some evidence that the patterns of group development frequently found are an integral part of the creation of personal change. The developmental sequence of the successful groups was similar to the findings of Lundgren and Knight (1978), while unsuccessful groups showed a very different pattern. The case study presented earlier in the chapter also fits well into the pattern now delineated. Just as Marks found with her groups, the proportion of time devoted to interludes declined. In terms of Lundgren and Knight's findings, session two illustrates the initial encounter phase. Sessions four to twelve all appear to fit into their interpersonal confrontation, although it is evident that by session twelve most members would have wished they were into the mutual acceptance phase. This final phase was achieved in session fourteen. Just as reported by Lundgren and Knight, the trainers were at their most active in this phase.

Analysis of this group's development into episodes also indicates the important role of other events in the training laboratory in triggering episodes within the group. In the present case this occurred most obviously at the beginning of sessions four and seven. A substantial further proportion of the episodes arose at the suggestion of, or with encouragement from, the trainer and cotrainer. It is also evident that the development of this particular group was considerably influenced by the continuing tension between Chris and various others, particularly Richard. Chapters 5 and 6 will return to a consideration of trainers, group composition, and programme design as major influences on the outcome of the T-group.

Summary

T-groups seek to create a cultural island characterized by high levels of self-disclosure, focus on here-and-now behaviour, and feedback on one another's behaviour. No one of these elements by itself has been shown to relate to the successful outcome of groups. Most probably the types of feedback and self-disclosure shown in groups evolve as the group climate develops. Earlier theories that an initial confrontation with the leader is a prerequisite for a successful group are not supported by recent data. The data do suggest that a period of some kind of confrontation may be required for group success, but this need not occur early and it need not necessarily involve the leader. It is probable also that this confrontation not only needs to occur, but needs to have an outcome which does not destroy the group's cohesion if the group is to succeed.

CHAPTER 3
THE EFFECTS OF TRAINING[1]

In the preceding chapter some of the typical events occurring during sensitivity training were described, but only passing reference was made to the lasting effects of these events. This chapter will review what we currently know of such effects. The principal obstacle in the path of such a review is the diversity of current training practice. A willingness to innovate has always been a central value of sensitivity trainers; indeed the method only arose because of the willingness of a group of trainers to adapt their design in mid-programme. Such innovation has both strengths and weaknesses. Where trainers innovate in order to adapt a method to a new training goal or a new population of trainees, there is much to be said for it. Where innovation seems to be more of an end in itself or an attempt to follow ephemeral fashions, there may be less to say for it. Either way, the rate of change means that if researchers are to make valid statements about the effects of groups, they must make clear what is and what is not included in a definition of sensitivity training.

Sensitivity training is here defined as a process which (a) occurs in small groups; (b) involves the examination of interpersonal relations among those present; and (c) extends its membership to include those *not* undergoing psychotherapy. Each of the elements of this definition have some ambiguity. Although sensitivity training does typically occur in groups with eight to twelve members, many variations are found. For instance, cocounselling is a procedure with many similar elements, in which most of the time is spent in pairs. Variants are also found in which the size of the groups is

1. This chapter is a revised and updated version of 'Controlled studies of the outcome of sensitivity training', which first appeared in *Psychological Bulletin*, 1975, *32*, 597–622. Copyright © 1975 by the American Psychological Association. Reprinted by permission.

..1 greater. For instance, some leaders within the Rogerian tradition and others using the Tavistock approach have, in recent years, devoted substantial proportions of their programmes to meetings of groups of forty or fifty, or even larger.

The examination of interpersonal relations among those present is certainly a key element in sensitivity training, but it does not make sense to exclude approaches in which this occurs only for part of the time. For instance, in many of the encounter approaches substantial time is also devoted to exploring fantasies and to reexamining or reexperiencing one's past relations with others. Studies which explicitly identify the approach studied as being one of those discussed in Section 3 will not be considered in this chapter. Studies which are considered here are those which the researchers describe as T-groups, sensitivity training, personal growth groups, or encounter.

The third element in the definition is still more problematic. A number of distinctions were proposed during the sixties between sensitivity training and psychotherapy, but these have not stood the test of time. The description of sensitivity training as 'therapy for normals' (Tannenbaum et al., 1961) has led to Schutz's (1967) categorization of his encounter group members as 'normal neurotics' and to Lieberman and Gardner's (1976) report that 426 people who enrolled for programmes at five personal-growth centres showed just as high reports of stress and psychiatric symptoms as 89 applicants to five private clinics. Of course not all sensitivity training is as therapeutically oriented as is implied by these authors. Organizational development approaches in particular are much more focussed on work behaviour and organization functioning. But in terms of definitions one cannot sensibly exclude the more therapeutically oriented formulations. Thus sensitivity training *can* be therapy where participants are encouraged to seek therapeutic benefits from it, but it need not be so. Where being a client in therapy or counselling is a prerequisite for gaining admission to a group, it seems more appropriate to refer to such activities as group therapy and group counselling.

There is some evidence to suggest that the issues explored above are not simply a matter of pedantic definition. It could very well be that the label by which an activity is designated will influence who actually volunteers to attend, and what expectations they bring with them. Studies have shown that groups run by university counselling centres attract volunteers who are more disturbed than nonvolunteers (Haase and Kelly, 1971; Olch and

Snow, 1970). On the other hand groups run by university psychology departments show no such differences between volunteers and nonvolunteers (Sheridan and Shack, 1970; Cooper, 1972(a); Cooper and Bowles, 1973; Gilligan, 1973; Seldman and McBrearty, 1975). Student volunteers from psychology courses are found to be *more* self-actualized (Nell and Watkins, 1974) and less authoritarian (Kuiken et al., 1974) than nonvolunteers. Hoerl (1974) found volunteers from the general public to be more flexible.

Discussion of the diversity of sensitivity training underlines a further point. The range of approaches encompassed by the definition outlined may very well have different outcomes. Thus it cannot be meaningful to ask researchers whether sensitivity training works or what are its effects. The best that one could hope for would be a description of the effects which the various approaches *can* achieve. It is highly unlikely that the elements included in the definition are themselves enough to make certain such effects. What is required is analysis at two separate levels. Firstly, in the present chapter there is a consideration of what effects sensitivity training *can* have. Subsequent chapters then seek an understanding of the circumstances which would make it more likely that these effects would in fact arise.

Early studies

One of the earliest substantive studies of the effects of T-groups was that by Miles (1960, 1965). He studied the effects of a ten-day residential NTL programme on thirty-four elementary-school principals. Two control groups were also employed. Respondents were asked to describe any changes they had noted in themselves eight months after the training. Job associates of trainees and controls were also asked to report on perceived changes. A system of content analysis was devised, based on scoring of verified changes, that is those which were reported independently by two or more respondents. Miles found verified changes for 72% of trainees but only for 17% and 29% of his two control groups. The areas in which verified changes were most markedly greater for trainees were 'the areas of increased sensitivity to others, equalitarian attitudes, skills of communication and leadership, and group and maintenance skills' (Miles, 1965).

The methods developed by Miles were employed by several subsequent investigators (Bunker, 1965; Boyd and Elliss, 1962; Valiquet, 1968; Moscow, 1971). Each of these studies found greater verified change among trainees than controls, with never less than 50% of trainees showing change and never more than 37% of controls. The types of change found varied somewhat from those reported by Miles, but were broadly similar. In reviewing these studies, Campbell and Dunnette (1968) concluded that they provided the firmest evidence then available for the effectiveness of sensitivity training. As they pointed out, these studies do have some evident weaknesses. The most obvious of these is that the observers reporting on change know perfectly well who has attended training and who has not. Further difficulties are the unorthodox manner in which these researchers recruited their control groups, and the use of measures collected only after training.

With the current availability of a broader range of studies, Smith (1975) has suggested ways in which it is now possible to be more demanding of research studies. In this way, the risks that misleading conclusions will arise from a review of the data should be reduced. A first step in this direction is to examine only studies which utilize a measure both before and after training. The advantage of this procedure is that after training it may be that trainees will have forgotten how they were feeling before the programme. This might be the case particularly with studies using long-term follow-up, such as the verified change studies. Such measures are required both from trainees and from untrained controls. A second step in making research more precise is to require that the training experience last for a sufficient length of time. Little is known about how long is in fact needed for the achievement of this or that training goal, but it is clearly unreasonable to compare groups lasting say ten hours with those lasting fifty hours without expecting some difference in outcome. In this review, only studies of groups which met for at least twenty hours are included. Such meetings might of course be intensively focussed as in the cultural island model, or they might equally comprise ten two-hour meetings on a once-a-week basis.

These limitations still leave almost a hundred studies for examination. The criteria employed by researchers have quite properly varied widely, since the types of group they have studied have also been diverse. In examining these studies one further distinction is important. Most of the studies have tested to see whether a particular effect is present immediately after training. A smaller proportion have then studied also whether such effects persist or not. The more numerous studies of immediate effects will be examined in the first part of each section, subdividing between a series of different types of measure.

Global measures of self-concept

Researchers have frequently studied whether or not participants feel more favourable towards themselves after a group experience. The most commonly used measures have been semantic differential rating scales. Significantly more positive self-ratings have been obtained in five studies (Cicatti, 1970; Larson, 1972; R. Lee, 1969; Lieberman et al., 1973; Miller, 1970), but not in three further studies (Krear, 1968; Sutherland, 1973; Parker and Huff, 1975). Two of these unsuccessful studies also included a measure of self-percept based on card sorting, but this also showed no change.

Six further studies included ratings of self on a more restricted range of scales, and all showed more favourable self-image after the group was over (Alperson, Alperson, and Levine, 1971; Berzon, Reisel, and Davis, 1969; Hewitt and Kraft, 1973; Insel and Moos, 1972; Solomon, Berzon, and Davis, 1970; Solomon, Berzon, and Weedman, 1968). A slightly different procedure was used by Shapiro and Ross (1971) whose subjects were asked to select from a list of 171 adjectives those which best described them. After the group, trainees selected significantly more positive adjectives than did controls.

The evidence thus shows that after group experience, participants saw themselves more positively in twelve out of fifteen studies, whereas controls did not. Six of these studies also included follow-up measures testing whether this change persisted. Alperson et al. (1971) found that among high-school volunteers, the effect had disappeared two months after a marathon group experience. Cicatti (1970) reports regression of the changes found three months after student groups, but fails to mention on which measures this occurred. Solomon et al. (1970) worked with vocal rehabilitation clients, but they also found that the gain in self-evaluation had disappeared after six months. By contrast, Lieberman et al. (1973) found that members of eighteen student encounter groups still evaluated themselves as more adequate than did controls six months after the groups ended. Likewise, Larson (1972) found that after six months, trainee United States Air Force noncommissioned officers still evaluated themselves more favourably than did controls. Furthermore, Shapiro and Ross (1971) found that one full year after training, the differences between trained and untrained supervisors in a school for delinquent girls were still present. The loss of significantly enhanced self-evaluation at follow-up is apparently frequent but not inevitable.

Psychometric measures

A second group of studies concerning global measures of self-concept have preferred the use of psychometric instruments to the ratings so far discussed. Fourteen reports are available which used the Tennessee Self-Concept Scale (TSCS), of which only three detected any significant change. There is some difficulty in interpreting these studies since few of them make clear which of the various scale scores on TSCS were computed. Eleven studies (Vosen, 1967; Brook, 1968; Becker, 1971; Livingston, 1971; G. McFarland, 1971; H. McFarland, 1971; Scherz, 1972; Poe, 1972; Cirigliano, 1972; Norton, 1973; Sherrill, 1973) all found no effect. The three remaining studies also found no effect on the test's main score, referred to as 'total P'. Young (1970) found increases on seven subscales of TSCS after three-day groups for students. Follow-up data showed some persistence of change, but this was most marked on the Self-Acceptance Scale, which was not one of those which changed immediately after the group. Ware and Barr (1977) found increases on subscales entitled Self-Criticism, Self-Satisfaction, and Personal Worth, but these differed significantly from controls only for one of two groups studied. Reddy (1970) found an increase on a scale entitled Number of Deviant Signs. Since this scale is usually used as an indicator of maladjustment, Reddy concludes that group members may have been adversely affected. Since Reddy's subjects showed no change on other scales entitled General Maladjustment, Personality Disorder, and Neurosis, this possibility is by no means established.

The TSCS studies contrast markedly with those using ratings and semantic differentials. It is unlikely that most of those choosing to use ratings were studying successful groups, while most of those choosing to use TSCS were studying unsuccessful groups. A more plausible hypothesis would be that the TSCS, at least where only its total P score is computed, fails to detect changes which are picked up by rating scales. This could be because some of the items on TSCS refer to one's experience of self in specific settings outside of the group such as family, on which there would be no reason to expect change during a group. In contrast, semantic differential ratings are context-free and therefore more likely to reflect a person's feelings at the time of testing.

A number of other psychometric tests of self-concept have been employed, with mixed results. Rubin (1967(a), (b)) measured self-acceptance through a sentence completion procedure. Codings of sentence completions were significantly more self-accepting after training. Zullo (1972) used the Offer Self-Image Questionnaire in assessing the effects of a three-day retreat for senior high-school students. Significant changes were found on the scales for social relations and morals. The latter change was still present after four months. King (1976) measured self-acceptance among teacher training students with the Lesser Scale. Increases were found after a weekly group for a term and these were still present three months later. King et al. (1973) obtained a similar effect with undergraduate groups. Innis (1971) found no change on the Berger Acceptance of Self Scale, and Lieberman et al. (1973) found no change on the Rosenberg Self-Esteem Scale. This latter finding is particularly interesting because it was obtained from the same sample who *did* show significant increases in self-ratings of adequacy. This supports the view that some self-concept measures are better able to detect the changes which occur than are others.

Of the twenty studies using psychometric tests of self-concept, only seven have detected change. Three of these studies provide follow-up data and all of these give evidence for the persistence of change.

Self-ideal match

An alternative approach to the measurement of self-acceptance is to obtain separate ratings of self and ideal self and study their convergence. Although some critics have pointed to difficulties in the interpretation of such convergence, a number of studies have used this method. Gassner, Gold, and Snadowsky (1964) reported two studies of student workshops. In the first study enhanced self-esteem was found equally among trainees and controls; in the second no change occurred in either condition. W. Lee (1970) obtained a convergence of self and ideal percepts with two groups of elementary-school teachers. The convergence differed from an untrained group, but not from a further control who received didactic instruction. Peters (1970) studied six groups attending a ten-day National Training Laboratories programme. Self and ideal ratings converged to a highly significant degree, whereas in a rather dissimilar control group they did not. Lieberman et al. (1973) found that self and ideal constructs tended to diverge in their sample, but the effect was not quite significant. Sigal et al. (1976) studied the effects of groups integrated within the school curriculum for tenth-grade students. They found complex effects, using mostly the Miskimmins Self-Goal-Other Test. Divergence between self and goal tended to widen. On the other hand, Shapiro and Gust (1974) did obtain convergence of self and ideal among counselling graduate students.

Three of the six studies do thus find convergence of self and ideal percepts. The effect can scarcely be seen as a reliable effect of group experience, since two substantial studies showed movement in the reverse direction, and two of the other studies found significant convergence among some of their controls. It seems likely that groups can influence not only trainees' feelings about themselves, but also the kinds of ideal self to which they aspire. The variability of the findings obtained could derive from the type of ideal which different groups construct.

Of the forty-four studies which included some type of global self-concept measure, twenty-one detected change. Nine of these included follow-up measures among which six found persistence of change. The actual percentage of studies detecting change appears to depend more on the type of measure employed than the type of group studied. It is concluded that group members do rather frequently feel more positive or accepting of themselves after groups. These effects are most readily detected by ratings and by the Lesser Self-Acceptance Scale. Whether or not these global feelings about oneself are associated with more specific changes will now be examined.

Specific aspects of self-concept

A wide variety of specific changes in self-concept have been anticipated. The studies will be examined in a series of subsections which will focus on the self as locus of causality, prejudice and openmindedness, orientation towards participative behaviours, and other aspects of personality.

The self as locus of causality

Participants in sensitivity training are frequently encouraged to take responsibility for their own actions, for instance by seeking out feedback or by caring for others in the group. Several measures have been employed which seek to assess whether trainees increase the degree to which they see themselves as active, causal agents in determining their behaviour, rather than seeing themselves as pawns of others or of environmental pressures. The most widely used instrument of this type has been Shostrom's Personal

Orientation Inventory (POI). The POI was designed as a measure of self-actualizing behaviour and it yields two major scales, Inner-Directed Support and Time Competence. The first of these derives rather directly from the conceptualization of oneself as the locus of causality and this scale comprises most of the items in the test. Increases in inner-directedness on POI have been reported in seven studies (Alperson et al., 1971; Lavoie, 1971; Trueblood and McHolland, 1971; Mitchell et al., 1973; Margulies, 1973; Kimball and Gelso, 1974; Gilligan, 1974). In a further ten studies there was either no increase in inner-directedness (Khanna, 1971; Bellanti, 1972; Poe, 1972; Klingberg, 1973; Shapiro and Gust, 1974; Pacoe et al., 1976; Ware and Barr, 1977) or an increase among both trainees and controls (Treppa and Fricke, 1972; Jeffers, 1972; Sherrill, 1973; White, 1974). In many of these studies there were also increases detected on one or more of the subsidiary scales of the test, but since the test items for many of the subscales overlap one another, the statistical procedures employed by these investigators are not appropriate.

Among the studies using POI, seven included a follow-up measure. Alperson et al. (1971) noted that approximately half the change found was no longer present after two months. Lavoie (1971) found the significant effect she had detected was gone after one month. Both Kimball and Gelso (1974) and Gilligan (1974) found that after four to six weeks the changes they found were still present, but that controls had meanwhile increased their scores so that the difference between trainees and controls was no longer significant. Treppa and Fricke (1972), Khanna (1971), and Bellanti (1972) continued to find no difference between trainees and controls on inner-directedness at follow-up. Khanna (1971) did however find a significant change on the other main POI scale, Time Competence, which was still present six months after training.

POI has proved a popular test with researchers into groups. However, the frequency with which it shows increases among controls both during and after groups suggests that whatever it measures is somewhat volatile, easily appearing, and as easily disappearing. The study by Jeffers (1972) used a Solomon four-group design, whereby half the subjects completed post-measures but no pre-measures. The findings supported the conclusion that changes on POI can be triggered simply by completing the test. This triggering might be particularly potent among those who attended groups, since the content of the items is close to issues often salient in groups.

Some further studies have employed other measures also related to the conception of self as causal. Insel and Moos (1972) obtained responses to the question 'Who am I?'. Responses were coded for external referents, defined as descriptions of oneself verifiable by reference to external sources, and internal referents which are those only verifiable by reference to one's internal state. They found significantly more use of internal referents after a group for graduate students. Kassarjian (1965) found no increase on a measure of inner-directedness. His conception of inner-directedness appears to derive more from examination of the source of one's values, rather than Shostrom's emphasis on inner-directedness as self-awareness. Rotter's Locus of Control Scale provides one further relevant measure. Diamond and Shapiro (1973) reported significant increases in perceived internal locus of control among students after group experience. Ware and Barr (1977) found no such changes in the student groups they studied. Katz and Schwebel (1976) found no change during a group-based management training programme, but increases in internality among both trainees and controls subsequently. Katz and Schwebel also used the Harrison and Oshry Problem Analysis Questionnaire to measure how far managers saw their work problems as caused by themselves. Both trainees and controls showed significant increases. Rettig (1978) used a sentence completion test after a student group and found increased use of personal explanations of why one's behaviour works out as it does, and decreased use of situational explanations.

The evidence presented in this section is less compelling than that in the previous section. Of twenty-four studies concerning the self as locus of causality, ten have detected increases not shown by controls. All of the seven follow-up studies are based on POI and only one or perhaps two of these gives evidence for persistence of change. It appears that an enhanced sense of personal causality, at least as measured in these studies, does quite frequently occur but tends to be a transient effect. One possible reason for this might be that the tests employed mostly rest on *generalized* expectancies about personal control. If trainees learn in a group to exert increased personal control over their behaviour in some specific situation or with some specific person, these tests would most likely not detect the change.

Prejudice and openmindedness

A number of investigators have hypothesized that trainees will become more open to new experience and less prejudiced against the alien or unfamiliar. Such changes are difficult to define and still more difficult to measure. There is good reason to expect that group members will become more open to experiences similar to those which they experience in sensitivity training, but less reason to expect them to become open to other types of novelty or change. If the changes to be expected depend on the nature of the trainee's specific experience, we should expect rather low generality of the changes found. For instance, one might anticipate that race prejudice might change in groups focussed on interracial encounter but not in groups with other goals.

The more global measures used are examined first. Decreases on the California F Scale are reported by Carron (1964), Khanna (1971), and Parker and Huff (1975). Kernan (1964) and Adams (1970) found no such changes. Carron's significant effect owed more to increases in his control group than to decreases among trainees. The trainees were supervisors in the chemical industry and the effect had disappeared seventeen months after training. Kernan's (1964) negative effect was based on engineering supervisors. His post-measure was not collected until ten weeks after training was over, so there is no conflict between this finding and Carron's. Khanna (1971) found that decreases in F Scale scores of Tennessee school teachers were still present six months after training. On the other hand Adams' (1970) null finding was also obtained with school teachers. Parker and Huff (1975) report significant reductions in F Scale scores after groups for students. Very few of these studies give actual mean scores for their samples, so it is impossible to judge whether the variability of the findings might be because some samples were initially much more prejudiced than others.

An allied measure, the Rokeach Dogmatism Scale, has been used in three further studies. Adams (1970) used the Dogmatism Scale and failed to obtain any effect. Poe (1972) also found no effect, but H. McFarland (1971) reported significant decreases in dogmatism in groups of student teachers. However, after the students had completed their teaching practice the change was no longer present. Insel and Moos (1972) reported no changes on the Wilson-Patterson Measure of Conservatism after a student group, whereas Parker and Huff (1975) found that their student groups did show changes on this measure, as well as on the Breskin Test of Rigidity. Hoerl (1974) used the Flexibility and Tolerance of Ambiguity Scales of the California Psychological Inventory, with members of three-week residential groups at the Center for the Study of the Person. No increases were found, but Hoerl was interested to note that volunteers for the groups already scored far higher on these scales before the groups than did non-volunteers.

Haiman (1963) designed an openmindedness scale which included many items from the F and Dogmatism Scales but had half the items reversed to take account of possible bias in responses. He found significant increases among student groups. Weissman, Seldman, and Ritter (1971) predicted an increase in preference for novel, complex, or ambiguous stimuli. A sharp increase was found after a student group, but an equally large effect occurred among controls.

One further global measure is the Marlowe-Crowne Social Desirability Scale, which measures the degree to which respondents seek to give conventional, socially desirable responses. Significant effects were obtained by Jeffers (1972) and Ware and Barr (1977), but not by Sutherland (1973). All of these investigators employed student groups. Katz and Schwebel (1976) also found change towards less socially desirable responses among management training groups, but these changes occurred equally for controls both at the end of training and two months later. There are thus fifteen studies which have used one or more global measures of openmindedness. Seven of these have detected significant change. Only four of these studies included follow-up measures, one of which did find a persisting effect.

More specific measures of openmindedness are those which are in some way designed to measure changes which might be anticipated as a result of a particular training design. Perhaps the most obvious such measure is that of attitude towards group training procedures. Miller's (1970) subjects rated the concept of sensitivity training more favourably on a semantic differential following training. They were also more favourable towards the concept of being praised. Lieberman et al. (1973) found more favourable attitudes towards the safety of encounter groups and also greater endorsement of the values which the investigators delineated as encounter group values. The principal change here was towards increased openness to making changes in one's own behaviour. Six months later, neither of these changes had persisted, although the belief in the safety of groups approached significance.

Young (1970) predicted changes in trainees' conceptions of human nature. Using Wrightsman's Philosophies of Human Nature Scale, he found significant increases on the Trustworthiness Scale after student groups. Kleeman (1974) used the same scale, also with student groups, and obtained increases on the scales measuring strength of will, altruism, and independence. Both of these studies included follow-up measures. Young found the effect no longer present, whereas in Kleeman's sample the differences between trainees and controls widened and changes on the Trustworthiness Scale were now also significant. Shapiro and Diamond (1972) reported increases in hypnotic suggestibility among three student groups. The tester was ignorant of which of the students he was testing had actually attended groups. Shapiro and Gust (1974) obtained a similar effect, but it was significant for only one of two populations of students studied.

Six studies have been reported which focus specifically on the effects of multiracially composed groups. Innis (1971) studied five groups in Texas, each of which had six white and two black members. Semantic differential ratings were made of a variety of concepts. The only significant change was on ratings of civil disobedience, but Innis fails to make clear in which direction the change occurred. Krear (1968) studied marathon groups in racially imbalanced schools. Semantic differential ratings became more favourable to the concepts of authority and family, but showed no change on the concepts of community and racial integration. Rubin (1967(a), (b)) studied eleven-day residential groups for professionals in New England. Eight of the fifty participants were black. Prejudice was measured by the Harding and Schuman Human-Heartedness Scale. Control data were obtained by asking fourteen of the participants to complete the scale ten days before the course and again at the start. The remaining thirty-six trainees showed a significant decrease in prejudice after training. Hull (1972) found increases in world-mindedness in student groups which also contained foreign students. Controls included both all-American groups and students who did not attend groups at all. Smith and Willson (1975) studied multiracial weekend workshops in England. One workshop comprised white teachers and black parents of children attending their schools. Interviews conducted before and three months after training indicated that teachers became more favourable towards the parents, whereas the parents became more critical of the teachers. A second workshop, involving whites and Asians, showed no lasting effect.

Lieberman et al.'s (1973) study at Stanford University included four groups which were specifically set up as black-white encounters. The wealth of measures used in this study casts some light on the views advanced in this section. Lieberman et al. found no change on global measures of openmindedness, either with the mixed groups or with the all-white groups. The measures used were the F Scale and scales testing for suspiciousness of others and militancy. At the same time they *did* find significant changes in their four interracial groups on a questionnaire specifically oriented towards race questions. These changes were increased endorsement of black separatism and increased mistrust of the other race.

Significant changes are thus reported in ten of the twelve studies using more specific measures of openness. Five of these include follow-up measures, among which three found persisting effects. Although every one of the studies of interracial groups detected significant effects, these effects were very diverse, ranging from greater acceptance to greater militancy. Since the measures were different, one cannot be sure that these are opposed effects rather than different aspects of a more global change which occurred in all the multiracial groups. In interpreting these findings, one should bear in mind that they mostly involved groups in which blacks were a small minority. Scores were usually not reported separately for the different racial groups, and none of the studies included a control in which multiracial groups undertook activities other than sensitivity training. All of these points underline how little is yet known of the effects of multiracial encounter.

This section has shown that specific measures of openness to others or to new experience are much more likely to detect significant changes after groups. The changes found also appear much more likely to persist. There do appear to be some circumstances under which the more global measures also show change, but it is not possible to say whether this is due to some distinctive quality of the trainees in these studies, or whether it derives from the training designs employed.

Orientation towards participative behaviours

Sensitivity training is frequently a participative rather than a passive process. One may expect that trainees would come to see their participation in group settings in a different light as a result of this. Behaviours in the T-group are often construed in terms of leadership or control, expression of friendship, self-disclosure, and so forth. This section is concerned with tests which reflect these aspects of the trainee's self-percept. The most widely used test has been Schutz's (1958) Fundamental Interpersonal Relationship Orientation–Behaviour (FIRO–B) which asks people to describe how they prefer to express inclusion, control, and affection behaviours to others and how much of these behaviours they like to receive from others.

Twelve studies have employed this test, of which nine have detected significant training effects. The changes reported are not homogeneous. Early studies in England (Smith, 1964; Cureton, 1968) found convergence between expressed and wanted scores on particular scales. More recent American studies (Terleski, 1971; McFarland, 1971; Zullo, 1972; Klein, 1973; Jacobson and Smith, 1972; O'Connor and Alderson, 1974) have all reported increases on some of the FIRO–B scales. Increases have been noted for expressed affection (three studies); wanted affection (three studies); wanted inclusion (three studies); expressed inclusion (one study); and expressed control (one study). The remaining studies using this test have presented their data in a manner which does not make it clear whether changes attributable to training occurred (Schutz and Allen, 1966) or no effects due to training were found (Weissman, Seldman, and Ritter, 1971; Lieberman et al., 1973; Kaye, 1973). Four of these studies included follow-up measures of which only one (Jacobson and Smith, 1972) found that the effects had persisted.

The overall impression given by the FIRO–B studies is that changes, at least in recent groups, are most strongly focussed on the giving and receiving of affection. It is particularly interesting that the Lieberman et al. study, which detected changes on many measures, showed no effect on FIRO–B. One possible explanation might be that changes detectable by FIRO–B are quite specific to the culture of particular groups. Thus a highly affectionate T-group might generate changes in FIRO–B Affection Scales, whereas a group with more conflict might not. The Lieberman et al. study included a much larger and more varied sample of groups than did the other studies using FIRO–B. It might therefore be that Lieberman et al.'s sample included groups showing moves in various directions on FIRO–B and yielding no overall change. In any event, the existing follow-up studies do not offer much confidence that the changes are much more than temporary adaptations to the culture of sensitivity training.

Another instrument which relates closely to matters of concern in T-groups is the Jourard Self-Disclosure Questionnaire. This asks people to indicate to whom they disclose various kinds of information about themselves. Solomon et al. (1970) adapted the measure and found that group members reported increased willingness to disclose to others after a nine-day workshop. Cicatti (1970) found increases in self-disclosure to others outside the group during weekly student groups. Increases were in disclosure to best friend of the same sex and to closest faculty member. Gold (1968) found no overall change in self-disclosure. There was an increase in disclosure of personality items, but this was no longer found after three months. Scherz (1972) also found no change after student groups. Walker et al. (1972) found that self-disclosure scores decreased after groups for women, many of whom were nuns. Drawing on material from follow-up interviews, the authors propose that there had been no actual decrease in self-disclosure but that the women now construed their behaviour as less self-disclosing than before, because they contrasted their usual behaviour with what had occurred in the groups. Hurley and Hurley (1969) have also shown that the Jourard Questionnaire does not predict actual self-disclosure in groups. These studies are consequently perhaps best interpreted as measures of attitudes towards self-disclosure, rather than providing any very direct guide as to changes in self-disclosing behaviour.

T-group leaders exemplify a particular approach to group leadership. One might consequently look for changes in attitudes towards different styles of leadership. Carron (1964) found decreases on the Initiating Structure Scale of the Fleishman Leadership Opinions Questionnaire among chemical industry supervisors. This change was not found seventeen months later. Kernan (1964) found no change in the same test among engineering supervisors. W. Lee (1970) found changes towards more participative leadership on the Minnesota Teacher Attitude Inventory among elementary teachers. No effects occurred for untrained controls, but similar changes were found among teachers who took classes in human relations. Adams (1970) found no change on this test. Miles (1960) also studied schoolteachers, but obtained no change on the Leader Behaviour Description Questionnaire or a Group Participation Scale. Gassner et al. (1964) reported highly significant changes on a Democratic Leadership Scale after student workshops. Bolman (1970) found that managers attending group training showed increased endorsement of 'confrontation of interpersonal issues' and decreases on 'use of formal power' and 'endorsement of pyramidal values' (i.e., belief in hierarchical authority). These changes were still present four weeks later, but at this time the managers were still attending a course together and had not yet returned to their jobs.

This section has shown that measures of orientation towards participative behaviour do frequently change after groups. Of the twenty-four studies reviewed, sixteen detected favourable effects. Of the seven studies with valid follow-up data, only one found that the effects had lasted. The rather generalized tests employed in these studies thus appear to detect effects which are transient rather than lasting.

Other aspects of personality

The three preceding sections have examined changes in various aspects of self-percept. Further studies have been undertaken which do not fit readily into any of these sections. Leary's Interpersonal Checklist has been used in four studies. Treppa and Fricke (1972) found an increased desire for dominance, whereas White (1974) found no change. Kaye (1973) found reductions in submissiveness and hostility, while controls became less loving. Each of these studies concerned student groups. Kaye's findings were still present eight months later. Khanna (1971) also obtained changes on the Interpersonal Checklist, but fails to indicate whether they were significant.

The groups of Filipino women studied by Lavoie saw themselves as more assertive, cheerful, and venturesome on Cattell and Eber's Sixteen Personality Factors Questionnaire and more sociable on the Gordon Personal Profile after training. These effects were gone after one month. Two studies using the California Personality Inventory (Flannigan, 1970; Vail, 1971) showed no change. Shapiro and Gust (1974) report enhanced scores on the Teachers' Counselling Questionnaire and on the Taft Experience Questionnaire among counselling students. Kleeman (1974) found increases on self-ratings of self-determination, self-affirmation, self-motivation, and empathy after student groups. The first two of these changes were still present after two months. Pfister (1974) found increased understanding of self as rated on the Edwards Personality Inventory among police attending groups. Martin and Fischer (1974) obtained ratings on the Adjective Checklist after student groups in Canada. Trainees saw themselves as more dominant and heterosexual, but less succorant, deferent, abasing, or unfavourably adjusted. Bloom (1975–6) conducted sensitivity training for the elderly. No change was found on two tests of mental ability and an index of activity level. In other studies no change was found on anomie (Rubin, 1967(a), (b)), ego-strength (Kimball and Gelso, 1974; Adams, 1970), Bendig's Scales of Hostility (Uhes, 1971), the Constructive Personality Change Index (Solomon et al., 1968), the Choice Dilemma Questionnaire (Poe, 1972), the Eysenck Personality Inventory (Insel and Moos, 1972), a Thematic Apperception Test, Machiavellianism, and the Guildford-Zimmerman Temperament Survey (Kernan, 1964).

Pollack and Stanley (1971) used a sentence completion test to assess students' ability to confront aggressive and sexual stimuli. Codings of responses showed improved coping after groups. A similar finding was that by Kuch et al. (1972) who obtained reduced 'unhealthy' responses to a forced-choice Rorschach test after a counselling group.

Lieberman et al. (1973) obtained several further measures as a part of their project. Group members reported significantly more growth experiences on a 'life-space' questionnaire after attending groups. They also rated more highly the level of their coping with their current personal dilemmas. Finally their descriptions of others changed in the direction of a factor which the authors term 'leniency'. None of these changes was sustained six months later.

The measures described in this section are diverse and it is not always easy to see why researchers selected some of them. Of the twenty-four studies mentioned, twelve did detect changes after training. Two out of four follow-up studies showed persistence of change.

Perceptions of others

The term *sensitivity training* implies that one of the major goals of training is that one should develop a more perceptive or accurate understanding of others. Surprisingly few studies have tested for such effects. Gassner et al. (1964) obtained ratings of the 'way others usually act' after student workshops. Such ratings were found to converge with self-percepts equally for trainees and controls. Innis (1971) found no change on Berger's Acceptance of Others Scale after a one-week workshop.

These two studies contrast with others where the subject is asked to rate specific others. Lieberman et al. (1973) found no change in ratings of one's best friend or of the environment in which one lives after training. Hewitt and Kraft (1973) assembled four-person discussion groups of mixed trainees and controls before and after training. No change was found in the perception of controls by trainees. Larson (1972) found a significant increase in semantic differential ratings of their subordinates by Air Force noncommissioned officers who attended training. This effect was still present six months later. Harrison (1962) found that one group of management trainees increased their use of interpersonal constructs to describe nontrainees. A second group did not differ from controls. Harrison's procedure was also used by Lieberman et al. (1973) who found no change after training.

Danish and Kagan (1971) developed an Affective Sensitivity Scale, in which the subject is asked to infer the feelings of characters on video tape. Improved scores were found after a ten-day training programme, while controls showed no change (Danish, 1970). Norton (1973) also used this scale, working with student groups, but no effect was obtained.

This section provides very little support for the view that sensitivity training leads to changes in perceptions of others not present during training. Only three of the eight relevant studies showed any change. Two of these were undertaken within work organizations, while none of the studies which failed to find effects were located in organizational settings.

Perceptions of trainee behaviour by others

Changes in the behaviour of the trainee may be examined in two ways. Either one may create some kind of temporary test situation in which the trainee's performance is assessed, or one may ask the trainee's customary associates to report their perceptions of everyday performance. The first procedure can reduce observer bias, but the second offers a more direct test of whether changes are actually evident in everyday settings.

Performance tests

A number of the tests employed related to the learning of communication skills. Heck (1971) asked teacher trainees to describe in writing how they would explain a problem to a twelve-year-old. Responses by those who attended groups improved, as did those of others who undertook programmed tasks. Controls showed no change. Bellanti (1972) used a counselling simulation interview. After training, trainees were higher on accurate empathy, unconditional positive regard, and congruence. This effect was not found three months later. Elliott (1978) used a video tape version of the Carkhuff Indices of Communication and Discrimination Test. Scores on communication rose, while those on discrimination did not. Norton (1973), using the same test, found increases on gross facilitation, empathic understanding, and the discrimination of facilitative communications. Each of these studies used students. Pacoe et al. (1976) found increases on measures of both empathic communication and facilitative discrimination among medical students.

Solomon et al. (1968, 1970) studied vocational rehabilitation clients. Ratings were made of interviews before and after training. Increases were found, particularly on motivation to work. Dua (1972) compared individual counselling with group sessions. Ratings of anxiety within a group discussion fell for those attending groups. Argyris (1965) obtained codings of executives discussing case studies. Changes in rated behaviour were noted for those attending groups. Unfortunately Argyris indicates that the coder for the trainees' post-test was different, whereas the same coder continued to code the controls. The study must therefore be judged inconclusive, since the changes found could easily be due to the changed coder.

Becker (1971) found no change in the physical distance maintained by subjects while performing a task before and after training. Powell (1972) found no improvement on a decision-making exercise based on the film *Twelve Angry Men*. Finally Hewitt and Kraft (1973) brought trainees and controls together for a one-hour discussion before and after training. Controls saw no changes in trainees' behaviour.

The evidence from performance tests indicates that changes are frequently found on such tests. Of the eleven studies which permit a conclusion, eight found positive effects. Only one of these included follow-up data and these indicated fade-out.

Observation of everyday performance

Perceptions based on everyday performance are available from fifteen studies. Five of these concern teachers. Schmuck (1968) reports on an extensive programme which appears to have involved more than one hundred hours of training. Children in classes taught by sensitivity trainees showed increases in the influence they perceived themselves to have. Various other changes were also detected but these were found also among those who had other forms of training but no groups. G. McFarland (1971) found that after 2½ days of training for the teachers, children in their classes perceived a significant increase in attempts by the teacher to include them. Khanna (1971) asked students to use the Leary Interpersonal Checklist to describe their teachers. After training, the teachers were seen as less hostile and more accepting. W. Lee (1970) found no change in the manner in which teachers were perceived by parents and by administrators after the teachers had attended training.

Geitgey (1966) investigated sensitivity training for student nurses. The nurses were perceived more favourably by patients and by instructors. The instructors also rated the nurses' relations with patients more highly.

Chambers and Ficek (1970) evaluated a marathon group for girls in a residential training centre. The girls were assigned to training or the control group by decision of their counsellors. One month after training the counsellors perceived more positive changes among trainees than controls. Since the counsellors were instrumental in assigning the girls to training in the first place, they might well have preferred to see more change among trainees than controls.

Larson (1972) obtained semantic differential ratings from the subordinates of noncommissioned officers in the Air Force. No changes were found after training. Pfister (1975) investigated the impact of sensitivity training for the police. Citizens involved in nonadversive contacts with the police were asked to make ratings on the behaviour of the police officer they had dealt with. After training, significantly higher ratings were found on confidence, warmth, sincerity, understanding, acting as a co-worker on a common problem, and accepting the citizen as an individual. Controls did not show these changes. Cohen and Keller (1973) obtained data on the impact of a management development programme. Trainees' supervisors saw increases in human relations behaviours but these changes did not achieve significance overall. Significant effects were found only where the leadership climate was high on consideration and low on initiating structure, that is where human relations behaviour was to some degree already present. Katz and Schwebel (1976) obtained peer evaluations of middle managers in a management development programme. Peer evaluations increased equally for trainees and controls, both immediately after training and two months later.

R. Lee (1969) asked roommates of students to complete the Barrett-Lennard Relationship Inventory as a description of trainees and controls. The students who attended groups were seen three weeks later as higher on empathy, unconditional positive regard, and congruence. Cicatti (1970) also found change among students using the Barrett-Lennard measure, but fails to make clear who completed the instrument with regard to whom. Lieberman et al. (1973), as well as Parker and Huff (1975), also obtained ratings from close associates of students who attended groups, but neither study detected changes. Cooper (1972(a), (b)) compared health service consultation records of students who did and did not attend groups. No immediate difference was found, but controls saw doctors more frequently one year after the groups.

The studies based on observations of everyday performance provide some quite strong evidence for the visibility of sensitivity training effects. Eight studies showed significant effects while six did not. In addition the Cooper study found an effect which was assumed to be adverse and which occurred among controls but not trainees. Of the five studies including follow-up data, three showed persistence of effect.

This section has indicated that of twenty-six studies involving observer perceptions of trainees, seventeen have found at least some effects favouring trainees. It should of course be remembered that in many of these cases the observers were well aware who had attended groups and who had not.

The current situation

The studies described in the preceding pages are impressively numerous, and offer some support to the enthusiasm of practitioners for these methods. Of the 177 tests of immediate effects of training which have been reported, ninety-six (54%) detected significant effects. These tests are by no means independent of one another, since many studies employed several outcome measures. In fact the number of separate studies providing these tests is ninety-one. Twenty-eight of these studies included follow-up measures, which provided fifty-two tests of the persistence of effects. Seventeen measures (33%) did show positive effects.

While the studies reviewed do employ somewhat more sophisticated research measures than those used in the early evaluation studies of groups, there continue to be numerous ways in which the findings could be misleading. Some of the most obvious of these sources of error are perceptual biases in observers of trainees; the use of control groups which are not closely equivalent to trainees; the use of measures which do not reflect sufficiently closely what happens in groups; and the use of measures which are prone to test sensitization, i.e., effects attributable simply to the completion of the form within the training setting. The measures which are most vulnerable to test sensitization are those in which trainees rate some aspect or other of their own self-concept, and it is precisely these measures which have been most frequently used.

Although these sources of error are certainly present, there is little evidence that the more tightly controlled studies are any less likely to come up with positive effects than the less tightly controlled ones. In many ways the most systematically designed study has been that by Lieberman et al. (1973). These authors concluded that about two-thirds of participants showed positive effects at the close of the group, reducing to about one-third at their six-month follow-up. While these figures are expressed in terms of proportion of group members showing change, rather than proportion of measures showing change, the conclusions accord well with the conclusions of this review. *A good deal of measurable change does occur after groups, but there is a substantial fade-out of these effects in subsequent months.*

The form in which these findings have been expressed is that of mean changes in scores on the various measures employed by researchers. Means are probably the most useful single way in which to summarize a pattern of change. However, changes in means may conceal how much variability there is in the changes found. Some critics of sensitivity training argue that while *on average* there may be positive effects, there are nonetheles harmful effects for a minority of those who attend. Studies relevant to this possibility are considered in Chapter 11, where the evidence is shown to be less than compelling. A more firmly based critique of the use of means is based on the likelihood that means conceal the fact that some people show changes after groups, while others do not. By aggregating together everyone's change scores, we may make it more difficult to understand why those who do change do so, and those who do not do not.

The use of mean changes may also conceal the fact that different people have changed in different directions on a particular measure. While such multidirectional change is often dismissed as random, there is no certainty that it always is so. Different trainees' individual learning needs may vary and the changes they achieve may relate to these needs. Lennung (1974) made a study of groups for Swedish managers based on this line of argument. He found that the variability of scores on various psychometric scales was much higher among the managers who had attended training than among those who were controls. The difficulty with this approach is that it limits the possibility of summarizing very clearly just what changes have occurred.

A final difficulty with the use of means is that they imply that the scale upon which one is seeking to detect change is fixed and immutable. As Golembiewski et al. (1976) have argued, some of the changes arising in groups may not be of this type, but rather may involve trainees changing the concepts or framework they employ in perceiving their feelings or behaviour.

The weight of data supporting the occurrence of change in various kinds of mean scores, as well as the limitations to their interpretation outlined above, imply that what is now required is not simply more data, but answers to a series of more specific questions. These questions centre on the need for clearer theorizing as to what occurs in groups. We need to know why the changes which occur in groups do occur and why they sometimes do not. If this question could be answered, it should prove possible to make the effects of training more consistently predictable. We also need to know why the effects so frequently do not persist. Insight into this question might also imply different types of training design. Finally we need to know how far the mechanisms of effective sensitivity training are unique, and how far they underlie the widening range of other group-based training methods. Exploration of this last question will be reserved for Chapters 7–10. The most urgent issue concerns the search for a theory of why personal change occurs, to which we now turn.

Summary

At the close of sensitivity training, participants feel more favourable towards themselves than previously. They frequently also feel more personally able to control their actions, more open to new experiences, and more concerned with giving and receiving affection. They show no tendency to perceive others who did not attend training in a different manner. Their own behaviour is often perceived by others as changed. Changes most frequently noted are improved communication skills and more warmth and concern. Follow-up studies show that these changes do not all persist. The effect which shows the strongest persistence is a more favourable evaluation of oneself.

CHAPTER 4
LEARNING PROCESSES IN GROUPS[1]

Views as to why learning or change might arise in groups have been expressed by a very wide range of theorists, encompassing all the main theoretical standpoints from within psychology and some from sociology also. This chapter will examine a range of these views, giving greater emphasis to those which do lead to the possibility of empirical test.

Perhaps the most obvious way to commence one's search for an adequate theory of learning in groups is to ask members of groups who have benefitted from their attendance what they found most helpful. Yalom et al. (1967) made a start in this direction using a small sample of therapy group members. Members were given sixty statements typed on cards and asked to sort them into piles, depending on how well each statement described what they had found most helpful about the group. The researchers categorized the sixty statements into twelve general areas, and the results showed that the most frequently selected items were from the areas which the researchers termed *interpersonal input, catharsis*, and *cohesiveness*. Interpersonal input items mostly referred to feedback received from others, catharsis items referred to self-disclosure to others, and cohesiveness items referred to the warmth and acceptance of the group. Rohrbaugh and Bartels (1975) also employed Yalom et al.'s list, but studied a larger sample, including both therapy groups and sensitivity training groups. Factor analysis of their data showed that the dimensions adopted by Yalom et al. were not very homogeneous with regard to responses to different items supposedly on the same scales. Nonetheless, the most frequently endorsed

---

1. Parts of this chapter are adapted from Smith (1980(a)). By permission of John Wiley & Sons Ltd.

G.P.P.C.—E

items were very similar to those obtained by Yalom et al. Sherry and Hurley (1976) also found interpersonal input and catharsis to be the two most frequently endorsed categories.

The finding that feedback, self-disclosure, and acceptance are seen by group members as central to their learning is important, but does not of itself establish that these *are* the central mechanisms of learning in a group. To assume that this was so would be to assume that learning processes are at all times carried out at the level of conscious awareness. The only study so far available, which compares reports of which learning mechanisms were felt to be most important by members with independent measures of learning, is that by Lieberman et al. (1973). In this study of encounter groups, the most endorsed sources of learning were feedback from others, universality (learning that one's problems were not unique), receiving advice or suggestions, understanding previously unknown parts of oneself, and cohesiveness. However, only the last three of these were used more frequently by those who showed high change on the independent measures of learning. According to this study, at least two of the mechanisms most frequently endorsed by members – feedback and self-disclosure – are not in themselves sufficient to sustain change. The Lieberman et al. findings suggest that more fruitful formulations of the change process are likely to be those which incorporate some reference to the warmth and acceptance of the group, and some reference to understanding or thinking about one's behaviour. We shall return to this view later in the chapter, having considered each of the principal views of how learning occurs in groups.

Behavioural approaches

While learning theory has had a major role in the history of psychology, its impact on theorists of sensitivity training has mostly been less overt. Many of those most active in studying sensitivity training in the sixties (Miles, 1960; Bradford et al., 1964; Schein and Bennis, 1965) saw the receipt of feedback as the central element in learning. The origins of this model lie in the theories of Kurt Lewin, who saw training as a 'laboratory' within which the individual can develop and test out new skills in relating to others. One of the central facets of this conception is that the creation of an adequate laboratory requires the creation of a 'cultural island' upon which such learning could be engendered. Once the laboratory is established, it is expected that individual trainees will obtain for themselves the feedback available in reaction to their various behaviours. Learning is thus individualized; what one takes out is dependent upon which aspects of oneself one expresses, thereby laying oneself open to feedback and to subsequent change.

Learning theory is by no means monolithic. Considerable movement can be observed in the manner in which learning has been conceptualized by theorists over the past few decades. While many of the early theorists saw learning primarily in terms of the repeated reinforcement of certain very specific fragments of behaviour, some of the more recent approaches (e.g., Bandura, 1974) envisage processes of social learning whereby one might acquire a lengthy behaviour sequence by the process of imitating another person. Such modifications in learning theory certainly make it easier to envisage how processes of feedback could enable someone to show behaviour change in a group. Diamond (1974) provides an analysis of change in groups expressed in the terminology which has achieved widespread currency within the field of behavioural approaches to therapy. Change is seen as contingent on a process of mutual reinforcement and mutual punishment.

Such generalized formulations are not easy to test. Exchange of feedback is clearly a central procedure in many groups, and participants report it to be important. But the studies reviewed in Chapter 2 showed that the feedback available in a group changed over time, just as it no doubt does in the rest of life. The key issue in learning may not be the availability of feedback, but whether or not we choose to listen to it. The willingness to listen to feedback may well vary, not only in terms of the motivational state of the receiver, but also in terms of how the feedback is expressed, its timeliness and its content. A theory of learning which simply specifies feedback as the source of learning is thus too crude. What is required is greater specificity as to the context and content of that feedback. A number of studies address themselves to this question.

A series of experimentally controlled studies was undertaken by Jacobs and others, using short-term experiences lasting from one to six hours. The results are of some interest, but require cautious interpretation since the feedback given and received under such short-term circumstances may differ from that employed in longer groups. Participants engaged in a series of structured group activities, and were then asked to give to selected others in the group written feedback of a particular kind. According to the design this feedback was to be either positive ('Your effectiveness and attractiveness is enhanced by your being . . .'), or negative ('Your attractiveness and effectiveness is hindered by your being . . .'). In formulating the feedback, the senders were asked to select suitable items from a list with which they were provided. Items on the list had been pretested to ensure that they were all perceived either as positive or negative. In variations of the experiment (Jacobs et al., 1973(a); Jacobs et al., 1973(b); Jacobs et al., 1974; Schaible and Jacobs, 1975; Jacobs, 1977), feedback was either anonymous or identified, couched in terms of observed behaviours or of one's own feelings and received once during the experiment or twice. It was found that feedback receivers strongly preferred and rated as more accurate the positive feedback they received. They also saw positive feedback as more desirable and more likely to lead them to change their behaviour. It was found that where feedback was positive, it had most impact when it included both descriptions of the feedback receiver's behaviour and the feedback sender's feelings. On the other hand, where the feedback was negative, the most effective version had only a description of the receiver's behaviour. Findings about the sequencing of feedback were more confused, with the data not making it clear whether it was better to precede positive feedback with negative or vice versa.

At one level these results are unremarkable – people have been shown to prefer compliments to criticism. In other ways they are of greater interest. It appears that effective positive feedback is different in kind from effective negative feedback, a distinction which appears nowhere in theories concerning sensitivity training. It is also apparent that the sequencing and timing of feedback have a lot to do with its effectiveness, but the studies are poorly designed to explicate this aspect, since the groups were so brief. Longer-term groups are rather likely to contain a blend of positive and negative feedback, but if the Jacobs finding that 'positive feedback is the greater motivator toward change' were shown to hold under longer-term conditions, it would be an important one.

The study by Miles (1965) provides a field test of some of the ideas generated by the Jacobs research. Miles studied school principals attending a residential ten-day laboratory. During the first week and again during the second, ratings were made of the feedback received from other group members. Ratings of feedback during the first week proved not to correlate significantly with any of the measures of subsequent change collected by Miles. Ratings of feedback during the second week were significantly related to ratings by the group leaders and by trainees themselves as to who had learned most. Those seen as changing most were those who rated their feedback as clear, strong, and helpful. However, there was no relationship between whether or not feedback was pleasurable and the amount of learning. Furthermore, measures of follow-up change were not related to any of the feedback ratings. It must be concluded that, although the receipt of feedback did have a substantial relation to learning during the programme, the durability of the changes achieved is better explained by other variables. One of Miles' most striking findings was that in his sample, anticipation of change, as expressed before the programme, was negatively related to subsequent actual change. As Miles points out, the most likely explanation of this is that the school principals who were most strongly constrained in their jobs very much wished to make changes but were unable to do so, whereas those who were less constrained had less wish to change before attending the programme, but found it easier to apply what they did learn during the group. Thus the receipt of feedback during the group would be a necessary condition for subsequent change, but not a sufficient one. The Jacobs research may tell us something about who will leave the group most wishing or intending to make subsequent changes, but the linkage with the achievement of those changes is a more tenuous one.

Approaches stressing insight or understanding

Many theorists see the achievement of insight into the behaviour of oneself or others as central to the purpose of group training experiences. This is particularly true of those who have been influenced by psychoanalytic thinking. The outcome of groups whose leadership is explicitly analytic in orientation is explored more fully in Chapter 7, but the notion that change subsequent to group experience is contingent on insight is widely diffused, and requires some discussion here. In the previous section, the postulation of feedback as a learning mechanism had two implicit assumptions. One is that prior to the receipt of feedback, the group member is assumed to be in a state of ignorance; the other is that the member will welcome the feedback at least some of the time and learn from it. Insight-oriented theories of change partially agree and partially disagree with these assumptions. They agree in so far as they see the group member as initially ignorant in some respect or other. They differ in that they assume that the member will resist feedback, because that feedback will most likely threaten the member's defensive system of assumptions about interpersonal relations. Thus, groups need to be structured in such a manner as to make that resistance explicit, and to enable the group leader to comment on it with sufficient frequency that members come to see how they are evading an enlarged conception of what is occurring. This should occur most readily where leaders are relatively inactive and decline to go along with procedures which the group may devise to lure them out of an interpretive role.

The consequences of the insight-oriented theorists' position is that most empirical studies which they undertake are case studies of the dynamics and development of particular groups, as perceived by group leaders or researchers. Little weight is placed on the perceptions of group members, other than as a basis for interpretation by the leader. For instance, the studies reviewed previously by Jacobs and her colleagues would be seen as illustrating the defensive processes at work in the groups studied. The fact that positive feedback was preferred would be seen not as showing that such feedback was more effective, but that it was less threatening and therefore more acceptable. Validation of the insight-oriented theorists' position (e.g., Gibbard et al., 1973) must thus be sought not by the study of members' perceptions of what occurs or what is useful, but through consideration of whether the interpretations advanced are coherently derived from descriptive materials concerning the groups under study.

This type of research procedure is a relatively self-contained one, which is not easily integrated with other approaches. The fruits of it are explored more fully in Chapter 7, but within the present chapter it is concluded that other approaches offer the possibility of drawing on a wider range of data concerning what is learned in groups.

Approaches stressing the social context

Theorists in sociology from G.H. Mead onwards have stressed the manner in which personal identity derives from the social context within which we are located. A theory of sensitivity training utilizing such an approach needs to take notice both of the context from which group members come to groups, and of the manner in which people relate to one another in the training setting. Back's (1972) study of the encounter movement is conducted within such a framework. Back sees the function of encounter experience as largely cathartic. He is unimpressed by the findings of evaluation studies concerning long-term effects of groups, but considers that short-term group experience proved so compelling during the 'boom' years of the early seventies because groups offered precisely what was lacking in many of our everyday lives: excitement, intimacy, a clear sense of purpose, and so forth. While an analysis along these lines clearly has some cogency, the closer reading of evaluation studies afforded by the previous chapter indicates that there are *some* lasting effects of training after all. It is the context which is able to generate these which must be more clearly analysed.

The context of T-group learning is one of intense involvement. With residential group programmes in particular, meetings are most usually found by members to be highly involving. Events within the group occupy the centre of the stage, whether those events be actually focussed on relationships of those present, or whether they also include self-disclosure by group members about other aspects of their lives. A theory which focusses primarily on the context of learning would thus stress factors such as involvement and trust as central. Golembiewski and McConkie (1975), for instance, have argued that trust is the key variable in group processes. According to this view, no amount of feedback in a group nor any amount of insightful interpretation will guarantee a lasting effect unless there be also trust in the group. Trust is seen as a state in which the group member is aware that others in the group are in a position to say or do something which may harm them, but has confidence that this will not occur. The consequences of high trust would be that the group member would be more likely to become involved, more likely to seek feedback from others, and more likely to risk self-disclosing statements. Friedlander (1970) showed that in a sample of groups within an organization undergoing training, those with high trust were the ones in which change persisted.

While few researchers in groups have made studies of trust development, some studies are available which examine the intensity of members' involvement in their groups. Lieberman et al. (1973) identified members of their groups who occupied what they termed the VCIA role (value, congruence, influence, activity). VCIA members were those who had values which accorded with the group and became influential and active in them. It was found that VCIA members were particularly likely to be high learners, especially where their central role in the group occurred in the later part of the group. Archer (1974) tested a similar hypothesis. He found that in the groups he studied, those members who achieved a relatively high status in the group showed increases in self-esteem, whereas those who achieved a low status showed decreases in self-esteem. In neither of these studies is it suggested that these effects are due to different personality patterns of those who achieve high or low status. Indeed, Lieberman et al. point out that since the effect is found more strongly for those holding the VCIA role late in the group, it is much more likely to be an effect of the group context than of the personality that the individual brings to the group.

High involvement and status in the group do not come about in some arbitrary manner. Most likely they come about because the group makes opportunities for certain individuals to contribute to the group behaviours which others value highly. One such behaviour is likely to be a certain amount of self-disclosure. As detailed in Chapter 2, Lieberman et al. found that, considering all types of self-disclosure, there was no significant relationship between self-disclosure and lasting change. However, more detailed analysis revealed that those showing lasting change were more likely to have self-disclosed about present feelings in the group, feelings of happiness or pride, and feelings of fear or weakness. High learning was also associated with self-disclosure which led to some kind of personal insight about oneself. Thus the difficulty in relating self-disclosure to learning may derive from a difficulty in defining what is and is not self-disclosure. In the context of the group it appears that disclosure related to present events in the group was effective in generating learning, whereas self-disclosure about more general aspects of one's life was less so.

Concepts such as trust, involvement, and self-disclosure are closely related to the conception which Carl Rogers (1970) has of learning processes in groups. Rogers sees learning as arising from the development of a context of care and acceptance within a group. As he sees it, this will develop of its own accord given time, but the leader may facilitate this process by offering a model of caring, listening, involvement, and empathy. The Rogerian facilitator would avoid making interpretations of group or individual behaviour, and would also not impose any particular structure either on a group or on a training programme as a whole. The Rogerian facilitator thus seeks to influence the way the group develops but not to control it. Studies showing trust, involvement, and self-disclosure to be related to group outcome can therefore, in a general sense, be seen as supporting the Rogerian model.

Progress review

The varied theoretical positions so far sketched out briefly in this chapter all leave something to be desired. Each one selects some particular facet of group experience and asserts that this facet is the key one. What each position fails to address is the question of *why* that particular facet should be selected as critical. Once one adopts one of the positions so far touched upon, it is not difficult to find a certain amount of empirical evidence in support of that position, as has been shown. However, the evidence is fragmented and can usually be reinterpreted in terms of one of the other theoretical positions. For instance, one might argue that highly involved VCIA members would not only be more self-disclosing but would also be more likely to attract feedback from others. Thus, data relevant to involvement might well prove not to contradict hypotheses about the role of feedback in learning.

A second difficulty is that in seeking a theory of change in groups, one can very easily fall into an implicit assumption that there is only one mechanism by which change arises in groups. Studies which have used multiple criteria of learning (Miles, 1965; Lieberman et al., 1973; Smith, 1971; De Julio et al., 1977) have shown that those who learn most on one criterion frequently do not do so on another. It could well be that there is a whole range of different ways in which people may learn from one another, some of them more frequent than others.

The remaining sections of this chapter will be devoted to a more extended presentation of theories which attempt to explain why change which arises in groups is maintained afterwards. It is argued that predicting durability of change must take precedence over all other theoretical predilections, since the purpose of almost all groups is the creation of such change. This shift in emphasis requires a reformulation of the questions already discussed. If this line of thinking is adopted, the question ceases to be 'How do group members respond to feedback, trust, interpretation, involvement, etc?' and must become instead 'Why should feedback, etc. lead to long-term changes in the feelings or behaviour of trainees?'. Answers to such questions may well suggest that of the range of possible ways of changing, some are much more likely to be durable than others. If this proves to be so, it will be further argued that it is the durable forms of change which are more interesting, both theoretically and practically.

Learning how to learn

Schein and Bennis (1965) propose a model of change which lays some stress on learning through feedback, but which identifies in addition the trainee's prior need to learn how to learn. By this they mean that before group members can start to benefit from the potentialities of the group, it is necessary for them to understand the bases of learning in that setting. For instance, they need to learn that paying attention to one's feelings and to the here-and-now behaviour of others is important, as well as taking risks in seeking and giving feedback to others. These aspects are referred to as the *metagoals* of training. The distinction between metagoals and actual learning is in some ways helpful, in that it reduces a confusion which is apparent in the feedback model of group learning. Somehow, under the feedback model, the trainee's learning was seen as free and unconstrained and yet at the same time dependent on the need to give and receive feedback in a particular specified way. The Schein and Bennis model clarifies this by acknowledging that the metagoals are provided by the staff, rather than arising spontaneously. They analyse why it is likely that participants will accept these metagoals. Basically they see acceptance arising from the fact that, in the training setting, existing models of learning are disconfirmed whereas the new model of learning provides psychological safety in an uncertain setting. The Schein and Bennis theory postulates that the persistence of what is learned after training is determined by how well the new learning fits in with the trainee's own personality, and how well it fits in with the trainee's relationships at work and at home.

This model provides a challenging characterization of learning in groups. Regrettably, very few researchers have conducted their studies with its hypotheses directly in mind. This may well be because the model comprises various elements, some of them more amenable to test than others. Perhaps the model's most distinctive feature is the assertion that learning how to learn in a group must precede the actual process of substantive learning. This way of formulating the process does not appear promising, as it implies that learning how to learn and actual learning are logically separate, so that what is learned is not in any way affected by the prior learning of how to learn. An example will illustrate the unlikelihood of this. Suppose a participant attends a group with the intention of increasing skills in working with others. If this person learns in the group that they frequently ignore the feelings of others and that there is value in attending closely to here-and-now behaviour, these learnings are likely to provide the major basis for change after the group. In other words, in this instance and probably in many others, the learning how to learn is not a precondition to learning, it *is* the most substantial learning arising from the experience.

The concept of learning how to learn has high potential as the basis for a model of change, because it measures up well to the criterion formulated earlier – it has implications for the durability of change after the group. If participants acquire from the group a new way of learning from situations, we may expect that they will try this out in other settings which are important to them. Whether or not this new mode of learning is sustained will then depend on the nature of these other settings.

One of the most readily testable of Schein and Bennis's propositions is that which concerns what causes people to learn how to learn, namely the concurrent experience of disconfirmation and of psychological safety. A similar view has been advanced by Harrison (1965), who sees change in more cognitive terms:

> . . . for integrated cognitive growth, a person should at all times have both a 'castle' and a 'battlefield'. By a man's castle we mean that area of his life in which his cognitive equipment is viable and effective. By the battlefield we mean a set of experiences in which the individual is confronted with discon-firming and dissonant phenomena.
>
> (Harrison, 1965, p. 105)

The castle and battlefield of Harrison's model can readily be equated with the presence of trust and of feedback in the group. However the difference between the Harrison and the Schein and Bennis models and those outlined earlier is that these latter models require the simultaneous presence of both elements. Elsewhere in Harrison's formulation he labels these elements *support* and *confrontation*, and these terms will be the ones employed in subsequent discussion here.

Person-environment fit

One element in the Schein and Bennis model was their emphasis on how the durability of group effects was dependent on their relevance to the trainee's circumstances back at home and at work. Kolb and Fry (1975) have elaborated a model of change which treats the fit between the person's style of thinking and their environment as the central element. Kolb and Fry's model is built around a psychometric test, the Learning Styles Inventory. This categorizes people's learning styles as either concrete or abstract, and either reflective or active. Depending upon the combination of their prefer-ences on these two scales, people are designated as *accommodators* (active-concrete), *convergers* (active-abstract), *assimilators* (reflective-abstract), or *divergers* (reflective-concrete). Kolb and Fry suggest that each of these styles of learning is appropriate to some types of occupation. Preferences for one or other style arise in childhood and are accentuated through school and further education. Accumulation of particular types in a particular occupation would occur partly through work in that field, encouraging the development of the most relevant style of learning, and partly through those who found this style uncongenial leaving for other occupations.

Kolb and Fry see group experiences as the realm of the diverger. In an informal study at Massachusetts Institute of Technology, they found that the business students who chose to attend a T-group tended to be divergers, and that after the group their scores had moved further towards the divergent pattern. Other data collected by Kolb and Fry showed that among graduates divergers tended to be arts students, and that divergers are more interested in interpersonal relationships than others. Kolb and Fry would expect that those most likely to attend groups would be divergers, that divergers would learn more from groups, and that learning would be best sustained in settings where divergent thinking has some usefulness.

Steele (1968) studied the relationship of personality to learning in groups. He proposed that those who scored high on intuition rather than sensation on a test known as the Myers-Briggs Type Indicator would be more at home in a group. The distinction between those who prefer sensation (i.e., information directly available to the senses) and those who prefer intuition seems close to the concrete-abstract dimension of Kolb and Fry's model. Steele showed that intuitive group members were indeed more actively involved in the groups, but the relation to measures of change was only weak and there were no follow-up measures. He concludes that personality measures alone are unlikely to be successful at predicting who learns from a group.

The model of Schein and Bennis suggested that one of the key properties of a group may be that it can induce people to transcend the limitations of their particular learning style and acquire new modes of learning. In terms of Kolb and Fry's model, one might find that trainees who were not divergers learned how to learn in a divergent manner. Such change would be more substantial than that involved in divergers who simply continued to learn within their established mode. This line of thinking would suggest that those who learned most might be those who were initially most at odds with the group setting. Findings of this kind were obtained by Harrison and Lubin (1965), who found that group members categorized as work-oriented rather than those categorized as person-oriented tended to be seen as learning more. However, the effect did not achieve statistical significance in their small sample.

The person-environment fit model of Kolb and Fry is of some interest, but is difficult to evaluate. If it were the case that each person's learning style were fixed and immutable, the implications would be clear; groups should only be conducted for certain types of people, and other types of training experience would be appropriate for those who more readily learn in other ways. However, learning styles are clearly not immutable and some theorists (e.g., Schein and Bennis) see the modification, or at least diversification, of learning style as central to the purpose of groups. The empirical evidence relevant to these issues is insufficient to provide the basis for any adjudication.

The learning of personal responsibility

This section takes up themes already expressed but formulates them in a more direct manner. This directness derives from the models of change advanced by some of those most active in the development of encounter groups. The central element in this model is the conceptualization of learning as the creation of experiences in which trainees accept responsibility for their feelings and behaviour. As Perls et al. (1951) put it:

> One cannot on any ground take responsibility for what one is not in contact with. This applies to happenings in distant places, of which perhaps one has never heard, but it also applies equally to events taking place in one's own life if one is not aware of them. If one makes contact with them and becomes intimately aware of what they are and how they figure in one's functioning, then one becomes responsible for them – not in the sense of now having to assume some burden which was not there before, but rather in the sense of now recognising that it is oneself who determines in most instances whether they shall or shall not continue to exist.

The procedures employed by Perls and others to teach personal responsibility are a good deal more direct than those envisaged in the learning how to learn model. Although there may be much in common between the essence of learning how to learn and the taking on of personal responsibility, the participant who is learning how to learn is mostly seen as relying on indirect teaching. Clients in Perls' Gestalt therapy receive very direct guidance once they have accepted a contract to 'work' with the therapist. For instance, the client may be told to attend to present feelings, to accept nonverbal behaviours or body postures as expressions of feeling, to say 'I' rather than 'we', 'it', or 'one', to say 'and' rather than 'but', and 'won't' rather than 'can't'. In all such ways the taking of personal responsibility for one's present responses is encouraged.

The personal reponsibility model is a model of change in self. It is assumed that once one has learned to take responsibility for a particular aspect of oneself, this process will continue outside the training setting. A sharp differentiation is thus made between the learning of personal responsibility and its application. In the learning phase very detailed and precise instruction is provided, while in the application phase such instructions are not available. In practice the two phases are unlikely to be so sharply differentiated. Within the training setting there is likely to be an element of paradox. If I do accept responsibility for my actions, there is no particular reason why I should wish to continue accepting instruction. If I do not accept responsibility I am more likely to carry out instructions, but the instruction will have failed in its purpose if I do so.

The delineation of the paradox at the centre of the personal reponsibility model in no way diminishes its potential usefulness. It may very well be that the sharpness with which this model is formulated permits the identification of a paradox which underlies all approaches to group training. Even where the learning model utilized does not provide for such direct teaching by the group leader, the leader's very presence implies that that setting is somehow more real or more important for learning than is everyday experience. The trainee must then wrestle with the paradox that the setting is both real and artificial. If I see the group as more real than the rest of life, I make it artificial by separating it from those other aspects of life. If I see it as artificial and unlike life, I deny the reality of potential learning implied by the leader's presence.

The role of experienced paradox in inducing change is only now beginning to be explored. In addition to Gestalt therapists, various others have developed approaches to therapy in which the client is instructed to sustain or even amplify his symptoms (Frankl, 1971; Watzlawick et al., 1974; Haley, 1977). The importance of paradox in evaluating the personal responsibility learning model is that it provides a potent source of hypotheses as to why that model might induce lasting change. Just as learning how to learn may rest upon the concurrent experience of both support and confrontation, so may the learning of personal responsibility rest upon the concurrent experience of instruction and autonomy. The author's own theory of learning in groups is closely related to these viewpoints, but before presenting this it would be appropriate to consider other sources of thinking concerning development in the awareness of self.

Awareness of self

The majority of changes after group experience that were reviewed in the previous chapter comprised changes in trainees' perception of themselves. To be sure, there were also changes in how trainees were perceived by others, which provides some reassurance that the changes in self-percept obtained do have consequences visible to others. Nonetheless, changes in self-percept appear to be a central component in change after groups.

The study of one's awareness of self has a long history both within psychology and outside of it. Carl Rogers is said to have made the concept of self a central component in his theory of personality because clients so frequently referred to their self in the course of talking with him. Sociologists such as Mead (1934) have distinguished different aspects of self such as the 'I' who continuously experiences consciousness, and the 'Me' who is able to stand apart and be aware of the person it is who experiences the 'I' experiences. They stress the role of others' reactions in the creation of one's self-concept. In a similar manner, Rogers (1951) argues that the child's awareness of others' reactions leads it to learn to tell lies to itself and to others in order to sustain a conception of self which is consonant with the demands placed on us by others.

The difficulty with formulations of self-concept is to structure them in such a manner so as not to create a whole series of subselves or subpersonalities within the self. While such fragmentation has some intuitive appeal, it goes against the unified quality which is to be found in most people's behaviour. If one asks people to describe themselves, they are usually very willing to do so, for example by sorting cards on which are written self-descriptive statements into piles which are more or less like oneself. Such procedures, which have frequently been used by Rogerian researchers, have some usefulness, but what they do not tell us is how aware people *normally* are of themselves. Instead they tell us how people describe themselves when attention is drawn to them.

Findings using somewhat more indirect methods are available from attribution theorists in social psychology. Jones and Nisbett (1971) asked students to explain why they behaved in certain ways and why their friends behaved in certain ways. They showed that friends were seen as behaving as they did because they had a particular personality. On the other hand explanations of one's own behaviour were more frequently couched in terms of the environment and situational pressures. Jones and Nisbett suggest that this effect arises because in the case of oneself, one is aware of how one has behaved in numerous previous settings, so that the variability of one's own behaviour is all too evident. In the case of friends, the range of settings in which one has observed them is more restricted, so it is much easier to see them as having a unified personality.

The Jones and Nisbett data suggest that reflecting upon one's behaviour may lead one to see oneself as weak or inconsistent. Duval and Wicklund (1972) go so far as to postulate that objective self-awareness (i.e., the awareness of oneself as an object) is an aversive state. In a series of experiments they showed that simply placing a mirror on the wall of a psychology laboratory made it more likely that people would blame themselves for failures in various hypothetical circumstances which the experimenter asked them to evaluate. This tendency did not occur when the experimenters distracted the subjects' attention from themselves by giving them other tasks to perform concurrently. Duval and Wicklund's formulation has required some subsequent revision. Wicklund (1975) acknowledges that where positive feedback is received, objective self-awareness may be a positive state, although he believes this to occur only rarely. Davis and Brock (1975) showed that when subjects were in front of mirrors or cameras, positive feedback enhanced their degree of self-focus. Duval and Hensley (1976) present evidence suggesting a strong link between focus of attention and the attribution of causality. In other words, their proposal is that where we attend to our own behaviour we see ourself as causal, whereas when we attend to the environment we do not see ourselves as causal.

Jones and Nisbett's (1971) proposal is of course rather close to this hypothesis. One study which helps point up the linkage between these ideas and the effects of groups is that by Storms (1973). Storms made video tapes of conversations between two people (whom he termed *actors*), each of whom was watched by a separate observer. He found that, as predicted, the observers were more certain in their ratings of the actors' behaviour than were the actors themselves. The observers saw the actors' behaviour as caused by the actors' personality, whereas the actors saw their behaviour as caused by the situation they were in. Storms then created a reversal of the experimental situation through the use of video tape. In this condition, each actor was asked to watch the video of himself, while each observer was asked to watch the video showing the conversation partner of the actor previously observed. Under these circumstances the pattern of ratings was reversed. After the actor had watched himself on video, he saw his behaviour as more personally caused. After the observer had watched the video of the conversation partner, he rated the situation as more important in determining how the actor had behaved. Thus, by a reversal of the attention of actor and observer, Storms achieved a complete reversal in the perceptions of causality about the actor's behaviour. His study supports the view that one way to enhance people's sense of personal causality is to make them more aware of their own behaviour.

Langer (1978) has advanced an intriguing critique of some aspects of attribution theory. She suggests that in everyday life many of our actions are not based on thought, but on the application of well-learned routines which are triggered by events similar to those we have experienced many times before. Children, she suggests, frequently do think out what to do in a particular situation, which is why they are often slower than adults. However, with increasing age, an ever larger proportion of situations are assumed by us not to require such active thinking. Thus particular behavioural routines, once learned, may be performed dozens or hundreds of times without our ever reviewing them. In her view, then, the proportion of situations in which we actively enquire whether we can or cannot cause a particular behavioural effect is low. A variety of empirical studies supports her view.

Implicit in Langer's view is the idea that the situations in which one does not need to think about oneself are those in which one is receiving no evidence that anything has gone wrong. By contrast, if something does go wrong, the reactions of both oneself and others will soon start one thinking. This provides the opportunity for a further differentiation of one's perception of self and others. While one's own feelings of inadequacy or failure are readily available, those of others are less frequently made visible. By faulty sampling one may readily learn to see oneself as having more of almost any negative quality than others. Clinical applications of attribution theory (Strong, 1970; Valins and Nisbett, 1971; Storms and McCaul, 1976) mostly explore the manner in which clients blame themselves for failures or deficiencies which they see as uniquely caused by their own inadequacy. The treatment favoured by these theorists consists of enabling the client to discover that others frequently experience a similar difficulty when faced with the same circumstance. Thus they strive to temper the client's negative feelings with more positive and supportive ones.

In nonclinical settings people may only be willing to sustain attention upon themselves if that turns out to be a pleasant rather than an unpleasant experience. Taylor and Koivumaki (1976) asked people to make ratings as to why they themselves or various others might behave in particular ways. They found strong support for the view that favourably evaluated behaviours are seen as personally caused, whereas unfavourably evaluated behaviours are seen as situationally caused. One might therefore expect the effect obtained by Storms (1973) only to hold where the experience was a pleasant one.

This excursion into theories of self and of causal attribution leads to the conclusion that the experience of the self as causal rests on two circumstances: (1) something occurs which leads the individual to focus attention on self rather than others or the environment; (2) the focus of attention on self proves to be more pleasant than unpleasant.

A typological theory of change

The possibilities of building linkages between some of the theories of change in groups examined earlier and the attributional perspective introduced in the previous section appear excellent. It was argued earlier that some of the more promising formulations of learning in groups were built around the notion that the experience of paradox is central to change. The prerequisites were expressed as safety plus disconfirmation (Schein and Bennis), or support plus confrontation (Harrison). One might expect that, initially in a group, members will employ well-rehearsed strategies for relating to and getting to know strangers. Quite frequently such procedures will be challenged by other members or by the lack of support for them from the leader. In this way group members are likely to quickly become self-conscious. The somewhat slower, but highly predictable, growth of warmth and cohesion in the group will provide the support and safety which are required if the group is to meet the second condition for the experience of self as causal. The developing procedures of feedback and self-disclosure will provide further instances of both support and confrontation.

Smith (1976(a)) has advanced a theory which seeks to specify what will happen both when the requisite mixture of support and confrontation is present and when it is not. The theory is expressed in terms derived from the work of Kelman (1958). Kelman distinguishes three types of social influence processes, which he terms *compliance, identification*, and *internalization*. Compliance is said to occur where person A has 'means control' over person B. In other words, B goes along with A's demand that B behave differently, because if not A has the capacity to administer punishments or to withhold rewards. Identification is said to occur where A is attractive to B. B goes along with A's preferences so as to sustain a rewarding relationship with A. Internalization is said to occur where B makes changes in behaviour because it is apparent that those changes would have some personal utility. B derives the idea of making the change from A, who is observed to have goals which are congruent with B's goals, but who is seen as able to achieve some of these goals more effectively than B.

The processes of compliance and identification are clearly instances of change which can be attributed to the influence of others. Kelman foresees that change based on these processes is likely to be strongly restricted by the reactions of others subsequent to the group. Only where the pressures for change concur, both during the group and afterwards, will these changes persist. By contrast, internalization is formulated in terms of B's *choice* to change. The prospects for the continuance of such change after the group are much greater.

Smith (1976(a)) proposes that compliant changes will occur where a group member is confronted by the perceived demands of another. For instance, a member may see the leader as requiring him or her to act in a particular way. Such change may be a relatively small component of change in groups, but it certainly occurs. In a similar way, change based on identification will occur where a member experiences support from another. In warm, cohesive groups this may be a much more frequent influence mode. The process of internalization is seen as the most important element in group learning, since it is predicted that this type of learning will persist more strongly than other types. Internalization occurs where the group member is influenced by those who are *both* supportive and confronting. The definition of internalization thus reflects the two-factor learning models discussed earlier. The use of the term confrontation in the definition of internalization requires some explanation. What is envisaged is not the type of overt demand which might characterize compliant influence. The confrontation is an *intra*personal one in which the individual is aware that there is some goal which they would like to achieve, and which some other member of the group evidently can achieve. Andrews' (1973) use of the term *challenge* might better capture its essence.

The three types of learning outlined in the Smith model may be seen as alternative ways of learning in a group, or possibly as types of learning likely to happen during different phases of group development. It is not envisaged that they would necessarily correspond to different personality types, since each is contingent on the availability of different patterns of social influence within the group. Korn (1975) has advanced a model of change with some similarity of conception, deriving it from more sociological sources. Korn sees change in a group passing from a stage where one is seen in the third person as an object (sociocentric), through a stage where one is seen as relating to others but only in such a way as to sustain one's self-concept (autocentric), to a final stage where one sees oneself as an active agent in developing and changing mutual relations with others (allocentric). Neither Smith nor Korn have undertaken empirical tests of the application of their theories to group development, but there does appear to be some resemblance between the different types of relationship each describes and the studies of group development reviewed in Chapter 2.

Smith (1976(a)) has developed measures of the type of influence processes experienced by participants during sensitivity training. The measures were based on ratings of how much different individuals in the group had influenced them, liked them, were trusted by them, and behaved in ways that made them tense. By use of these ratings, each group member's predominant mode of influence at the close of the group was determined. The study also included ratings of how much each person had benefitted from the group. Ratings were completed concerning oneself and all other group members. Ratings were also made by the trainers. Further ratings on the same scale were obtained by mail five months after training. The sample comprised 199 members of English T-groups. In analysing the data, those whose influence in the group had been compliant and those who had identified with others were grouped together and referred to as externalizers. It was found that at the end of the one-week groups, internalizers and externalizers did not differ in amount of benefit as rated by themselves and as rated by others in the group. However, the trainers saw internalizers as having benefitted more. After five months the ratings of benefit for externalizers had sharply decreased, both for self-ratings and for ratings by others where these were available. In contrast, the ratings for internalizers showed no significant decrease from those made at the end of the group. The findings were thus entirely as predicted; both types show change during the group, but externalizers show fade-out of the effects while internalizers do not. The fact that trainers could already distinguish internalizers from externalizers at the close of the group is presumed to be due to their greater experience and consequent awareness that not all change in a group is likely to be durable.

This study provides a firmer test of two-factor theories of learning in groups than was hitherto available, primarily because it included a follow-up measure. However, the evidence is still far from conclusive, since the study included no untrained control group. Smith (1980(c)) reported further data. In this study group members were asked to make ratings of change they had experienced both before and after training, thereby providing own-control data. Ratings were included for the amount of change in oneself, evaluation of change, and whether change was perceived as caused by oneself or by external factors. It was found that after the group, as compared with before the group, more change was reported, the change was more favourably evaluated and the change was seen as more personally caused by the trainee. When the sample was subdivided between those classified as internalizers and those classified as externalizers, it could be seen that the effects reported were almost entirely due to the internalizers.

A number of the outcome studies reported in Chapter 3 indicated that among the effects of groups are increases in perceived personal causality. For instance, some studies showed increases in inner-directedness as measured by the Personal Orientation Inventory, while others showed increased internal locus of control on Rotter's Scale. Rettig's (1978) measure was particularly close to the present conception. He found increased use of personal rather than situational explanations of one's behaviour. The main significance of Smith's findings is not that they extend the range of studies showing enhanced personal causality after groups, but that they relate these increases to a specific theory of what needs to occur within groups if the changes are to occur. One further investigation utilizes ideas which relate to this discussion. The study by Lieberman et al. (1973) includes a chapter by Allen, who studied the maintenance of change after the groups were over. She found that those who succeeded in maintaining change stressed the taking of personal initiatives, thinking out what one wanted to do and so forth, as might be expected of internalizers. Those who had failed to maintain change laid greater stress on the reactions of others subsequent to training, which is the pattern one might expect for externalizers. The search for further empirical data relevant to the Smith model is frustrated by the fact that so many of the published studies of groups are *either* evaluations of outcome *or* studies of process during training. Studies of group process will be explored in the subsequent two chapters, while this one concludes with a consideration of how much has been achieved in formulating a model of change in groups.

Critique

A great many theories of learning in groups have been propounded, only some of which have been treated in this chapter. As in other parts of the book, priority has been given to those which have been, or look as though they could be, tested empirically. From within this range it has been argued that theories which postulate enhanced personal causality show particular promise. This is because they propose that a single unifying framework can account for the diversity of changes found after groups. If a group member learns how to learn, i.e., discovers that by paying attention to relevant data his or her behaviour can be adapted to achieve the goals intended, a tremendous range of subsequent behavioural changes can become possible. In the light of this formulation, the views advanced by many authors that different people learn different things from groups must be seen as a kind of 'null hypothesis'. It remains true as a generalization only until such time as someone can successfully hypothesize what it is that links the various changes found.

How successful is the personal causality model in accounting for the data? Here the question must be divided into two parts. A number of theories converge on the notion that two separate factors are required to account for learning. A smaller number of theorists link this to the enhancement of personal causality. Two-factor theorists are somewhat vulnerable to the criticism that what they delineate may be only one of several ways in which people learn in groups. While the Smith model distinguishes some subsidiary styles of learning, which can sometimes yield learning which persists, there may well be quite other types of learning which occur in groups as well. For instance, Oatley (1980) finds the two-factor theory persuasive concerning learning about oneself, but postulates an entirely different mechanism for learning about others in groups. He sees this as occurring through the modification or change of the 'scripts' on which we rely in order to relate to others. Learning about such scripts would involve a greater degree of conscious insight than might be required for the simpler discovery that one could now behave in a way which had previously proved difficult. The investigations by Yalom and others with which this chapter began also suggested a range of different ways of learning. While it does appear that the learning mechanisms identified as most frequent by Yalom, such as inter-personal input, catharsis, and cohesiveness, would be encompassed by measures of support and confrontation, some of the less frequent mechan-isms would not. The evidence for the two-factor theory is also still rather scant. Further evidence is required from a broader range of groups, using more specifically focussed measures of change.

The proposal that enhanced personal causality underlies at least some of the variety of changes which are found after groups requires some scrutiny. The changes found are, of course, changes in subjective estimates of one's causality. Outside of the psychology laboratory, determination of objective causes for events is rarely practicable. The linkage between objective causality and subjective causality is not certain and may sometimes be at odds, but an increase in subjective causality must make more probable an increase in objective causality also. Those who do not believe themselves to be causal are unlikely to take initiatives to influence events. On the other hand, those who do see themselves as causal will do so, and consequently will at least sometimes *be* causal. To some degree, belief in one's personal causality is a self-fulfilling prophecy. De Charms (1968) reviews a number of studies which support the view that those who perceive themselves as 'origins' of their behaviour do indeed act differently to those who perceive themselves as 'pawns' of others behaviour.

In this discussion, belief in one's personal causality has been presented as a unitary trait. Such an oversimplification has also characterized, for instance, Rotter's (1966) work on the internal locus of control. In Rotter's case the oversimplification has not prevented the discovery of numerous empirical correlates of high internality. In terms of the individual's awareness of self, a unitary perception of one's personal causality is improbable. Most people are likely to be quite confident that they can cause themselves to behave in certain ways, such as greeting a stranger amicably for instance, but much less sure of their ability to control their feelings or behaviours in a less routine event. Enhancement of personal causality after training might therefore better be seen as an increase in the *range* of feelings and behaviours which the individual feels able to control.

A crucial element in the argument presented has been that enhanced personal causality is a function of events which lead trainees to attend to their own behaviour. Further clues as to the circumstances which lead people to do this may well be found in allied fields such as psychotherapy. Studies of those therapist techniques which are most effective both in individual and group therapy are worthy of consideration, and these can most usefully be considered in Chapter 5.

One further difficulty attends the use of causal concepts in the model. Some critics of attribution theory argue that while theoretical development in this field is an entirely worthwhile endeavour, enabling us to come much closer to the way people experience life, we still have not devised adequate ways of asking people about their intentions and perceived powers. For instance, people are on the whole not given to saying that they feel able to cause a certain event. Buss (1978) has argued that the clumsiness of this aspect of attribution theory arises from confusion of causes with reasons. People may find it easy to say what caused someone else to behave in a certain way, but they would usually expect to respond to enquiries about their own behaviour in terms of reasons rather than causes.

These various points imply some directions in which further thinking about models of change may prove fruitful. For the present, a further test of the usefulness of the two-factor theory is provided by an examination of studies of processes occurring within group training programmes. These will be explored in Chapters 5 and 6.

Summary

Numerous authors, from all the main theoretical positions in psychology, have advanced models of learning processes in groups. It was argued that the most useful of these are those which attempt to explain why change persists after the group in some instances but not in others. A more detailed discussion of the theories of Schein and Bennis, Harrison, Perls, Smith, and Korn shows some common elements. It is suggested that several of these identify learning as occurring where two paradoxical messages impinge on the learner, the messages being identified as support and confrontation. Where this occurs, the learner is seen as able to take greater personal responsibility for actions and therefore able to sustain changes subsequent to the group. A review of experimental studies undertaken by students of attribution theory supports the proposition that the conditions required for such increases in personal causality are that (1) the person attends to their own behaviour, and (2) the experience proves more pleasant than unpleasant.

Section 2

The Creation of Effective Group Work

CHAPTER 5
THE LEADER'S BEHAVIOUR

There is a wide measure of agreement that the leader is a key element in the creation of effective group learning experiences. This certainly does not mean that everyone is agreed as to what is the basis of that importance or how it may best be exercised. While some see the role of the leader in terms of active initiatives, others argue that many important events in groups occur not because of activities initiated by leaders, but because they do *not* initiate or respond to others in the conventional manner.

A basic level at which to start thinking about the role of leader is to consider studies of groups in which the leader function is deliberately omitted. Desmond and Seligman (1977) review a range of such studies, but few of them can truly be said to have dispensed with the leadership function. In many of the studies reviewed, the leader is replaced by a set of tape recorded instructions. The effectiveness of such groups is examined in Chapter 8, but for the present purpose they cannot be accounted truly leaderless, since the tapes do provide precisely structured statements as to what the group should spend its time doing. Most of the remaining studies reviewed by Desmond and Seligman concern the procedure used in some types of group therapy, whereby the leaders deliberately do not attend certain sessions of the group. This procedure has been shown to have positive consequences under some circumstances (and negative ones under other circumstances), but it too cannot be considered as representing a leaderless group. These groups do have known leaders, who are absent for a preplanned and publicly known duration. In short, it is not possible to shed light on what might happen in leaderless groups because the widespread belief that leaders, or some substitute for them, are essential has precluded any substantial study of leaderless groups.

There is a good deal of evidence that leaders are highly influential members of their groups. Lohmann et al. (1959) found that participants' perceptions of the leaders became more similar to the leaders' self-percepts. Vansina (1961) found that participants' personal goals became more similar to those of the leaders, as measured by a card-sorting task. Psathas and Hardert (1966) showed positive relationships between T-group norms and the manner in which leader interventions were coded by observers. Peters (1973) obtained measures of the degree to which participants identified with their leader, and showed that those who did so became more similar to the leader and were rated higher on personal learning by themselves and by others in the group. Both Luke (1972) and Smith (1980(b)) showed that leaders were rated as significantly more influential in their groups than were group members.

Since it appears clear that leaders *are* highly influential, the key question can be addressed of what is it that they do which achieves this effect? A number of researchers have used the technique of factor analysis to attempt to identify dimensions along which leader behaviour might usefully be classified. Lomranz et al. (1972) provided group leaders with descriptions of hypothetical situations likely to arise in groups, and for each one asked them to select which of three possible responses they would prefer. They found, as they had anticipated, three types of leader focus which were labelled as 'personal and interpersonal effectiveness and learning', 'personal and interpersonal expanded experiencing', and 'personal and interpersonal remedial experiencing'. While such a typology provides a straightforward, if obscurely phrased, division between a traditional T-group style, a newer encounter-oriented one, and a more therapeutically oriented one, it appears that the structured format of the researchers' questionnaire may have predisposed the appearance of just such factors.

Biberman (1977) undertook a similar study but offered trainers twelve alternative responses to each incident. He found six factors: 'directive behaviour'; 'question, reflect, process group issues'; 'psychoanalytic'; 'self-disclose, show affect'; 'explain or analyse'; and 'do nothing'. These two studies asking leaders what they *would* do contrast with others which were based on actual behaviour in various kinds of groups.

Lieberman et al. (1973) factor-analysed a wide variety of data concerning leaders from their extensive study. They concluded that four dimensions of leader behaviour were discernible. These were termed 'emotional stimulation', 'caring', 'meaning attribution', and 'executive function'. Long and Bosshart (1974) factor-analysed ratings by staff members at two Rogerian workshops as to which participants might make effective facilitators. Three dimensions were found: 'generalized interpersonal sensitivity', 'ability to express a full range of spontaneous feelings and emotions', and 'nondirective style'. Cooper (1977) factor-analysed ratings of trainers by participants attending groups in management training programmes. He found a large first factor which he termed 'openness and congruency', and subsidiary factors termed 'supportiveness', 'low-authority-profile', 'extraversion', 'tranquillity', and 'task competence'. Bolman (1971) extracted seven factors from participants' ratings of leaders in his sample. In line with Cooper, his largest factor was termed 'congruence-empathy', while the others were 'conceptual input', 'conditionality', 'perceptiveness', 'openness', 'affection', and 'dominance'.

Factor-analytic studies have rarely proved decisive in resolving research controversies. The researchers in the six studies using this method who have been cited were of course sampling different populations, but it is difficult to know whether the differences in the factors they found stem from this, from the range of items they chose to include in their data sources, or from their differing preferences as to how many factors to extract from their analyses. The four factors of Lieberman et al. (1973) will provide a suitable framework for discussion here, both because their sample was more diverse than that of the other studies, and because it rests on a wider range of data sources. Material which does not fall readily within this framework will be discussed later in the chapter.

Lieberman et al.'s own conclusions were that the most effective group leaders were those who scored high on caring and meaning attribution, and moderately on emotional stimulation and executive function. These conclusions are based on their overall index of change at the close of the group. In their case, as in that of most of the studies to be discussed, trainers are assigned a single score on a dimension. In some studies the score represents how the leader behaved *on average*, while in other studies it represents how he or she was perceived by members of the group at the end. Variations in the leader's behaviour over time, or in the timing of particular interventions, are likely to be a vital element in their effectiveness and will be discussed in due course.

Caring

Caring is defined by Lieberman et al. as 'a leader style (which) involves protecting, offering friendship, love, affection, and frequent invitations for members to seek feedback as well as support, praise and encouragement'. It is clearly synonymous with the support dimension in some of the theories of group learning discussed in the previous chapter.

Babad and Melnick (1976) conducted a rather direct test of the relation between liking by the leader and the outcome of group experience for the group member. They found that those whom the trainers liked most were seen at the end of the group as having learned most both by the trainers and, more importantly, by other participants. The subjects of the study were women students of occupational therapy in Israel. In a further study (Babad and Amir, 1978), similar findings were obtained and it was shown in addition, that group members were able to assess accurately which members of the groups were best liked by the leaders.

Long and Schulz (1973) studied weekend Rogerian workshops. It was shown that two groups in which the leaders were rated high on accurate empathy were more successful than two other groups in which the leaders were rated lower on accurate empathy. The criteria of group success were ratings of the depth of exploration and accurate empathy of group members during sessions. Sampson (1972) hypothesized that student groups where the leaders liked those members who were also the most popular among group members, would do better than other groups where the leaders preferred unpopular members. The hypothesis was supported in a sample of six groups. Bugen (1978) compared eight groups and found that those which achieved greatest cohesion were those whose leaders most expected that they would learn and grow from the experience.

There is some question as to whether it is more fruitful to treat caring as a broad category, including for instance expectancy of success, empathy, and genuineness as well as liking, or whether more useful findings may be obtained by using concepts which are less diffuse. Bolman (1971) argues for more specific concepts. In his study, ratings of one's own and of others' learning at the close of the group proved to be related to perceptions of the leader as congruent and empathic, but not to perceptions of the leader as affectionate. Babad and Melnick (1976) suggest that this may have been because Bolman asked members to make ratings of whether the leader liked the group in general, rather than whether the leader liked the individual member. This seems possible, but Bolman's finding appears securely based as very similar results were obtained in a further study (Bolman, 1973). Hurley (1976) has developed an extensive critique of Bolman's findings. In essence he argues that the different measures developed by Bolman rested on very few different questionnaire items for each of the concepts employed, so that one could have little confidence that each had been validly measured. Hurley goes on to point out that Bolman also overlooked positive correlations between many of the dimensions he differentiates, and concludes that Bolman's results are not inconsistent with the notion that the trainer's impact on the group derives from a single dimension which he terms 'acceptance/rejection of others'.

One other researcher (Cooper, 1969) has explored the usefulness of differentiating the leader's attractiveness and the leader's genuineness. He showed that those who found the leader attractive showed changes in behaviour in the direction of increased similarity to the leader during the group, but on follow-up measures collected some months later, no change was found. On the other hand, those who perceived the leader as particularly genuine showed no change towards greater similarity to the leader during the group, but did show significant change on the subsequent follow-up measures. This study was somewhat influenced by the Smith model of group learning outlined in the previous chapter, and its findings are consistent with that model. It differs from the previously described studies of group leaders in two ways – it differentiates two types of change, and it incorporates a measure of the persistence of change after the group is finished. In line with the Smith model, it finds that the type of changes occurring most frequently within the group are not necessarily those most likely to persist afterwards. Change within Cooper's groups appears to have been most strongly related to the process of identification based on the leader's attractiveness. Change which persisted after the group was related to the leader's level of genuineness, which implies that where a leader is experienced as genuine, there are better prospects for the establishment of internalization-based influence in the group.

Cooper's finding suggests that although the establishment of a caring relationship between leader and group may be necessary for the creation of an effective learning group, caring by itself is insufficient to guarantee a lasting outcome. A series of studies by Lundgren indicate some further qualifications concerning the manner in which a caring relationship develops through the course of the group. Lundgren (1971) made a case study of the development of two T-groups. In the first group, the group leaders were initially inactive and this led to an increasing amount of frustration and criticism of the leaders' role. After a resolution of this crisis, the group developed a cohesive and productive climate, which included warm relations with the leaders. In the second group, the leaders were relatively active and directive from the outset. Members were initially favourable towards the leaders, but this group subsequently showed lower ratings of cohesion and productivity than the first one. Lundgren concluded that the creation of a learning climate in the group may require an initial crisis in which the leaders are confronted. Not all subsequent studies of group development (see Chapter 2) have found this to be necessary, but it is certainly of some importance to note that the groups which finish up with the strongest caring relationship between members and leaders may not be those that start off that way.

Lundgren (1975) studied changes in the attitudes of members towards the leaders at different points during the group. He found that, in order to comprehend the development of positive attitudes to the leader, he had to take account of the personality of both member and leader. Positive attitudes were particularly found early in the group where both leader and member had high control needs, and late in the group where they had low control needs. Studying a somewhat larger sample, Lundgren and Knight (1977) obtained a different finding. In this case they found that attitudes towards the leaders became more favourable over time, except in the case of those leaders who were low on both the need to control others and the need for affection. Lundgren (1976) found that group members tended to be attracted to others in the group who disliked the leader more than they themselves did.

The Lundgren studies do not at first give a clear picture of the manner in which a caring relationship develops between leader and group. This may well be because the studies have encompassed a wide range of types of group, including weekend groups (Lundgren, 1975, 1976) and residential ten-day groups conducted by NTL (Lundgren, 1971; Lundgren and Knight, 1977). The shorter-term groups yielded findings which reflected more ambivalence towards leaders and stronger relationships between personality compatibility and the development of a caring relationship. The longer-term studies suggested that by the end of a ten-day group, the great majority of group members felt warmly towards their leaders, and personality measures were thus less predictive.

The studies of caring as a component of effective leader behaviour have been more numerous than conclusive. Where the leader is attractive to members and is seen to like them, there is certainly a short-term effect, but whether or not this lasts is unclear. The Cooper (1969) study suggests that it would not. Lieberman et al. (1973) do not report directly on the persistence of change in terms of the different dimensions of leader behaviour. Instead they chose to delineate a number of leader types, whose behaviour approximates different combinations of scores on their various dimensions. They found that most of the differences between the types arose during the groups rather than afterwards. Only one other study is available which tests the relationship between caring behaviour of the leader and changes measured at follow-up. In this study (Cooper, 1977), ratings were obtained from work colleagues of changes in relationships after training. Measures were obtained after six weeks and again after seven months. It was found that the amount of change after six weeks was significantly related to trainer supportiveness and to leader competence, which comprised ratings of ability, enthusiasm, influence, etc. After seven months these correlations with change were no longer present, although a significant amount of change had persisted. The relationship between leader caring and long-term change is thus at best not proven.

The leader behaviours discussed in this section are those most strongly advocated by Carl Rogers in his approach to both psychotherapy and encounter groups. A great deal of research has been undertaken in clinical contexts to determine the impact of *facilitative conditions* provided by the therapist, i.e., high empathy, high genuineness, and high unconditional positive regard. Many studies have found positive links between these variables and positive therapy outcome. However controversy persists, for instance as to how it is most valid to determine whether these conditions are present or not. Early researchers mostly employed judges, who were asked to make judgements on excerpts from the tape recorded therapy. More recently the view has gained ground that what matters most is not whether an 'objective' judge believes empathy, genuineness, or positive regard to be present, but whether the actual patients in treatment do so. The more recent studies therefore employ methods more similar to those reviewed in this section. Gurman (1977) reviews such studies and shows that of twenty-two studies with patients seen individually, twenty-one reported significant relationships between outcome, and some or all of the Rogerian facilitative conditions. On the other hand, in the ten studies of group therapy, only one clearly supported the Rogerian view, with several others providing weak support.

Gurman suggests that the reason for the much weaker support for Rogerian theory in groups may be that the outcome of therapy in groups does not depend simply on what the therapist does, but also on whether or not group members develop a climate of facilitative relationships with one another. Gurman's review thus concurs with the conclusion of this section: caring behaviour by the leader in groups may help the group's development, but by itself it is insufficient to assure a lasting positive outcome.

Emotional stimulation

Emotional stimulation, according to Lieberman et al., 'represents leader behaviour which emphasises revealing feelings, challenging, confrontation, revelation of personal values, attitudes, beliefs, frequent participation as a member in a group, exhortation, and drawing attention to self'. This dimension overlaps with, but defines in a somewhat broader manner, the confrontation dimension of the models discussed in the previous chapter.

Some of the encounter leaders in the Lieberman et al. (1973) study engaged in a great deal of emotional stimulation in their groups. On the whole, however, leaders tend to use emotional stimulation somewhat sparingly and perhaps for that reason its impact has received much less attention from researchers than has the caring dimension. The principal type of emotional stimulation by the leader to be investigated has been self-disclosure. Self-disclosure by group members as a component of learning has been discussed earlier, but here we are concerned specifically with self-disclosure by the leader.

Culbert (1968) undertook an experiment with two T-groups, in both of which were the same two leaders. In one group they were deliberately more self-disclosing, in the other less so. Ratings were obtained as to how many of each member's relationships in the group were characterizable as mutually therapeutic, i.e., empathic, congruent, and so forth. The high self-disclosing group did not generate a higher proportion of mutually therapeutic relationships, but those that were found tended to be more centred on the leaders. The level of self-awareness judged to be present in tape recordings of sessions was also studied. It was found that self-awareness rose faster in the high self-disclosure group, but ultimately both groups arrived at the same point.

A more extensive study was that by Hurley and Force (1973), who studied five residential eight-day groups. Members made ratings of how far their leaders were self-disclosing and how far their leaders actively sought feedback themselves. These ratings were then related to measures of member change six months after the programme. It was shown that those trainers rated highest on self-disclosure and feedback-seeking were also those seen by members as the most effective. Each group had two leaders and the scores for each pair were pooled. Gains shown by the follow-up measures on acceptance of self and acceptance of others proved to be strongly related to the ratings of leader self-disclosure and leader feedback-seeking, both early and late in the group. Unfortunately these results are not as clear cut as at first appears. The ratings of self-disclosure employed asked members to assess many other aspects of the leaders' behaviour including, for instance, defensiveness and concern for others' feelings. The measure cannot therefore be considered a measure of 'pure' emotional stimulation, but has elements of caring as well. Another difficulty is that Hurley and Force combined the scores of all members of any one group, so that in the end all they had were five sets of data.

Moss and Harren (1978) attempted to study leader self-disclosure in a more detailed manner. Self-disclosures were rated in terms of their social desirability, concreteness, level of affect, relevance to the here-and-now, congruence, and vocal intensity. There was no overall tendency for leader self-disclosure to lead to member self-disclosure. However, high-affect disclosure by the leader did have a significant impact and the type of leader disclosure had some effect on the type of member disclosure. No direct measures of learning were included in the study.

Lieberman et al. (1973) found that in their study the leaders whose groups were most successful tended to be at a medium level in terms of emotional stimulation. Some of this type of behaviour from the leader was useful, but it was equally possible for leaders to do too much of it as to do too little of it.

Of the studies reviewed in this section the only one which provides direct evidence that emotional stimulation, or more specifically self-disclosure, has a lasting effect is that by Hurley and Force, whose measures may have been clouded by other variables. The effect is not proven, although it remains plausible.

Meaning attribution

Meaning attribution, in the words of Lieberman et al. (1973), 'involves cognitising behaviour – providing concepts for how to understand, explaining, clarifying, interpreting, and providing frameworks for how to change'. This dimension was found to be positively related to change, with effective leaders doing a relatively high amount of it. Very few other researchers have investigated variables relevant to this dimension, possibly because the values often prevalent in group training programmes favour learning through doing, rather than learning through instruction. Bolman's studies (1971, 1973) included ratings of conceptual input by the leaders, but these were found to be unrelated to members' ratings of their own and others' learning at the close of the group. However, Bolman (1975) acknowledges that his measures may only have picked up certain kinds of conceptual input. For instance, one of the questionnaire items which people were asked to rate was 'he gives short lectures on concepts relevant to current problems in the group'. Effective meaning attribution may well prove not to be a matter of lectures, but of leaders explaining why they do what they do, how they see the group relating to their own or others' lives, or why it may be fruitful to set the group up in a particular way. Leaders who do these things may well be rated as more genuine (which Bolman did find to be related to learning). The evidence for the importance of this dimension thus rests at present entirely upon the findings of Lieberman et al.

Executive function

Executive function is defined in terms of 'behaviours such as limit-setting, suggesting or setting rules, limits, norms, setting goals or directions of movement, managing time, sequencing, pacing, blocking, stopping, interceding, as well as such behaviours as inviting, eliciting, questioning, suggesting procedures for the group or a person, and dealing with decision-making' (Lieberman et al., 1973). These authors found that in their sample a medium amount of executive function was most effective. This finding is in some ways unfortunate, since it makes it difficult to compare with other studies, most of which have contrasted high structure with low structure. However, a closer examination of the Lieberman et al. data shows (p. 237) that one of their groups was extremely high on executive function, while only three others exceeded the midpoint on the scale. In the extreme case, the leader employed structured exercises virtually without pause throughout his group. For this reason it is probably true that what other researchers refer to as high structure would approximate what Lieberman et al. considered to be medium structure.

Aron (1968) compared student groups of up to forty hours with directive leaders and with nondirective leaders. Greater change on the California Psychological Inventory and the Rotter Locus of Control Scale was obtained in the directively led groups. However the directive and nondirective leaders were different people, so one cannot be sure that the effect was due to the amount of leader directiveness. In a better controlled study, Pino and Cohen (1971) found that two leader-guided T-groups achieved greater self-disclosure than two group-centred ones. Each pair of groups had the same leader. The groups met for a total of nine hours. Levin and Kurtz (1974) compared three pairs of groups with each pair once again having the same leader. In the structured condition, a programme of exercises was followed, whereas in the unstructured condition the leaders were inactive and nondirective at least initially, and used no exercises. The groups lasted a total of eighteen hours. Participants in the structured groups rated themselves as more involved, showing more change, and experiencing more group unity than those in nonstructured groups. Ware and Barr (1977) compared structured and unstructured group experiences lasting a total of twenty-four hours. The structured format included exercises concerned with analysing one's goals, strengths, use of time, conflicts, etc. Both groups showed gains on the Shostrom Personal Orientation Inventory and the Tennessee Self-Concept Scale which were not shown by untrained controls.

These studies suggest that structuring of the group by the leader does often enhance learning. However, the studies which provide the strongest evidence for this conclusion have concerned relatively brief types of group work. It would not be a valid inference from these studies to conclude that all types of group work would be more effective if highly structured. Indeed, Cooper and Bowles (1975) found that in a sample of one-week management training groups, the more highly structured ones had more members perceived by other members as 'hurt' than did the less structured groups. A more plausible inference would be that brief training may *require* that the leader structures an event. Where greater time is available, a broader range of options are open depending on how readily a particular set of training goals may be approached through a structured or unstructured format.

Some further researchers have investigated the use of structure during particular stages of the group but not others. Crews and Melnick (1976) used structured exercises either during the first half or the second half of groups totalling twenty-four hours. Controls had unstructured groups throughout. Early structure was found in this study to increase anxiety and self-disclosure, presumably because the exercises were found confronting, as may have been the case also in the Cooper and Bowles (1975) study. Structure late in the group had no effect on anxiety or self-disclosure. There were no differences in the levels of cohesion ultimately achieved by the groups. Kinder and Kilmann (1976) ran twenty-three-hour marathon groups in which the leader provided structure either early, late, both, or neither. Change was measured on the Shostrom Personal Orientation Inventory. It was found that group members who scored low on the Rotter Locus of Control Scale did equally well in all conditions. However, those who favoured an external locus of control did best where there was structure provided early but not late. In this setting, the ideal training format thus depended on the personality of the group member.

Bednar and Battersby (1976) varied the type of structure provided by way of introduction to two-hour group workshops. It was found that the most effective introduction was one framed in terms of specifying the behaviours to be followed, rather than outlining goals or providing suggestions. These further studies suggest that structure may be particularly useful in the early stages of groups, and for people who prefer to work within an established structure. Although a number of studies have shown positive effects of increased structure, it must be borne in mind that none of them includes any kind of follow-up measure. Increased structure is likely to set up influence patterns involving compliance or identification with the leader. The risk of high structure is that learning will prove nontransferable from the group setting. This may be why, for instance, Kinder and Kilmann (1976) found that even for those who did well with high initial structure, low structure later in the group was preferable. This would presumably be because the low structure provides an opportunity for members to take greater personal responsibility for their actions once a safe climate is established in the group.

Combinations of effective leader behaviours

In the previous chapter a model of group learning was advanced which proposes that *both* support and confrontation are required if group learning is to be internalized and hence retained. It need therefore come as no great surprise to find that the evidence in favour of each of Lieberman et al.'s four dimensions, when considered on its own, is not compelling. Very few of the studies of leader behaviour have tested for the persistence of the effects they found. Within the group the effects most frequently found have been those due to high caring by the leader and the provision of high structure.

Lieberman et al. (1973) also believed that it would be most fruitful to look at the impact of their different dimensions of leader behaviour in combination. They devised six different types of leader to exemplify the particular combinations they found. These types were named *energizers, providers, social engineers, impersonals, laissez-faire,* and *managers. Energizers* were charismatic figures who were, above all else, high on emotional stimulation. They were also high on executive function and medium to high on caring. Energizers achieved a positive impact with some members but their groups were also characterized by high dropout rates and some members adversely affected. Among those for whom follow-up data were available, 29% of those who attended groups led by energizers were seen as deriving lasting benefit.[1] *Providers* were those who scored high on caring and meaning attribution and moderate on executive function and emotional stimulation. They achieved the most successful outcome at the close of the group and this success increased subsequent to the group. At follow-up, 49% were seen as benefitting. *Social engineers* were characterized as high on meaning attribution, particularly with regard to the group as a whole. They were moderate on caring and low on emotional stimulation. Their effect was moderately positive and at follow-up 28% were seen as still benefitting. *Impersonals* were moderately high on emotional stimulation and low on other dimensions. Their groups had few positive changers, high dropout rates and some members were adversely affected. Positive follow-up change was found in 36% of respondents but the response rate was particularly low, and therefore potentially misleading for this category. *Laissez-faire* leaders were low on all dimensions except meaning attribution. Their groups had a high dropout rate and few changers. Lasting benefit was reported among 25%. The one leader classified as a *manager* was high on executive function and low on all other dimensions. His group had no positive impact at the time, but showed 17% benefitting at follow-up.

This study has been fiercely criticized by some (Schutz, 1975; Russell, 1978) for including some leaders who had little previous experience of work with student populations, and others with extensive experience who were nonetheless widely thought to be incompetent. To the researcher, if not to

1. The percentage given here for lasting benefit is derived from the data in Lieberman et al., (1973), p. 248. Lieberman et al. do not, however, compute overall percentage in this manner.

the apologist for groups, such diversity is an advantage. The study indicates the clear superiority of providers as leaders, even though only three of the fifteen leaders fell into this category. Lieberman et al. stress how the diversity of leaders included makes it clear that the leader who is high on both caring *and* meaning attribution is superior to other leaders who are high on one dimension but not the other.

A number of other researchers have examined combinations of the conditions required for learning. Bebout and Gordon (1972) surveyed over one hundred student groups at Berkeley. They delineated six types of group drawing on characteristics of both the leaders and the group climate. The most successful groups were found to be those in which members were active and expressive and the climate was warm and empathic. In these groups the leader was helpful and close, but not highly salient. Somewhat less successful groups were those in which leaders and members shared equally in a climate of high warmth and empathy, but in which no negative emotions were shared. In the less successful groups no climate of warmth was found, and the leader tended to be more active, presumably in an attempt to improve the prospects for learning in the group. In some of these groups the leader was also rated as unhelpful, but the least successful of all group types had no distinctive leader role. The Bebout and Gordon study was not linked to any particular model of learning, and differs also from the Lieberman et al. (1973) study in that the leaders in the groups were fellow-students; nonetheless there are some interesting convergences in the findings. Both studies agree that the most salient, central energizer style of group leadership is only moderately successful. Both agree that the most successful style is a leader seen as helpful and accepting. However, the Bebout study included no measures relevant to the meaning attribution dimension of leadership behaviour.

Hurley and Pinches (1978) made a further study of the programme earlier analysed by Hurley and Force (1973). Statements made by participants as to which behaviours by leaders had been helpful or unhelpful were content-analysed. High leader effectiveness was found to be related to two overall dimensions which were termed *love* and *dominance*. Measures of dominance were somewhat more strongly related to positive change than were measures of love. However, the most notable finding was that when the dominance and love measures were combined, the correlations with positive change were much more positive than for either dimension alone. This finding is very clearly consistent with the two-factor learning model and there is little difficulty in seeing love and dominance as synonymous with support and confrontation.

Bierman (1969) advanced a two-factor theory of change in individual psychotherapy. He proposed that effective therapy requires two components, affection and activity. Where the therapist is inactive but warm and supportive, therapy is only moderately effective. Where the therapist is both active and supportive, therapy is highly effective. Where the therapist is active but not supportive, therapy will be harmful rather than helpful. In reexamining the Lieberman et al. findings, Russell (1978) argues that they fit the model proposed by Bierman. It certainly is the case that Lieberman et al. found two factors to be important but whether they are the same two factors as those envisaged by Bierman, by the Smith model of learning, and by Hurley and Pinches, is less clear. All these authors agree that an element of support or caring is crucial. However, it is less certain that confrontation (Smith), activity (Bierman), dominance (Hurley and Pinches), and meaning attribution (Lieberman et al.) can be equated. One could certainly envisage behaviours where a leader provided feedback to a member which would be included within all four concepts. But many forms of active or dominant behaviour do not count as meaning attribution, and would more likely be considered as relevant to Lieberman et al.'s other main factor, emotional stimulation.

This difficulty most likely derives from differences between theorists as to whether to concern themselves with concepts of high generality (e.g., activity) or greater specificity (e.g., meaning attribution). Lieberman et al. do not explain why they chose to extract four factors from their analysis of leader behaviour, rather than some other number. If they had chosen a lesser number, it is entirely possible that the items comprising meaning attribution would turn out to be to some degree associated with those comprising emotional stimulation, which would make it easier to relate their findings to the other models. There may be nonetheless distinct benefits to the more differentiated approach of Lieberman et al. One way of expressing their findings would be to say that they have shown that only certain kinds of confrontation by leaders are fruitful: those in which leaders explain or clarify what they or others are doing. Whether this cognitive approach is of equal value in all circumstances, or whether it turned out to be important because Lieberman et al.'s group members were students at a high-prestige university, must await further investigation.

The leader and the group

The discussion in this chapter so far has gone along with two assumptions that are frequently made, but are unlikely to be true. The first of these is that the behaviour required of an effective leader will be the same in every group. It could of course be argued that what is required of the leader might be considerably different in one group than another, depending on the culture and history of that group. Such a viewpoint would be consistent with the situational theories of leadership developed by social psychologists. In more individual forms of training or therapy, we can be certain that the relationship between leader and trainee will be crucial. In group settings even this is not certain. As the Bebout and Gordon (1972) results suggested, where a group has established an effective learning climate, the best leader intervention may be to do nothing. Where a group does not have such resources, more active leadership would certainly be required. One way of conceptualizing this problem would be to see it as the leader's task to provide whatever elements of an effective learning climate are missing from a group.

A second pervasive assumption about leadership behaviour in groups is that the leader is a free agent in providing this or that behaviour. We often think of groups as though they passively received whatever input the leader provides, without ever exerting any reciprocal influence over the leader. Closer analysis will suggest that this assumption too is often ill-founded. This section will consider what makes it easy or difficult to diagnose and carry through a line of leader intervention in a group.

Studies of the group's influence on the leader are scattered and not highly conclusive. Hurley and Force (1973) obtained ratings of leaders' effectiveness from participants in a series of groups. Where the leaders had worked in more than one group, it was found that members of each group tended to evaluate them at about the same level. No statistical tests of this effect were made, but it suggests that these leaders did not vary their behaviour from group to group. Biberman (1977) made a questionnaire survey of group leaders, asking how they would react to various hypothetical group episodes, and also what types of episode did tend to crop up within their groups. He found little relation between the leaders' preferred modes of response and the types of episode which occurred. This implies that the events occurring in a particular group are mostly *not* caused by the leader's previous style of intervention. In other words, it is not so much appropriate to ask how a leader creates a particular group climate, but rather to ask how a leader diagnoses and responds to the climate and events of the developing group. A more direct test of trainer-group influence is reported by Lundgren (1974). He found that in a sample of seven groups, leaders' ratings of how they saw themselves moved closer to how they believed group members saw them. However, these perceptions did not correspond at all well with the way that group members did actually perceive them. This study does show leaders as responding to feedback from their groups; it also suggests that communication from member to group leader may be somewhat distorted.

A further study of leader-group relations was made by Smith (1980(b)). His data were derived from thirty-one English T-groups comprising a mixed professional population, conducted by the Group Relations Training Association. On the basis of ratings made by members, these groups were divided into four types, depending on whether trust was relatively high or low in the group and on whether tension was relatively high or low in the group. The association between the successful outcome of the groups and the leaders' behaviour was then examined separately for each of the group types. The index of success was a composite of ratings by self, others, and leaders, both at the close of the group and five months later. Overall it was found that group success was correlated with ratings of the leader as influential and trustworthy. However, differences were also found in what was effective leader behaviour in the various group types. When tension in the group was rated as low, there was a strong positive relation between group success and the leader being perceived as behaving in ways that made one tense. When tension in the group was rated as high, this pattern was not found. In terms of the two-factor learning model, these findings indicate that leader supportiveness is always helpful, but that confrontation by the leader is only helpful where the group is not already confronting.

Although this study used quite different measures and samples from Lieberman et al. (1973), the findings seem highly compatible. While the Lieberman et al. view was that moderate emotional stimulation by the leader was most effective, the Smith study shows that the required level is a function of the group's own culture. In some of the Lieberman et al. groups, high emotional stimulation amounted to extended verbal abuse, with in one case the leader punching and throwing a cup of coffee at a group member (Lieberman et al., 1973, pp. 41–46). The groups in the Smith study were more within the NTL tradition, as illustrated by the case study of one of them in Chapter 2. Nonetheless it appears that in these groups too, there was sometimes too much confrontation as well as too little. If leaders are to optimize their effectiveness they must attend to the culture of their group. In the Smith (1980(b)) study, eighteen of the thirty-one groups were led by leaders who led more than one group. This makes it possible to test further whether different leaders do tend to create a particular type of culture in their groups. No evidence for this was found; the range of group types led by any one leader was no more homogeneous than in the sample as a whole. The conclusion is inescapable that leaders do not create the climate of their groups. Leader skill lies in tailoring one's interventions to the emerging culture of the group.

Leaders of groups frequently face certain dilemmas and it is worth discussing them in the light of the findings already presented. A particularly frequent dilemma is that of how to relate to one's coleader, where there are two leaders in the group. Frankiel (1971) made a study of this problem, using also the concepts of support and confrontation. He argued that the trainer-cotrainer relationship provides a model whereby the group is shown the type of relating to others which the leaders favour. If the goal is to create relationships in the group which are both supportive and confronting, then the trainer-cotrainer relationship must demonstrate this. Frankiel's data showed that groups with cotrainers were in fact less successful than those with a single leader, thereby underlining the difficulty of achieving this goal. The problem most usually arises because the leaders tend to conceal some aspects of their relationship with each other from the group. Within the group they may either ignore one another or maintain a supportive camaraderie. Between sessions they may discuss with one another criticisms of what each has done, or differences in how they perceive what is happening in the group, but this facet of their relationship is withheld from the group. Unless leaders can find ways of acknowledging at least some of these things within their groups, they are likely to be discouraging rather than encouraging the emergence of internalization-based influence. A further difficulty identified by Frankiel is that where there are two leaders, groups frequently encourage a role differentiation between them whereby one becomes supportive and the other confronting. The model advanced in the previous chapter clearly indicates that where this occurs, the result will be an increased level of identification and a decreased level of internalization in the group. The only way out of this difficulty is for each of the leaders to ensure that their relations with group members are characterized by a balanced level of both support and confrontation.

A second dilemma occurring from time to time in groups has to do with the group making a scapegoat of an individual member. In terms of the two-factor model, this also must be seen as a splitting of the processes of support in the group from the processes of confrontation. In seeking to preserve an orientation towards internalization in the group, the leader will need to find elements worthy of support and of confrontation both in the majority faction and in the scapegoat. To do otherwise is to collaborate with the process of splitting, with a consequent loss of learning opportunities. A specific and quite frequent instance of this type of behaviour within a group is where the scapegoat is in fact the leader. It was seen in Chapter 2 that attacks on the leader are a crucial phase in group development, particularly in those types of group where the leader is inactive and analytic in orientation. Such leaders would describe the process as one of counterdependency. Whatever the leader's orientation, a successful outcome when it is the leader who is the scapegoat rests on the leader's ability not to collude with the splitting implicit in the process. This may be achieved, sooner or later, by showing that one is not destroyed by the process of being attacked, that one is interested in and responsive to what is said, that leaders have their own feelings and vulnerabilities, and so forth. O'Day (1973, 1976) has made a series of detailed case studies of the relation of four leaders to their groups. He concludes that the capacity to tolerate attack is crucial to leader effectiveness. Of the four leaders studied, the first tended to respond to attack by direct counterattack, the second was a warm and kindly father figure whose style tended to suppress hostility, and the fourth was cautious, apologetic, and anxious. Only the third, whom O'Day terms an 'emotional protagonist', was seen as optimally effective. He was able to accept and respond to a wide range of feelings towards himself and others. His stance was one of encouraging the group to explore the feelings expressed more fully and not to be satisfied with an oversimple view of anyone's reaction to anyone else.

A third dilemma which occurs with some regularity is that of group members who are overly dependent on the leader. Not all leaders would agree that this constituted a dilemma to the same degree as those previously discussed. A teacher-learner relationship can often be a dependent one, at least initially, but sooner or later the dilemma arises as to how to foster greater autonomy for the learner. If this is left until after the group is over, the task is essentially one for the members to resolve on their own. By facing it during the group, there is a greater chance that it can be more satisfactorily achieved. In terms of two-factor theory, excessive dependency is support without confrontation. The leader's dilemma is to find ways of confronting the group member's dependence which do not destroy the motivation to learn which the member has invested in dependency.

The Smith (1980(b)) findings stressed the need for the leader to adapt his or her behaviour to the specific group culture. The consideration of the specific dilemmas which have been outlined illustrates some of the ways in which this may be achieved. The leader needs to be able to keep the processes of support and confrontation within the group in balance. Where confrontation is focussed on the leader, the leader must find ways of responding supportively. Where support but no confrontation is focussed on the leader, some measure of confrontation is required in response. These specific examples also bring out the point that for the support and confrontation to be effective, it must bear a close relation to preceding events in the group. For instance, where a group member is closely dependent on the leader, the leader's confronting response is only likely to be effective if it actually confronts the member's dependency. Confrontation concerning some other unrelated aspect of the member's behaviour is unlikely to be effective.

The studies reviewed in this chapter do provide some guidelines concerning effective leader behaviour in groups. These guidelines turn out to be reasonably consistent with the model of learning advanced in Chapter 4. The precision of the research studies of leaders still leaves a good deal to be desired. Few studies involve follow-up measures, and the concepts upon which they are based often prove too broad to provide a definitive set of prescriptions for leader practice. However, the choice a leader faces may be seen in sharper focus. Leaders' effectiveness is not only determined by what occurs within their groups, but also by prior decisions about the design of the programme as a whole. These will be discussed next.

Summary

Effective leaders are those who provide a high level of support or caring *and* who confront group members in appropriately judged ways. Such ways will frequently include various forms of meaning attribution, and sometimes also emotional stimulation and executive function. The leader does not typically have the power to determine the culture of the group, and leader skill lies in being able to judge what balance of support and confrontation to provide within a given context. The guideline for effective leader behaviour is to seek to ensure that support and confrontation are provided by the same source(s), whether those sources be members or leaders.

CHAPTER 6
THE DESIGN OF TRAINING PROGRAMMES

Discussions of small group training frequently lay heavy emphasis on the facilitative role of the group leader. Whether training effects are achieved through structuring or inactivity, through caring or through meaning attribution, the leader's intervention style is seen as critical. This chapter attempts to show that other factors, also potentially within the influence of the leader, have an equally large effect on the outcome of group experiences. These factors include the manner in which the principal learning groups in a programme are composed, the design of other types of session in a programme, and the basis upon which participants join a particular programme.

Group composition

Where T-groups last for a substantial period of time, they develop a quite characteristic culture of relationships. Although leaders seek to influence the development of this culture directly, it was argued in the preceding chapter that these attempts at influence need to be tailored to the particular culture of a group. The culture is not created solely by the leader, but by a complex interplay between the different members, the leader, the setting, and the group's early history.

A difficulty in developing adequate research into the effects of group composition has been the selection of suitable concepts with which to characterize composition. Some researchers have used nominal categories such as homogeneity or heterogeneity, while others have preferred to think in terms of the compatibility or incompatibility of members' preferred styles of relating to others. As Reddy (1975) points out, there is no necessary overlap between these sets of concepts. For instance, where two members both wish to exert dominance, their needs are similar or homogeneous, but incompatible. But where two members both wish to express affection in the group, their needs are similar, homogeneous, and compatible. Thus, in order to make clear the relationship between homogeneity and compatibility, one has to specify whether the behaviour one is considering is like dominance which seeks a reciprocal response from the other person, or like affection which seeks an identical response.

Very few of the studies which have been made of the effects of group composition report much about the behaviour of the leaders in the groups studied. One needs, therefore, to be a little cautious about assuming that the effects obtained are the result of compositional variables, particularly where the sample of groups studied is small. For instance, Lieberman (1958) compared two groups, one of them heterogeneously composed, the other composed to exclude members oriented towards affection. It was found that members predisposed towards counterdependency, who were present in both groups, benefitted more in the heterogeneous groups. Although this effect was attributed to the differing composition of the groups, other explanations are equally plausible. In a similar way, Harrison and Lubin (1965) found that a group composed of task-oriented members tended to show higher learning than a second group composed of person-oriented members.

Building on this study, Harrison (1965(b)) hypothesized that learning would be highest in those groups where there was some degree of incompatibility between members. He found that a group composed of members with preferences for differing levels of structure in the group was rated as learning more by observers than were members of five other groups, each of which had members preferring the same level of structure. In a similar way, Vraa (1974) compared three student groups, two of them homogeneous and the third mixed, with regard to preferences for how much one likes to be included in group activities. All three groups had the same two leaders. No measures of learning were obtained, but it was shown that each group did develop a culture reflecting its composition. Bugen (1977) also composed groups differing in how much they preferred to be included. He found that the most cohesion developed in the groups which comprised those who had low to medium inclusion needs.

Pollack (1971) studied a more extensive sample of student groups. The basis for composition was members' preferences for controlling others and being controlled by them. Four homogeneous groups showed less subsequent change on Schutz's (1958) FIRO–B Questionnaire than did twelve heterogeneously composed groups. This study is of particular interest since each of the homogeneous groups had a different type of member, some of them compatible with one another and others not so. For instance, one group had members all of whom wished to give and receive high levels of control, which would be a compatible group, while members of another of the homogeneous groups all wished not to control others but to be controlled by them, which would be highly incompatible. It was found that only one of the homogeneous groups achieved a high degree of change, which implies that the hypothesis that change is maximized by high incompatibility is not adequate.

Another study casting doubt on incompatibility as a predictor of change is that by Harrison (1965(c)). Harrison identified particular participants in an NTL training programme who were deemed likely to have difficulty in participating. These participants were then placed in groups composed so as to maximize their chances of learning. For example, passive, low-affect participants were thought likely to have difficulty, and were placed in groups with other members who were active and expressed high affect. This procedure appeared to work well. In other words, the learning of these particular 'problem' members was enhanced by placing them with others whose style would be likely to support them, rather than confront them. Harrison concluded that the compositional requirements of optimal learning comprise a mixture of support and confrontation, rather than a preponderance of either one.

Melnick and Woods (1976) review a broad range of studies of the effects of group composition. They conclude that while a number of studies of T-groups favour heterogeneous composition, there are an equally large number of studies concerning therapy groups which favour homogeneity. It will be argued here that closer examination of the studies of T-groups does not show them simply to favour heterogeneity, but rather to favour the provision of support and confrontation. In a similar manner it could be argued, although this point will not be pursued here, that effective therapy groups require not only the support they would derive from some kinds of homogeneity, but also an element of confrontation which is implicit in the acknowledgement that one is sufficiently distressed to be in need of some form of group therapy. One further study which sought to choose between support and confrontation as predictors of change was that by Stava and Bednar (1979). They contrasted what they termed a *dissonance* and an

interpersonal attraction condition with a further mixed condition. The dissonance condition contained four groups which were homogeneous for control needs. The interpersonal attraction condition contained four groups
with some who were high and some who were low on control needs. The
groups were based on tape recorded instructions (encounter tapes, see
Chapter 9) but lasted only six hours. No differences in outcome were
detected, but the various conditions did show different behaviour patterns.

The most systematic statement of the proposition that support *plus*
confrontation are required for optimal learning is found in the work of
Reddy (1972(a), 1972(b), 1975). Reddy sees the ideal group as composed of
two somewhat incompatible sections, each of which derives some support
or strength from those with compatible orientations, and some confrontation from those with incompatible orientations. Where the two sections are
of equal size, confrontation and support should be well balanced, whereas if
one section is much larger than the other, the majority will be oversup-
ported and the minority will be overconfronted. This formulation fits well
with the findings of the studies by Harrison (1965(c)) and Pollack (1971)
already described. Reddy's own studies include a direct test of his
hypothesis. Two groups on a five-day residential programme were composed in such a way as to contain subgroups which were mutually incompatible in terms of their preferences concerning affection behaviour. Two
further groups were compatibly composed. The greatest change on the
Shostrom Personal Orientation Inventory was found in the first two groups.
In another study, Reddy (1972(b)) investigated which members of six
further groups showed greatest change on the Personal Orientation Inventory. It was found, as predicted, that the highest changers were those whose
preferences concerning affection behaviour were opposed to the majority in
the group. Smith and Linton (1974) sought to extend Reddy's findings by
looking at preferences concerning both affection behaviours and control
behaviours. In a five-day training programme, three groups were composed
so as to be compatible for affection but not control behaviours, three groups
were compatible for control but not affection, and four groups were incompatible for both behaviours. The greatest change on the Personal Orientation Inventory was obtained in the groups incompatible for both
behaviours, but each type of incompatibility was associated with a distinctive pattern of change.

These various studies all favour the support plus confrontation model for
composition, but none of them provides any evidence that the processes of

support and confrontation do actually occur in the groups where they are postulated. Smith (1974) created sixteen one-day T-groups with varying compositions, and studied both the behaviours occurring within them and the patterns of influence which emerged. It was not expected that one-day groups would have any lasting consequences for members, but that what occurred within the groups would demonstrate whether the conditions for learning could be established in a predictable manner. Composition was based on members' preferences regarding control behaviour, and leadership was held fairly constant, there being two leaders each of whom took eight groups. It was found that the groups with the most incompatible composition showed a significant lack of supportive behaviours and scored high on a measure of compliance. The groups with the most compatible compositions scored high on supportive behaviours and on a measure of identification. Groups scoring high on a measure of internalization were, as predicted, those with some support and some confrontation. These findings are consistent with those later obtained by Stava and Bednar (1979), but they differ in so far as these authors did not include a condition combining support and confrontation.

Of the various studies of group composition, the one which most satisfactorily disposes of the possibility that the leaders in some way biased the findings is that by Andrews (1973). He studied an NTL programme which contained five T-groups. The design employed by the leaders required them to rotate between the various T-groups every few hours, while the T-groups themselves remained intact throughout the programme. Andrews' research method differed from that used in many of the other studies. While Reddy, Smith, Pollack, and others all used the Schutz (1958) FIRO–B Questionnaire to compose groups, Andrews obtained members' behaviour preferences on the Leary Interpersonal Checklist. He then examined each group to see how many of the various possible pairs within it had incompatible preferences. He found that the groups with the highest proportion of 'high-challenge pairs' were those which reported the greatest number of critical learning incidents. These groups were also more highly evaluated by the leaders. This study did not test whether or not support-generating compositions also enhanced learning. However, it does provide firm evidence relating to the role of confrontation.

The empirical evidence concerning group composition is relatively clear; by deliberately composing groups according to specifiable criteria, the chances are increased that participants will achieve the type of gains on the

Personal Orientation Inventory or FIRO–B which were shown in Chapter 3 to be among the most frequently found effects of groups. None of the compositional studies have tested directly for the persistence of the changes found at the end of training, but since the changes do appear similar to those reported in other outcome studies, we may anticipate that there will be some persistence and some fade-out. The concepts employed by group composition researchers have mostly been closely related to those used in the two-factor model of group learning. Indeed, the terms support and confrontation were first popularized by Harrison in connection with his compositional studies in the mid-sixties. It therefore seems reasonable to anticipate that compositions yielding support and confrontation should induce more internalization-based influence in the groups, and hence more persistence of effects.

Although the evidence for systematically composed groups is quite persuasive, most leaders do not in fact compose their groups on the basis of FIRO–B responses. There are no doubt a number of reasons for this, including the laboriousness of scoring questionnaires under time pressure, the smallness of some programmes which precludes much choice of how to compose groups, scepticism or unawareness of research data, and so forth. Most often T-groups are composed by leaders so as to maximize the diversity of each group on the basis of more readily available information such as age, sex, and occupation. A few years ago, the author made an informal test of how close this procedure comes to approximating the compositions required by FIRO–B scores. In a mixed professional population of forty-three, members were divided into four T-groups on the basis of age, sex, and occupation. Examination of FIRO–B scores of members and leaders then indicated that, in this instance, it was only necessary to change the assignment of one member to a group in order to achieve the ideal composition. This suggests that, at least in relatively heterogeneous populations, the procedures currently used by group leaders are reasonably adequate, and that the time required to obtain test data would not usually be worthwhile. On the other hand, in a more recent project reported in the previous chapter, Smith (1980(b)) showed that groups led by the same leader often have a different culture from one another. If groups are normally composed in such a way that differences are effectively minimized, the source of such variation is somewhat puzzling. Harrison (1965(c)) offers one plausible suggestion which he terms the *multiplier effect*. Although groups may start off relatively similar, he suggests that they may rapidly multiply any small differences between them. Suppose, for instance, that in one group a particularly assertive member starts by attacking others or the leader. This initiative may elicit assertiveness from others in the group also. In another group the first initiative might be a more friendly, supportive one, which would also elicit supportiveness from others. In this way, each group creates a shared history, each drawing perhaps on a relatively similar stock of group members, but highlighting different facets of themselves. Effects such as these place a practical limit upon the extent to which leaders can create rather than react to the development of the group, unless they choose actually to structure each session.

The role of the primary learning group

Numerous other choices face the leader of a group training programme. These choices cannot be presented here in terms of what is or is not appropriate, since the whole point of training design is to achieve some kind of matching between a specific set of training goals and an overall experience which can hope to achieve these goals. What can be presented is some information concerning what the choices are most frequently seen to be, and the research data showing how some of these choices have worked out in particular circumstances.

One of the most basic choices a leader faces is deciding how long a group needs to last if it is to have a reasonable chance of success. In reviewing outcome studies of groups then available, Smith (1975) chose to examine studies of groups lasting twenty hours or more. It was found that a higher proportion of groups of less than twenty hours' duration failed to achieve significant effects. Above this arbitrarily fixed cut-off point, there was no greater probability of significant effects with increasing duration, no doubt because once the group had lasted as long as twenty hours many other variables had more to do with its success or failure than simple duration. Somewhat longer ago, Bunker and Knowles (1967) showed that NTL programmes lasting three weeks achieved a greater impact than those lasting two weeks. It was noted that this could not be due to the effect of the T-groups since roughly the same amount of time had been spent in T-groups in the two-week programmes as in the three-week ones. The greater impact must, therefore, have been due to the other elements in the longer programme, which gave practice in applying what was learned to back-home situations.

In some ways the Bunker and Knowles finding is by now an academic one, since three-week programmes have long since ceased to be available. The trend of the past decade has been towards ever shorter programmes. Since twenty hours of T-group time can be comfortably accommodated within a one-week programme, this may be no bad thing. Beyond some point however, it must be the case that increasing brevity means that the goals of what can be achieved must be scaled down. The only study which has attempted to determine the effects of duration in a more systematic manner is that by Handlin et al. (1974), who compared student groups lasting four, twelve, and twenty hours. Each group had the same three leaders. No outcome measures were used, but codings of group interaction were made. The twelve-hour group appeared most effective, but since only one group of each type was employed, this might just as easily have been an effect of composition as of duration.

In the absence of firmer data, the required duration of a group remains an intuitive judgement. Factors which one needs to weigh up include whether or not group members already know one another, whether they are already familiar with group methods, whether they share a common background, and how specific are their learning goals. A positive response to each of these criteria implies the possibility of a shorter experience being fruitful. The success of rather short group experiences may also prove dependent on variables which differ from those shown to be important in longer groups. Lubin and Smith (1979) found the development of six-hour student groups was unrelated to variations in leaders or in group composition. The degree of structure provided may be more important.

Linked to the question of the duration of a group is that of whether meetings should be intensive (for instance, over several days residentially) or extended (for instance, once or twice a week). Practical circumstances may dictate one's choice here, but it is worth considering also the properties of each type of training format. Smith (1975) showed that among studies of groups meeting periodically, 58% found significant effects, whereas among groups meeting intensively the figure was 81%. Most of the periodic groups were composed of students, but this did not account for the differences found, as success rates in student and nonstudent groups were similar. Intensive groups thus have a better chance of creating positive effects, but the more crucial question is whether these effects will last. Advocates of periodic groups often argue that they give trainees a better chance to integrate what they learn into everyday living. Two studies provide empirical data relevant to this point. Lieberman, Yalom, and Miles (1973) set a time limit of thirty hours for the groups they studied, but left the leaders free to choose whether to meet intensively, periodically, or a mixture of the two. They found that after the groups there was a significantly positive correlation between meeting intensively and high gain. These researchers do not present a correlation between intensity of meeting and their measure of follow-up change, but the data they provide enable one to be calculated. From after the group to follow-up, the correlation obtained falls from +0.57 to +0.48, indicating a continuing advantage for the groups which met intensively. The data provided by Lieberman et al. enable one to see why this might have been so in the case of their sample. The groups which met intensively tended to be those whose leaders were high on caring and meaning attribution. Hence, unless one wished to argue that it was the intensity of meeting which enabled the leaders to achieve an optimal role in these groups, one should not expect that intensive meetings would always prove able to sustain change. The more parsimonious explanation is that these groups showed lasting benefit because the leaders were able to establish within them the conditions for internalized change. The relative importance of intensity of meeting in facilitating this remains an open question.

Bare and Mitchell (1972) also studied different intensities of group meeting. They compared groups of adults meeting intensively, periodically, or a mixture of the two. The groups lasted twenty-five to thirty hours, and fifteen different groups were included in the sample. After training, groups of all kinds showed greater change as rated by self and others than did untrained controls. However, the effects were much stronger for periodic groups and groups with a mixture of periodic and intensive meetings than they were for intensive groups. Follow-up measures showed that after three months only the periodic and mixed groups now showed greater change than controls. If the ratings made by trainees themselves are excluded, leaving those made by close associates of the trainees, the mixed groups were the only ones showing a continuing significant change at follow-up. Bare and Mitchell do not provide much information on the type of groups they studied, beyond stating that they were a 'conventional, verbal' type of sensitivity training. On the face of it their findings contradict those of Lieberman et al., since intensive groups were found to be inferior. However, in both studies the differences found at follow-up were already in evidence in the measures obtained at the close of the groups. The findings obtained do not seem to be due to some kind of differential fade-out of learning, but to the success with which learning conditions were established in the groups in the first place. The findings from the range of studies reviewed by Smith (1975) suggest that it is on the whole easier to set up the conditions for effective group learning where a group meets intensively. But the findings of Bare and Mitchell indicate that it is not always so.

One of the reasons why intensive meetings may be advantageous is that is makes more practicable the inclusion of a variety of activities in a training programme, whereby members of several different groups may meet one another in order to augment or complement what is occurring in their separate groups. Such joint activities are not necessarily employed, even where a number of groups are meeting concurrently and intensively. For instance, in both the Lieberman et al. and the Bare and Mitchell studies, no such contact is referred to, and marathon groups frequently meet from start to finish without interruption. Within the traditions of group training associated with National Training Laboratories (NTL) and also the Tavistock approach (see Chapter 7), the design of a series of different types of session within a training programme is seen by leaders as a crucial way of linking the primary group learning experience to events outside the group. Such emphasis on design can be seen as an attempt by leaders of intensive, residential programmes to build linkages with trainees' back-home environments and with facets of their experience which do not find direct expression in their primary learning group. Advocates of groups meeting periodically might argue that group members can do this themselves, where the group does not have the artificiality created by short-term intensive meetings. Advocates of intensive groups would respond that by systematically designing such activities, one may do better than by leaving them to chance.

Smith (1976(b)) investigated how extensive the patterns of influence were among leaders and participants on a residential sensitivity training programme. The programme comprised sixty participants, six leaders, and six coleaders. During the five-day programme, about twenty-two hours were spent in separate T-groups and there were a further nine hours of scheduled activities of various kinds. It was found that at the end of the week, members rated themselves as having been influenced by an average of six other members of their T-group, the two leaders of their T-group, and one further person in the workshop, who was about equally likely to be another member or another leader. This implies that the great majority of learning on this particular programme should prove explicable in terms of events within each separate T-group. Nonetheless, 13% of participants identified their *principal* source of influence as lying outside their own T-group, so for these people at least the structure of the larger programme was in some way crucial. Sources of influence outside one's own group tended to be rated high on liking and trust, but not on behaving in ways that made one tense. Smith concluded that influence sources outside one's group played a primarily supportive role in this programme. The group leaders were not asked to complete these ratings, but had they done so, most likely the ratings would show that group leaders also obtain support from those outside their groups, particularly other leaders.

The benefits to be derived from having more than one group concurrently in a training programme are not limited to the provision of mutual emotional support. No doubt such support would occur within any design which actually permitted a certain amount of contact between members of different groups. Further possibilities are events intended to affect the way the various T-groups develop, events which enable members to stand back from and conceptualize what they are experiencing, events which illuminate relations between rather than within groups, and events which direct attention towards one's back-home setting and the creation of change within it. Many of the structures most frequently employed by group leaders contribute to more than one of these goals, so that it is not possible to discuss them one at a time.

The structuring of alternate sessions

Evidence was reviewed in Chapter 5 indicating that a certain amount of structuring of the primary learning group by the leader is related to positive outcome. Such structuring has been especially associated with some exponents of encounter groups, and studies of the outcome of certain structured forms of encounter are reviewed in Chapter 9. This section is concerned with the practice, more salient among group leaders in the NTL tradition, of leaving the primary learning group with an open agenda, but staging additional sessions which are much more tightly structured by the leaders.

One difficulty arises immediately. It is difficult to devise appropriate ways of evaluating a structured experience which is embedded within a context of a much more extensive training programme. It is not reasonable to expect the structured experience by itself to have a lasting impact. Its function is to augment and sustain effects of the programme as a whole. For example, one procedure group leaders have quite frequently employed is to have different T-groups observe one another's sessions for thirty minutes to an hour. The intentions of such an exercise can vary, but might include gaining practice in group observation, testing out how far the problems faced by one's own T-group are unique, picking up ideas about what is or is not safe to do in T-groups, experiencing intergroup defensiveness, seeking to find ways of giving constructive feedback to the other group despite these difficulties, and so forth. The most straightforward way to test the impact of this procedure, which is often referred to as the *fishbowl technique*, might be to record observations of T-group behaviour before and after such interventions. Unfortunately no such study has been published. White (1974) compared two regular T-groups with two further groups, which spent half of their meeting time using the fishbowl technique. During these sessions the group divided in half and took it in turns to observe one another. White found some evidence that the fishbowl groups developed more slowly, but despite the fact that the groups lasted for twenty-four hours, it was found that neither type of group showed more change in self-concept than untrained controls.

Another procedure for giving feedback to a whole group is the use of video recordings. Just as feedback from the fishbowl procedure might be received by a group either as providing an opportunity to learn and innovate, or as an attack upon themselves, so video may be seen as a resource or as a threat. While a number of published descriptions of the use of video are available, little systematic research has been reported. These is, nonetheless, little doubt that video can be a potent source of change where a group is open to its use. Walter and Miles (1974) studied changes in self-acceptance in student task groups whose behaviour was video recorded. He found that a weekly ten-minute playback enhanced self-acceptance among one group who were given no instructions as to what to observe. However, another group who were instructed to observe various aspects of group process and their own behaviour, showed less increase in self-acceptance than did controls. One might speculate that this was because the uninstructed group obtained some reassurance from what they saw, whereas the instructed group became self-conscious or defensive.

Feedback may also be presented to groups by way of completion of questionnaires, which are processed and fed back to group members. Myers et al. (1969) showed that T-group members who received feedback as to the sociometric structure of their group after every session, showed increasingly accurate estimates of their own status, while members of other groups did not. Extensive use has been made of some types of instrumented feedback of this kind, particularly in organizational development programmes, which are discussed in Chapter 10.

A different type of structured session is that which is intended to provide explicit teaching about small groups and ways of learning within them. Such sessions typically involve a brief lecture followed by discussion and one or more illustrative exercises. The exercises are most typically not carried out within separate T-groups, but in ad hoc groups set up for the purpose and varying from session to session. Hipple (1976) investigated the differences in outcome of two group training programmes for students, one of which included substantial cognitive input and the other of which was largely given over to T-group time. Each programme lasted twenty-five hours and the students who volunteered to attend were randomly assigned to one or other programme. Rather few differences were found between the effects of the two programmes. The follow-up measures collected six weeks after training did, however, show that those who attended the programme with heavy emphasis on T-groups became more trusting, warm, and affectionate as perceived by their friends. Since there were no control groups in this study, it is not possible to know whether either of the programmes was particularly successful, but it does appear that whatever advantage there was lay with the programme maximizing T-group time.

The amount of time devoted to explicit teaching in training programmes has declined over the years, and the proportion in Hipple's high cognitive input programme (52% of the total time) is now probably rather unusual. Other studies of theory inputs into group training programmes have examined how well founded are some of the points most frequently put over. One exercise which has been very frequently employed compares the properties of one-way and two-way verbal communication, by having a 'sender' describe a pattern of rectangles on a sheet of paper to an audience of 'receivers'. The conclusions usually drawn are that one-way communication is quicker and more satisfying to the sender, whereas two-way communication is slower but more accurate, and more satisfying to the receivers. Group leaders have often used this simple exercise as support for participative styles of teaching and of management. Group work, it is argued, may be slow and sometimes frustrating, but the time is well spent because the ultimate product is of higher quality. More sceptical participants sometimes speculate that this demonstration is in some way 'rigged' to give the right answer. Tesch et al. (1972) made empirical studies to determine whether this might be so. They found that the two patterns of rectangles normally used are in fact equally difficult to describe. They also found that while the experiment is normally done with one-way communication first, this does not explain why people do better with two-way communication. However, they did show that where two-way communication occurs first, subsequent one-way communication is enhanced. The exercise does, therefore, have some validity, but should not be used to argue that two-way communication is under all circumstances preferable.

Another frequently used exercise is the moon-shot exercise, derived originally from materials used by NASA in training astronauts. Group members are asked to decide individually a rank order priority of fifteen items available after an imaginary disaster on the moon. Members are then required to reach a group decision as to the priorities, and it is almost always found that the group decision approximates more closely the rankings provided by NASA experts. This exercise is said to illustrate the creative and problem-solving potentials of group work, but critics argue that it too may not be valid (Bradford and Eoyang, 1976; Slevin, 1978). The evidence certainly shows that on this particular task, groups do better than individuals, but this may rest on the fact that this is a field in which few people have much expertise. The demonstration also needs to be used in a way which makes clear how much of the effect derives from simple averaging, and how much from members' responses to one another. Properly used (Hall, 1979), the exercise can show not that group procedures are always more effective, but that they are better under a more specific set of circumstances which can then be discussed.

Other topics frequently covered either by short lectures or structured exercises are more closely linked to members' experiences during training. For instance, there may be coverage of helping processes, ways of giving feedback, stages in group development, models of what occurs in groups such as the Johari Window, and nonverbal communication. In each case research data are available which underpin the coverage given by group leaders, but this will not be detailed here as it is touched upon in other chapters.

Exploration of intergroup relations was at one time seen as an important issue in training programmes. T-groups or separately composed groups were engaged in some kind of conflict with one another, and then required to explore ways of resolving such conflict. Such an approach was particularly used by Blake and Mouton (1962), who subsequently designed structured training programmes for use in organizational contexts, and experimented with the resolution of real-life conflicts such as those between unions and management (Blake and Mouton, 1965). Intergroup conflicts certainly have a very powerful effect on intragroup processes. The growing emphasis on more personal types of learning in groups during the past decade has meant that some group leaders do not wish for the kind of disruption of the possibilities for personal learning which intergroup events may entail. In terms of two-factor theory, they risk encouraging a split between intragroup support and extragroup confrontation, which may reduce the prospects for personal learning. However, some kinds of inter-group contact may help in enhancing supportive processes within groups, where these are developing too slowly. A range of more specialist designs have also been developed in recent years, which treat the processes of conflict and intergroup negotiation as the primary focus. In one instance of this, known as the *power lab*, participants are arbitrarily assigned to high- and low-power groups, with the high-power group receiving better accommodation, more food, and a larger say in how the time shall be structured. Another instance is the *mini-society*, in which groups representing different segments of society participate in a workshop and must negotiate with one another over such practical issues as purchasing and preparation of food, child care, and so forth. A third instance emphasizes the development of individual bargaining skills. No empirical data are available on the impact of these designs, although a number of case studies indicate that they do vividly portray the issues.

A further difficulty with the incorporation of intergroup conflict into a programme is that a separate leader's group may be required, in order to resolve disputes in a manner which enables the rest of the programme to proceed. This can be done easily enough; Johnson and Lewicki (1969) describe how an intractable dispute on a hot summer day was quickly resolved by the leader's statement that everyone could go swimming when negotiations were complete. But such strategems must have a marked effect on the leader's subsequent role in the T-group. Suspicions that he is really manipulating the groups behind the scenes are given some reality value. Tavistock group leaders make extensive use of intergroup and large group events, and it is most likely no coincidence that they do maintain a highly separate staff group. Their approach is examined in Chapter 7.

Training programme designs quite often incorporate one further feature – the use of alternate groups. Such groups usually only meet for one or a few sessions. They are intended to augment or highlight some issue which it may be less easy to initiate in the T-groups, but they are usually scheduled with the hope in mind that once the alternate group has aired the issue, it will be raised also in subsequent T-group meetings. This possibility can be explicitly encouraged, as for example when alternate groups are composed of one member of each of the T-groups present, and asked to compare how each group is developing. Since the T-groups are usually composed to maximize heterogeneity, alternate groups may also be established which are homogeneous with regard to some attribute such as personality, age, sex, or occupation. A number of studies have shown how members' behaviour differs in newly composed homogeneous groups, but few have examined subsequent effects on behaviour in the main T-group. An experimental study by Aries (1976) illustrates the effects obtained when members meet in single sex or mixed sex groups. She found that in the mixed setting, men spoke more personally and addressed individuals more, while in the all-male groups they tended to be competitive and status-oriented. Women shared a great deal with one another in the all-female groups, but in the mixed groups they let the men dominate.

Another type of alternate group is the pair. Pairs may meet once or a number of times, and may be charged with the task of helping one another learn from their respective T-groups. Andrews (1975) experimented with the composition of pairs in a workshop, following his earlier study of group composition. He found that the most successful pairs were those composed to maximize interpersonal challenge, but his pairs did not meet until late in the workshop. In line with two-factor theory, he suggests that the success of this exercise rested on the fact that a high level of support already existed within the workshop community.

The range of design opportunities open to group leaders is enormous. The choices which are made are frequently intuitive and we have seen that research studies provide few guidelines as to which might be most effective. Leaders may also sometimes overlook the fact that the provision of free time in residential programmes is a vital element in design. Free time provides opportunities for participants both to relax and to initiate activities of their own, which may well contribute to the goals of the programme. Free time is often also partly used by leaders to hold staff meetings, which have a key role to play in providing support to them. One possible reason why even the research which has been done is somewhat inconclusive, may parallel the findings reported earlier by Lieberman et al. that processes such as self-disclosure and feedback were not strongly linked to outcome. It may not matter so much exactly what the programme is; what may be more important is *how* it comes across, and whether the staff show themselves open to criticism and willing to adapt to members' expressed needs. If they show themselves both supportive of members and willing to confront differences with them, then the alternate sessions may well augment T-group meetings rather than interfere with them.

The viewpoint that programme design is something which should arise collaboratively between leaders and group members is most strongly held by Rogerian group leaders. In residential Rogerian programmes, the very minimum of advance planning is undertaken by the leaders. This may amount to obtaining a physical location for the programme, ensuring that a range of group leaders are present, and provision of food and accommodation for those who come. Programme design thus becomes the responsibility of all those present, and normally such programmes start off with everyone in a single large group attempting to decide how the time shall be structured. Typically, after a period of some frustration, a design is arrived at which includes both small and large groups. The strength of this type of 'no-design' design is that each participant is clearly responsible not just for their behaviour within a small group designated by the staff, but within the programme as a whole. Proponents of this approach would argue that it maximizes the possibility of internalized learning, by requiring of participants that they act in such ways as will meet their needs. Advocates of more tightly structured designs would argue that this degree of flexibility may well meet the needs of those who have the self-confidence to face up to it, but that others may be more helped by the support of a more imposed structure. It is certainly true that a Rogerian design leaves open the *possibility* that a small (or large) group may be set up which has nonoptimal composition, insufficient meeting time, no leader, and so forth. Rogerians would argue that though this may be so, the flexibility of their programmes can ensure that if any of these things proves to be problematic, the learning community of the programme as a whole provides a forum in which people can seek to rectify them. Tightly structured designs may also prove to be inappropriately structured, and in such cases they may be harder to modify than Rogerian ones. In Rogerian designs, even more than in others, the actual activities engaged in may be, to some degree, secondary to how people feel about the way in which they participated in setting them up and carrying them out.

No research studies are available contrasting the Rogerian style of programme design with more structured styles. Just as was shown to be the case *within* the primary learning group, it may turn out that different design styles suit different personality needs. One leader who has attempted to follow this line of thinking to its logical conclusion is Pagès (1975), whose 'flexible structures' design is intended to mirror the types of structure which participants seek at different stages in a training programme.

Meeting the participant's needs

It is a truism to propose that however well a training programme is designed, it cannot succeed unless that design in some ways connects with the trainee's current needs. One of the best indices that a programme is meeting someone's needs is if that person becomes actively involved in it. The most active members have frequently been seen as benefitting most (Miles, 1965; Snortum and Myers, 1971; Archer, 1974; Lieberman et al., 1973; Levenberg and Spakes, 1975; Babad and Melnick, 1976). Such involvement is no doubt partly a function of personality, and those who are highly involved have been shown to be less dogmatic (Davis et al., 1972), more oriented towards economic, political, and theoretical values (Poppen, 1972), and having values congruent with those exemplified in the group (Lieberman et al., 1973).

By far the most extensive investigation of the personality of those who learn most in groups is included in the Lieberman et al. study. The characteristics found to be most useful in distinguishing high and low learners were their values and their attitudes towards others. High learners placed a low emphasis on having new experiences for their own sake, and a high emphasis on achieving personal change. They saw themselves as being not as personally adequate as they wished and lacking in opportunities to create change. Miles (1965) also found some linkage between personality and learning in the group. High learners were more flexible and had a greater need for affiliation.

Whether or not these personality attributes are linked to the persistence of change has been little studied. Lieberman et al. do not analyse their data in this way. Miles (1965) did so however, and found no relationship between personality factors and the persistence of change. In his sample of school principals, change was more strongly linked to organizational factors.

The position to be argued here is that the problem of meeting participants' needs is not much helped by identifying individual personality types who benefit most from groups. A wide variety of people come to groups, and what is important to clarify is how to assist them in making linkages between everyday experience and their group experience. The most straightforward way in which to undertake this is to ensure that potential group members are fully informed as to what the group will be like. To those who have not previously participated in any kind of experiential group work, this may not be easy. Written descriptions tend to convey more to those who already have some experience on which to draw. Some attempts have been made in recent years to evaluate ways of orienting prospective group members. D'Augelli and Chinsky (1974) found brief, cognitive inputs followed by exercises involving feedback and self-disclosure to be effective. Zarle and Willis (1975) used relaxation exercises as a preparation for an encounter group. Silver and Conyne (1977) compared the impact of a structured programme of encounter exercises lasting forty-five minutes with a video tape of a group. Both these groups also received a short account of the Johari Window. When compared to controls who received no orientation, it was found that the participative experience induced favourable attitudes towards attending groups, whereas the film was found rather alarming. The need for such preparatory experiences may be particularly great where the experience itself is relatively brief. With longer groups there may be a certain amount of initial confusion, but this does not pose such great risks to the long-term goals of the group.

The evidence showing how widespread is the fade-out of effects generated by groups, suggests that factors in the participant's back-home setting have been too much overlooked. Even where group leaders have succeeded in staging a programme which meets the member's needs, and the member returns home intending to initiate particular changes, fade-out still frequently occurs. The most plausible hypothesis is that this occurs because of social influences in the back-home setting which run counter to those established within the group. If we are to take account of these, we must know more about them.

Moscow (1969) studied the work relationships of managers attending T-groups. He found that those who sustained the greatest amount of change after training were those whose relationships with others were neither very good nor very poor, but somewhere in between. He reasoned that those with very good relationships had no incentive to change, while those with very poor relationships may have found it too difficult to carry through a change unilaterally. Miles (1965) found that the school principals who sustained most change after groups were those who had been principals longer and were more powerful (i.e., had more subordinates). Cohen and Keller (1973) found that change after training groups for managers was only sustained where the trainees' superiors had favourable attitudes towards human relations.

Smith (1979) asked group members to make ratings of a wide range of types of relationship in which they were involved. The most sustained changes after the groups were found in three types of relationship; those with persons much older than oneself, those with work associates of the same sex and age as oneself, and opposite sex relationships. Different kinds of change were described for each of these relationship types. This implies that some relationship types may be much better able to incorporate the types of change generated by group experience than others.

A further study in progress by the author seeks to study this issue in a more systematic manner. It is reasoned that the type of social influence processes which are most salient in the group member's back-home setting will have a large effect on the type of continuing impact a group will have. Participants at six NTL training programmes were asked to describe six relationships, including those with both work and nonwork associates, which were currently important to them. These relationships were described by use of the same rating scales employed in earlier studies by the author, so that it was possible to characterize each participant's back-home relations as tending towards a pattern of compliance, identification, or internalization. Two possibilities may be envisaged for change after a group; either the participant's pattern of influence relationships will change, or it will remain the same and thereby condition the manner in which other effects of training are expressed. Complete sets of responses (before and after the group, and a follow-up measure five months later) were received from 119 participants. Before training fourteen of these were compliant, fifty-nine showed the identifier pattern, and forty-six were internalizers. Five months later, only two (14%) of those who were originally compliant were still so, whereas thirty-nine (66%) remained identifiers and twenty-nine (63%) remained internalizers. Examination of the various change scores showed that those who had been initially compliant made the most marked changes. Evidently for some of this small subgroup, the group experience provided a sufficient stimulus to trigger a radical change in their pattern of relating to others. Those who were initially identifiers showed the lowest rate of change on most measures. They were relatively pleased with the benefits they had derived from the experience, but did not see this expressed in changed relationships with others. Those who were initially internalizers showed an intermediate level of change, and this was most marked for changes in relationships with others.

The finding that those from compliant settings are those who make the most spectacular changes fits in well with the findings of Cooper (1977). He found that managers showing the greatest change after groups, as perceived both by themselves and by work associates, were those who had been required to attend by their organization. While such findings may initially appear to contradict the common-sense view that volunteers would learn more, this need not be so. Volunteers are likely to be better informed, may already have some of the skills to be learned in groups, and may have been in groups before. The changes they show may be more subtle and less visible to others. According to this analysis, compliant members, or those who are required to attend, do not change *because* of their compliance, but because when they arrive at the group they find the style of relationships within it so much preferable to their normal ones that they subsequently initiate large changes.

The ultimate outcome of the experience for these group members would thus rest not only on the pattern of their back-home relationship, but also on what happens to each person during the group. It is the interaction between these two dimensions which requires much further analysis. The findings reported do indicate, however, the way in which the back-home environment channels and constrains the effectiveness of a training design. Many of these constraints are unknown to the group leader, at least initially. We may speculate that it will turn out to be those from compliant back-home settings who benefit most from the provision of structure, both within the group and in the programme as a whole. On the other hand, it will be those who have internalizing back-home relations who will most readily grasp the opportunities for self-directed learning. Identifiers may prove to be those for whom periodic groups are more effective than intensive ones, since more intensive meeting may only serve to strengthen their tendency to seek out warmth and affection and avoid confrontation.

This chapter concludes a sequence which has explored the different aspects of the design and conduct of sensitivity training. The next four chapters will consider a somewhat wider range of group work, and consider how far the conclusions so far formulated may apply also to them.

Summary

The most effective way to compose a T-group is in such a way as to maximize support and confrontation. The presence of more than one group in a training programme provides a wider range of design options. While there is little firm evidence for the usefulness of particular designs, theory inputs, exercises, and alternate groups may all serve to support the T-group's development. The proportion of T-group time required may not be crucial, at least above about twenty hours, but intensive meetings are usually preferable to periodic ones. Preparatory orientation may sometimes be useful, and effective design needs to be based on a full knowledge of the background and goals of the participants.

Section 3

The Varieties of Group Experience

CHAPTER 7
THE INTERPRETIVE APPROACHES

Most approaches to small group training envisage that the leader will do a certain amount of interpretation of what occurs. Lieberman et al.'s (1973) phrase *meaning attribution* captures the flavour of the way in which the leader's comments are likely to be seen as more definitive than those of others. Most sensitivity trainers do not see this function as their main one, stressing instead the manner in which they seek to encourage participant autonomy and the notion that anyone's perception in the group provides equally valid data for further examination. Such an assumption rests on the basis that group members do have an adequate capacity to perceive what is occurring. Where a group is composed of those whose perceptual abilities are subject to substantial distortions, the assumption may no longer be a tenable one.

It is most likely no coincidence that the interpretive approaches to group work have developed most strongly among those whose experience has strong links with the clinical field. Not all clinicians favour interpretive approaches, but the arguments for such an approach have often been found more persuasive in that field. The origins of interpretive approaches to group work are thus linked with the evolution of group therapy, and the application to such groups of theories derived from the psychoanalytic tradition. Two such approaches will be examined in this chapter, the Tavistock model, which arose in England during the 1940s, and transactional analysis which developed in the United States in the 1960s.

The Tavistock model

The origins of the Tavistock model are to be found in the work of Bion and others during World War II. Experiments were undertaken in the use of therapeutic communities for the treatment of psychological casualties from the war. The basis of this work was the British School of Psychoanalytic Theory, in particular the object-relations theory of Melanie Klein (e.g., 1959). This theory explores the origins of our orientation towards others in early childhood experience. It was envisaged that therapy would seek to create a setting in which the individual's most basic defence mechanisms would become explicit, thus making possible both insight and personal change. Bion's experiences in conducting such groups, first with patients and later with students and others, were written up as a series of papers appearing during the late forties and collected together as a book in 1961. Bion's descriptions of his own behaviour in groups show that he was largely passive. He describes the manner in which members nonetheless reacted to his behaviour in a variety of patterned ways. The assumptions which any individual chooses to make about the leader, in the absence of any firm basis for such assumptions, are seen as indicative of that individual's defences. While individuals vary in terms of which assumptions they place most reliance on, Bion was more impressed by the way in which the group as a whole seemed to shift from one set of basic assumptions to another over time. Thus Bion's approach is sharply contrasted to others, who have seen psychoanalytic group therapy as a setting in which the focus is essentially on individuals rather than the group. In Bion's terms, the group faces a choice between *work* and *emotionality*. *Work* is seen as occurring where the group faces up to the task of studying its own behaviour and does so without making spuriously based assumptions. *Emotionality* takes one of four forms, each of which involves the importation of basic assumptions about the group, which have no basis in reality. The four basic assumptions are termed *dependency*, *fight*, *flight*, and *pairing*. *Dependency* is most typically expressed through a belief in the leader's great wisdom and ability to guide the group through all difficulties. *Fight* is expressed in the assumption that involvement, attack, and questioning are the best way for the group to solve its difficulties. Conversely, *flight* is the assumption that evasion and denial will best preserve the group. Finally, *pairing* is the assumption that the group's problems may be overcome by turning the group into a series of pair relationships. Bion noted that each of these basic assumptions had high valency for a group at particular times, although he did not propose any particular sequence of group development.

Bion's reports did not lead to any rapid development in the use of his approach to group work. Further developments were triggered by visits to England in the mid-fifties of Americans who were actively developing T-group methods. This encouraged the holding of the first Tavistock Group Relations Conference in 1957 (Trist and Sofer, 1959). The central element in the conference was meetings of study groups, whose function is analogous to that of T-groups. From the first, however, other elements were given more importance than they were in the T-group laboratory. Application groups were utilized, in a manner resembling the early use of action groups in Bethel. Other elements which quickly evolved were inter-group events and large group or institutional events. Within Bion's conception, work occurs where the group resists assumptions which have no place within it. Thus, each element within a Tavistock training design has a 'primary task' and the work group is the one which addresses itself to that task. The diversification of groups within the Tavistock conference legitim-izes work on a variety of aspects of group behaviour. An intergroup event permits the formation of a number of groups, and then looks at the basic assumptions they make about one another. In a large group or institutional event, the focus is on relations between the staff group and the total conference. Categorization of behaviour can only be done in relation to the specified primary task. For instance, if one group in an intergroup event spends time discussing the attractiveness of another of the groups, this might be seen as pairing. But if one study group spends time discussing the attractiveness of another of the study groups, this would be a flight from their task.

Tavistock leaders, or consultants as they prefer to be known, do not see it as their main task to teach group members to use the Bion categories as a diagnostic framework. As often as not, in making interpretations to the group, they do not even use Bion's terms. Interpretations will be phrased in terms of what has actually happened in the group, rather than using Bion's more abstract labels. For a Tavistock consultant the primary task is to show, by example, an adherence to the precept of work rather than emotionality. Consultants will strive to behave 'in role' at all times, despite whatever inducements the group may offer in an attempt to get them to behave in a manner which legitimizes their current basic assumption. This striving may, at times, cause the consultant to behave in ways which the group finds baffling or mysterious, such as not responding to direct questions, remaining impassive in the face of general merriment, or leaving the room exactly at the moment the session is scheduled to end.

Bion's model has been examined from a philosophical standpoint by Sherwood (1964). Sherwood's critique is primarily addressed to the difficulty of how one might test whether Bion's view of what is occurring in a group is a correct or fruitful view. Bion's own writing makes light of such difficulties, suggesting for instance that where only a few members show a behaviour, others must share the assumption exemplified by that behaviour, since otherwise they would stop the others from behaving in that way. Further, Bion posits that where group members do not contest his interpretations, they must at some level accept them. Sherwood is unconvinced and argues that it might be better to work from transcripts of groups, so that interpretations of events could be compared in a more scientific manner. Whether the consultant is or is not able to provide interpretations which are objective or uncoloured by the culture of the group is thus a crucial question. No attempts at empirical studies seeking to test this point have been reported.

The detached and relatively passive style of the consultant has more in common with the approach of the early T-group trainers than the more active styles which have arisen in recent years. There were indeed some attempts to use Bion's ideas in the analysis of T-group behaviour. Stock and Thelen (1958) report a series of studies based on the measurement of Bion's basic assumptions. However, the measures which they employed focussed mainly on individuals, so that Bion's concepts were reinterpreted as personality traits. It was found, for instance, that those who benefitted most from groups were those who scored high on pairing and fight in response to projective tests. Coding systems were also devised, which enabled the level of work and of emotionality in the group at any one time to be assessed. In common with the approach of Tavistock consultants, leaders themselves were not seen as active creators of the group experience and perhaps for this reason their behaviour was not studied.

Tavistock consultants, particularly those in England, see it as very important that any research study of their approach should encompass it in its entirety, rather than singling out one particular element for study, as has so often occurred with T-groups. Very few empirical studies of this kind have been undertaken. For the most part, descriptions of what occurs in the Tavistock conference still rest on generalized accounts provided by group leaders, e.g., Rice (1965). The first genuinely empirical study of Tavistock method (Higgin and Bridger, 1964) was in fact a case study of an intergroup experience, rather than a total training event. Higgin and Bridger chart the manner in which relations between three groups developed over a series of sessions. The staff consultant group formed a fourth element in the exercise. The study provides a clear illustration of the types of interpretation employed by Tavistock consultants, but it is not always so clear which of these were shared with participants at the time.

Klein and Astrachan (1971) have made a more systematic exploration of the theories underlying both T-groups and study groups. They propose that the role adopted by the consultant in the study group clearly implies a hierarchy of authority, a differentiation between the consultant's adherence to the specified role of work on the primary task, and the group's emotionality. They find it unsurprising that study groups frequently focus their attention around authority relationships in general, and the rightness or wrongness of their consultant's comments in particular. By contrast, they argue, the T-group trainer minimizes the differences between leader and members, and thus provides an impetus towards the examination of peer relationships. Each approach, they suggest, has both strengths and weaknesses. In the Tavistock model, the consultant's rigidity and self-presentation as a blank screen facilitates the exploration of relations with authority and the fantasies and unconscious assumptions that underlie such relations. However, it makes less likely the focus on peer relationships, feedback, and self-disclosure which characterize the T-group. The strengths and weaknesses of the T-group are seen in the reverse manner, with peer relations highlighted and opportunity for learning about authority curtailed. As Klein and Astrachan wrily put it, the T-group is a love-in, while the study group more closely resembles making arrangements for one's own funeral. While protagonists of neither approach would much like such characterization, it does capture elements of the differences, albeit in cartoon form.

The contrast between the two positions is further illuminated by a paper by Pagès (1971). Pagès is a French group leader who, while not committed to the Tavistock approach, nonetheless works within a similarly psychoanalytic tradition. He joined the staff of an NTL T-group laboratory in 1969, and his article presents a unique view of the one culture viewed through the eyes of someone steeped in the other. Pagès proposes that the culture of the T-group laboratory alleviates basic personal and group anxieties, by offering a range of defensive satisfactions. These include love, closeness, the denial of conflict, and a sense of mystical union. He suggests that this artificially united community is sustained by the design activities of the staff, even if their rule over the community is a benevolent one. Pagès' analysis is dispassionately presented and has a good deal of cogency. Its implicit values are nonetheless such that most of those working within the T-group tradition would experience it as an attack on their approach. It illustrates in a more specific manner the point which Klein and Astrachan sought to make: that the adoption of either approach tends to undermine the concurrent utilization of the other.

A number of the studies of group development reviewed in Chapter 2 were conducted by group leaders in North America, who had no direct link at the time to the developing Tavistock tradition, but were nonetheless influenced by psychoanalytic thinking. The studies by Mills (1964), Mann (1967), Dunphy (1968), Gibbard and Hartmann (1973), and Farrell (1976) all fall into this category. It will be recalled that these studies did actually find a different pattern of group development to that found in the studies of T-group development. The main difference was that these studies found substantial evidence that there was a stage in the group involving conflict with the leader. There was not total agreement as to when in the group's history this occurred, but all the studies did find such a phase. In 1965, the first American Tavistock conference was held and since that time a number of empirical studies have begun to appear, examining further the distinctive quality of the study group (Klein, 1978).

Harrow et al. (1971) studied two groups of Yale students. One group experienced a five-session T-group followed by a five-session study group, while the other group followed the reverse sequence. The groups were not aware that there was to be a change of group style half-way through. Ratings completed by members showed that study group consultants were seen as more distant, less emotional, less friendly, less gratifying, and more authoritarian. T-group trainers were seen as more emotional, flexible, open, close, pleasant, friendly, satisfying, and unauthoritarian. Some, but not all of these differences, also carried over into members' perceptions of others in their groups. T-group members were seen as more trusting, open, satisfying, friendly, sensitive, and close, while study group members were seen as more rigid and inhibiting. Harrow et al. found that members' ratings of their own behaviour did not differ between the two settings. A similar study is reported by Morrison and Thomas (1976), who studied two groups of juvenile court staff. Each group had one day of study group and one day of T-group meetings. Very similar findings were obtained for perceptions of leaders and groups, but in this study it was also found that members perceived themselves differently in the two types of group. In the study groups they rated themselves as less favourable, less potent, and less active. Butkovich et al. (1975) studied a group which had a T-group leader for one of its sessions and a study group consultant for another session. They found that more comments were made to the leader in the study group sessions. In the T-group session there was more member-member aggression, and more discussion of interactions and feelings. The study by Kohler et al. (1973) of an intergroup event is also interesting. It was found that after an intergroup event, consultants to the study groups were seen as more sensitive and close, and less authoritarian and powerful. These various recent empirical studies suggest that the differences envisaged between T-groups and Tavistock groups do occur in a consistently measurable manner. The study group appears to be a considerably less comfortable place to be in than the T-group. The Kohler et al. study suggests that one reason why it may nonetheless acquire a comfortable and homelike quality is because the other events within the Tavistock conference prove to be still more unnerving. This line of reasoning is consistent with Turquet's (1975) analysis of large group events within Tavistock conferences. He sees the principal dynamic in such settings as the individual's feelings of loss of identity.

While these studies may help to clarify what happens during a Tavistock conference, there is a most regrettable lack of evaluation studies. Not one study has been published which satisfies the criteria employed in Chapter 3, such as the use of a control group and repeated measures. Klein (1978) does review a number of studies, but most of them are unpublished and all of them lacked control groups. Doob and Foltz (1974) report follow-up interviews with forty out of fifty-six Belfast community leaders who attended a ten-day workshop in 1972. The first half of the workshop was based on Tavistock methods, which then gave way to T-groups. The workshop leaders were American. Doob and Foltz reported that the programme had generated substantial change, along with a certain amount of confusion and distress. The intention of creating continuing groups crossing denominational lines was mostly unsuccessful, but a number of strong linkages did persist. A critique of this project (Boehringer et al., 1974) delineated some of the misunderstandings which had arisen, and argued against the use of such approaches in politically sensitive situations.

A follow-up study was recently reported by Malan et al. (1976) of patients in group psychotherapy at the Tavistock Clinic. While there are numerous differences between the basis for such therapy and for group relations training conferences, common elements may also warrant an examination of the findings. Malan et al. followed up forty-two former patients. They concluded that the great majority of patients experienced their treatment as frustrating and depriving. A good deal of resentment was expressed at the lack of expression of care or consideration by the group therapists. A small minority of the patients had derived substantial benefits, and it turned out that these had very often already undergone individual psychoanalytic treatment. It was thought that having learned something of the ground rules for this type of therapy in individual treatment, they were better able to benefit from the groups.

Malan et al. conclude that more preparation may be necessary for those entering psychoanalytic group therapy, and that greater expression of care and concern by group leaders may enhance the effectiveness of treatment. It is not possible to know whether similar prescriptions might be in order for group relations conferences. It is possible that those attending conferences are better able to sustain the leader's impassiveness than are patients in therapy. What are certainly required are much more substantial studies of the benefits to be derived from this approach. The aura of mystery which often surrounds Tavistock consultants has too frequently extended to delineation of the intended effects of training.

One way of looking at the goals of the Tavistock model would be to focus on the heavy emphasis which consultants place on their behaving 'in role' at all times. To behave 'in role' is to make conscious choices as to how one wishes to behave at each point in time, and to act in accordance with those wishes. Such a goal has much in common with the achievement of personal control over behaviour discussed in earlier chapters. Thus, if this were seen as a major goal of the Tavistock approach, one might argue that the appropriate usage of this method would be to enable participants to learn increased personal control of their behaviour in face of authority figures. Since many settings in life feature authority relationships, this could be a substantial achievement. It remains for research to establish whether such learning does arise from the Tavistock approach.

Some indication of the variables affecting whether or not such learning does occur, is afforded by the work of Wright (1976). Wright compared the impact of four consultants who were instructed to be nonresponsive, i.e., to maintain an impersonal, affectless, and rational style of behaviour with four further consultants who were responsive, i.e., were permitted to let their feelings show through facial expression, eye contact, and so forth. Apart from these differences, all consultants' acted as observers of and commentators on group process. Wright's study was of one-day groups of students in New York. He found that responses to the two styles were different for men and women. Women were more active when there was a nonresponsive consultant and less positive towards other group members, while men were seen more positively by both sexes. While such findings are of some interest, they still fall short of providing measures of what is learned during the experience.

A more than usually frank insight into the manner in which one consultant operates is given by Mann (1975). Mann discusses the range of ways he finds open to him as responses when he, as group leader, is attacked by a group member. These range from delight through concern, silence, patronizing responses, and anger to interpretation. In discussing the last of these he writes:

> I find rereading the transcript of an old group to be a painful process. There is some solace in recalling how strange the leader role was to me and how much I was oriented to my internal image of the mysterious, unflappable and brilliant analyst/leader. There is some solace in discovering that the group gradually weaned me from my stylised affection of the professional. But the transcript is scattered with interpretations which are basically teasing, partisan, cute, smug, and unhelpful. (Mann, 1975, p. 261)

In discussing how the consultant may best help the group through the painful sequence of competition and rivalry, which he finds his behaviour often highlights, he suggests:

> If we stay within the leader theory, it follows that one way out proceeds via the path of far greater self-awareness and self-control on the part of the leader. In their effort to construct the perfect blank screen the psychoanalysts work exceptionally hard to understand the sources of their own countertransference, the better to remove themselves from the set of disturbing factors blocking the patient's progress. The (group) leader can try to become aware of and to transcend his or her own hang-ups. Or leaders can be selected partially on the basis of their relative lack of malice, moralism, or whatever. The would-be perfect master has a lot of work to do internally, as most of them make very clear. So does the would-be group leader. (p. 267)

Transactional analysis

Transactional analysis was developed by the Californian psychoanalyst Eric Berne. First published in his book *Transactional Analysis in Psychotherapy* in

1961, it became widely known as a result of a series of more popularly written books such as *Games People Play* (1964). Berne seeks to make easier the discussion of behaviour in groups and elsewhere, through the provision of simple descriptive taxonomies. His terms derive in a general way from psychoanalytic ones, but the adaptation is a rather free one. Berne distinguishes five types of social interaction: rituals, pastimes, games, intimacy, and activity. These types are ordered in terms of their complexity. Intimacy and activity describe states in which the individual behaves in an autonomous and direct manner. The goal of transactional analysis is to enhance these states. Much social interaction is however given over to rituals, pastimes, and psychological games, in which behaviour is either repetitive and unfulfilling, or self-defeating. Within each of these types, each participating individual's behaviour is categorizable as representing various possible ego-states. Those states which Berne differentiates are usually referred to as parent, adult and child. 'Parent' behaviour is that in which individuals imply that they know better than someone, and is exemplified by the expression of rules and prescriptions as to how others ought to be. 'Child' behaviour occurs where one assumes that others know better and are needed in order to gratify the emotions, wants, and feelings which one has. 'Adult' behaviour occurs where neither of these assumptions about others is present, and is expressed through the use of rational decision making as to what one wants to do, and intellectual analysis of the behaviour going on around one. Social interaction between two parties involves a sequence of transactions, and the categorization of these is what is known as *transactional analysis*. Since transactions involve at least two parties, it is clear that a transaction may be either complementary, where the assumptions of either party are congruent, or crossed, where they are not. Berne distinguishes two types of parent behaviour, critical and nurturing parent, with the first of these characterized by self-defeating games. Likewise there are two types of child behaviour, free child and adapted child, where the latter shows a loss of spontaneity and is engaged in various manipulative games. Transactions may also be ulterior, that is to say the individual pretends to be in one state while actually being in another.

Berne describes a very wide range of 'games' which occur in everyday transactions. He also suggests that the games which each one of us favours, tend not to be randomly selected but to accord with our individual life scripts, which are acquired during childhood. Thus, transactional analysis provides a detailed and sometimes elaborate taxonomy for the description of behaviour. Like Bion, whom he quite frequently quotes, Berne envisages an ultimate free or unconflicted state in which one makes autonomous and unconflicted choices. Also like Bion, he gives relatively little attention to this target state and focusses on the ways in which people may fail on their way to that goal. Unlike Bion, he is more concerned with the analysis of everyday life events than with what occurs in groups.

Contemporary transactional analysis has a much more didactic flavour than does the Tavistock approach. The teaching of Berne's method of classifying behaviour is seen as a central component of transactional analysis. Courses are organized on a hierarchical basis, with only those who have been accredited by the International Transactional Analysis Association being acknowledged as legitimate teachers. Central elements in most transactional analysis are the identification of games, either within the group or from participants' everyday lives, and work on delineating members' life scripts.

The sample of groups studied by Lieberman, Yalom, and Miles (1973) included two based on transactional analysis. As the authors found in a number of the groups they studied, the overt label did not provide a very good guide to what actually happened in the groups. The two transactional analysis groups proved markedly different. One of the leaders was highly active and operated primarily through summarizing and closely questioning members. His group mostly did not focus on here-and-now behaviour. He was an exuberant charismatic figure and his group was one of the most highly evaluated. The leader of the other group adhered much more closely to Berne's concepts. He saw his task as interpreting the games which individuals in the group played, which he did with a 'take it or leave it' air. He had never previously led a nonpatient group. This group was rated as one of the least successful. The variability found in this study is something one needs to bear in mind when considering the few evaluation studies of transactional analysis which have so far been conducted.

Since a large element of transactional analysis involves the learning of a diagnostic system, a useful first step in evaluating the method is to devise a measure of how well the diagnostic skills have been learned. Sowder and Brown (1977) prepared a series of video tapes of a secretary interacting with various people in the course of her work. Persons who were shown the tapes were then asked to classify her behaviour in terms of how long she spent in each ego-state (parent, adult, child), how time was structured (activities, pastimes, games, etc.), and the nature of the transactions (crossed, complementary, ulterior). It was found that those with more than two years of experience in transactional analysis made different codings of the secretary's behaviour than those with less experience. The secretary herself also underwent training and marked effects were found, in particular more adult ego-state, more activities, and less pastimes. Schaefer (1976) has developed a modified adjective checklist to enable studies of change in self-concept to be made with transactional analysis concepts, but no research on this has yet been reported.

Three adequately controlled studies of the effects of transactional analysis have so far been reported. May and Tierney (1976) studied a training programme for residents in a student dormitory. It was found that on the Omnibus Personality Inventory those who attended training showed significant change which was not shown by controls. There was an increase on the Aestheticism Scale and a decrease on the Complexity Scale. May and Tierney suggest that aestheticism scores rose because of the use of art and music during training, whereas complexity might have fallen because transactional analysis encouraged a more standardized way of construing interpersonal behaviour. However, the sample included only sixteen trainees so these effects may not prove to be reliable. Garber et al. (1976) studied a training programme for youths on probation. After ten weeks of learning, the principles of transactional analysis trainees showed changes not found among controls. These were an enhanced self-concept as measured by the Tennessee Self-Concept Scale and increased inner-directedness on the Personal Orientation Inventory. These tests have both been discussed in Chapter 3. The fact that changes on them are found in this study after transactional analysis, suggests that the effects of this type of training may not prove distinguishable from other types of group training. This study also found no change on the Jourard Self-Disclosure Questionnaire, a finding which is again consistent with others in Chapter 3.

Jesness (1975) made an extensive study of schools for delinquent boys in California. One school, the O. H. Close School, was organized around the application of transactional analysis, while another school used behaviour modification techniques and further schools used neither approach. In the O. H. Close School, transactional analysis was employed individually, in groups, and in large community meetings. It was found that both the experimental schools did substantially better than those with which they were compared. In the O. H. Close School, the parole violation rate fell from 49% to 31%, with the other schools showing lesser decreases. Reconviction rates also fell. Jesness argues that since both schools using widely differing approaches appeared to have some success, the success might not rest on the specific principles which guided the staff, but rather on the degree to which the boys felt cared for under each of the regimes. He presents data which support this view.

The Jesness study is impressive in the magnitude of the project undertaken, as well as the effects achieved. As a contribution to our understanding of transactional analysis it is, however, somewhat less useful. Inevitably the running of a school over a period of years involves many events not directly linked to transactional analysis, some of which Jesness touches on. His findings do not give us such a clean differentiation of the effects of transactional analysis as would studies of shorter-term projects.

Transactional analysis is currently employed rather widely, so that a more adequate range of studies will most likely appear in the next few years. So far the data are encouraging but fragmented. They give no indication that the effects of transactional analysis in groups are any different from other types of group experience.

Summary

Two differing interpretive approaches to group work have been presented. The Tavistock model rests on the role of the withdrawn, authoritative consultant. It may facilitate learning relevant to relationships with authority figures. Transactional analysis has a more didactic flavour. Each approach seeks to provide the trainee with increased autonomy from previous behaviour patterns (basic assumptions, scripts) through interpretation. Research evidence relevant to either approach is sparse. There is some evidence that Tavistock conferences do differ from other approaches, but no firm basis exists for conclusions about their effect. There is evidence that transactional analysis does have detectable effects, but no certainty that these effects are different from those of approaches discussed in earlier chapters.

CHAPTER 8
THE STRUCTURED ENCOUNTER

In Chapter 2, some emphasis was laid on how the group leader in most early forms of sensitivity training was largely inactive. The leader's inactivity was indeed seen as a prerequisite for the creation of the appropriate learning climate. The further development of group method has created for some leaders a more personally involving role, and Chapter 5 showed how this involvement can affect and enhance learning in the group. Enhanced leader involvement may include not only the expression of personal feeling, but also a resumption of more traditional leadership functions such as the structuring of group activities. In Chapter 6, it was seen that structured sessions in between group meetings and also the use of some structured activities within group sessions, may yield further benefits. But some leaders have taken this process much further, to the point where the entire time at the group's disposal is structured by the leader. These approaches are the focus of this chapter.

The convergence of techniques which gave rise to the structured encounter approach arose at Esalen Institute in California in the mid-sixties. The principal figures in this convergence were Will Schutz and Fritz Perls. Schutz was formerly a T-group leader, who became impatient with the constraints of that tradition, and sought to break out of it through the development of a range of nonverbal activities designed to give greater access to immediate feeling. Perls was a former psychoanalyst who, many years earlier, had started to formulate a therapeutic system built around a focus on here-and-now feelings and behaviour. The result of this convergence, *structured encounter*, is not easy to delineate. Confusion stems from the fact that not only does Schutz (1967) employ the term 'encounter', but so also does Rogers (1970) whose approach has much more in common with sensitivity training and has been described earlier. Many of the studies reviewed in earlier chapters have concerned encounter groups, but the authors of these studies have rarely made it clear what type of encounter was employed. The studies reviewed in this chapter will comprise the much smaller number which do make it clear that they refer to the approach here labelled as *structured encounter*.

Lieberman et al. (1973) also encountered the difficulty of accurately labelling the different orientations. In the seventeen groups which they studied, there was a steady progression from the leader who introduced no structured exercises during the thirty hours of meetings, to the one who introduced over eighty such exercises. A simple count of frequency does not serve to differentiate structured encounter from the other approaches, since some exercises may last for an hour or more, while others may be over in a minute or two. It does nonetheless appear that a high proportion of the Lieberman et al. leaders did rely heavily on structured exercises. This was particularly the case in the groups described as Esalen eclectic, eclectic marathon, Rogerian marathon, Gestalt, and Psychodrama, as well as those based on tape recorded instructions known as Encountertapes. In a critique of Lieberman et al., Schutz (1975) himself argues that many of these types of groups cannot be considered as instances of encounter at all. Terminological confusion thus continues unabated. The difficulty appears to stem from the fact that not just one or two of these leaders is eclectic, but that many of them are. For instance, the leader describing himself as Rogerian structured his group in a most unRogerian way, including the use of sensory awareness exercises, while one of the leaders described as using transactional analysis utilized some Gestalt exercises in addition. Some suitable word is thus needed to describe the overall range within which this eclecticism occurs, and Lieberman et al.'s choice of the word 'encounter' seems as good as any.

When Lieberman et al. compared all the groups using structured encounter with all those which did not, they found no significant difference in outcome. This was largely due to the fact that were large variations between one group and the next in each of the categories. It does therefore make sense to examine separately each of the various types of structured encounter, in order to see whether these variations might have been due to the approach employed, rather than to personal qualities of the leader or his particular group.

Open encounter

Open encounter is the phrase coined by Schutz (1967, 1971) to describe his approach. Two principal elements in the development of open encounter were his previous experience in working as a T-group trainer for nearly a decade, and his enthusiasm for body therapies, particularly bioenergetics (Lowen, 1967). The basis of bioenergetics is that one's feelings are not simply cognitions, but expressions of energy flow within one's body. Thus breathing, posture, gait, and so forth will all be expressive of feelings, only some of which may have been consciously verbalized. Schutz saw the possibility of enhancing and speeding up the development of T-groups through the use of structured exercises, which were designed to surface feelings which were already present in the individual but were not easy to express. These exercises were almost all nonverbal, and were undertaken either by the group as a whole or by pairs. Schutz showed considerable ingenuity in devising nonverbal activities which might be expected to elicit the various types of feelings present in the group. Some of the better known of these are detailed in Figure 3. Once the apparent usefulness of employing such leader-initiated exercises was established, Schutz and others rapidly extended the range of possibilities, drawing on a variety of existing traditions within the clinical field. Immediately fruitful sources included Gestalt therapy and psychodrama (to be discussed shortly), and others were the conjoint family therapy of Satir (1964), the use of various types of massage, the use of imagery and guided fantasy deriving from clinical approaches such as psychosynthesis (Assagioli, 1965) and laboratory experiments on imagery (Singer, 1974), and the techniques of body-oriented therapies such as bioenergetics (Lowen, 1971) and psychomotor therapy (Pesso, 1973).

For Schutz, the criteria as to whether or not to employ one of these structured exercises would be twofold. Firstly, does the exercise give the individual access to additional feelings? Secondly, does the exercise enable the individual to experience success in the expression of those feelings? Successful expression of feelings which had long since been suppressed might require the utilization of fantasy, the taking on of imagined roles, or the relinquishment of customary verbal controls over oneself. The consequent feeling would nonetheless have a situational realness which transcends the structure of the exercise employed to induce it. His approach originally involved the use of exercises entirely within the context of an ongoing group, which resembled a T-group. However, it quickly became apparent that the exercises could often have a powerful impact, even if employed with people who were available only for an hour or two, and who could not therefore expect to wait for appropriate moments to arise in the development of a group when particular exercises would seem appropriate. Exercises have frequently been used subsequently to demonstrate the nature of encounter, although they clearly demonstrate only a facet of what would be likely to occur in a longer-lasting group.

None of the reported research studies of groups have unambiguously identified their orientation as being that of open encounter. Schutz's influence has been widespread and it is very probable that quite a few of the studies reviewed in Chapter 3 referred to his type of encounter. There have, however, been a number of studies specifically co,cerned with assessing the effects of structured encounter exercises and these will now be examined.

Boderman, Freed, and Kinnucan (1972) conducted an experiment which was ostensibly concerned with extra-sensory perception. The subjects were asked to guess the suit of cards drawn from a pack by another subject. All subjects were women. In one condition of the experiment, subjects were asked to make some of their guesses while exploring the face of the other person with their hands. Face exploration is an activity which is sometimes employed in open encounter. It was found that the women who had explored one another's faces evaluated one another more favourably than those who were not asked to do this. In a similar experiment, Murphy (1972) asked students to solve a pencil and paper maze while holding either the hand of an unseen person or a wooden bar. The maze was actually insoluble, but it was found that the students' persistence in attempting to solve it was much affected by whether or not they were touching another person.

These experiments examine the effect of touching another person on one's feelings, but they do so in circumstances rather different from an actual encounter experience. Cooper and Bowles (1973) utilized the first of the series of Encountertapes, to be discussed more fully later in the chapter. This tape gives instructions for a two-hour introductory encounter session. Activities include introductions, giving first impressions, the Schutz break-in exercise, and the Schutz trust fall exercise done as a group. Cooper and Bowles asked nine students to participate in the exercises and a further nine to listen to the tape recorded instructions and discuss how they might feel if they did do them. Before and after this, they completed questionnaires concerning their willingness to disclose various things about themselves to others in their group. It was found that those who did the exercises became more willing to self-disclose, while those who merely listened to the tape and discussed it did not.

Snortum and Ellenhorn (1974) asked their subjects to participate in a sequence of fourteen nonverbal exercises. After each one, a set of semantic differential ratings was completed. There were eighty-seven subjects of mixed sex and age. It was found that there were highly significant variations in the feelings induced by the various exercises. Women experienced a wider range of feelings, from greater pleasure in some exercises to greater negative affect in others. In the paired exercises, men preferred to be with women but women enjoyed being either with men or with other women. Their strongest preference was to be with other women.

The Snortum and Ellenhorn study was done under rather naturalistic conditions, and indeed some of the subjects were at the time participating in groups. Walker (1975) studied the impact of a sequence of seven nonverbal exercises in a manner which was more tightly controlled by the experimenter, but therefore also more artificial. Subjects were paired by the experimenter either with a member of the same or opposite sex, who in all cases was a stranger. The subjects were 180 unmarried psychology students. Once paired, the students were asked to go through the sequence of exercises in a room by themselves, having been told that they would be observed through a mirror. Under these circumstances, it was found that after the experience subjects felt more anxious, depressed, distant, guilty, and angry, and less affectionate, relaxed, joyful, or sexually aroused. The findings of this study contrast with those of the previous three. They serve to underline that there is nothing automatic about the effect of nonverbal exercises; their impact is dependent upon the context within which they are employed. Walker also found that all-male pairs were the least comfortable.

Friedman et al. (1976) studied the use of a sequence of nonverbal exercises as a warm-up for subsequent group sessions. It was found that fifteen minutes of exercises left participants feeling significantly more extrovert than usual. Watching a film of a group for a similar period did not have this effect, but led participants to predict a higher subsequent level of self-disclosure. Control conditions of 'getting to know you' discussion, or of no activity at all did not have these effects. Dies and Greenberg (1976) report a similar study in which a thirty-minute warm-up preceded a 1½-hour group session. Groups whose warm-up activities included touching rated their groups more positively, and were more willing to take risks.

Lieberman, Yalom, and Miles' differentiation between groups with a

Figure 3.   *Examples of open encounter exercises*

Focus	Procedure
Group member feels excluded.	Group forms a circle excluding member, who attempts to break in.
Group member feels trapped, constrained.	Group forms a circle, with member inside the circle. Member attempts to break out.
Group members feel initially wary of one another.	Group mills around, without speaking, but communicating nonverbally.
Two members are unable to resolve a disagreement verbally.	They are invited to continue the conversation without speaking.
Two members find it difficult to make their feelings towards one another known.	Each stands at opposite ends of room and moves towards the other in whatever way feels right.
Two members are competing.	Various exercises including arm-wrestling, pushing one another around, etc.
Two members explore their trust in one another.	One falls backwards into the arms of the other.
One or more members explore their trust in the group as a whole.	Group forms a circle, while member stands in the centre and allows self to fall. Group continues to support the member so that they repeatedly rock from side to side.
Group expresses support to an individual.	Member lies on floor, eyes shut. Group raises member, rocking back and forth, and after some time lowers member again.
Exploring nurturant-dependent relationships.[1]	One member of a pair closes eyes while the other guides them on a walk for a few minutes, attempting to communicate without words or sight the sensory experiences which are available.
Mapping the social structure of the group.[1]	One member positions the others in a manner which portrays or 'sculpts' the relationships within the group.

1. These exercises were devised not by Schutz, but by Satir (1964).

high proportion of exercises and those without, found no difference in outcome, but some differences were obtained. The most consistent of these was that the exercise-based groups were more cohesive. With the exception of the Walker study, which was done under very different circumstances, these studies all suggest a similar conclusion: the effects of nonverbal exercises are to enhance warmth, trust, and cohesion within the group. The Walker study suggests that this will only occur if the exercises are set up in a manner which is felt to be permissible by participants.

There is room for considerable debate as to whether the enhancement of group cohesion will necessarily lead to greater learning within the group. Schutz himself would most likely argue that cohesion itself was not an integral part of the learning, which might arise from working through a particular nonverbal activity, but rather a side effect of the discharge of other more powerful and possibly painful feelings which are elicited by the exercise. A thoughtful critique of the use of nonverbal exercises is that by Argyris (1967). Some of the arguments he presents relate to the theories of learning discussed in Chapter 4. He follows Schein and Bennis (1965) in asserting that learning in a group occurs when the participant experiences a dilemma, and invents a solution to that dilemma. In the use of nonverbal exercises, what most typically occurs is that the participant experiences a dilemma and the solution is then provided by the group leader in the form of an exercise. In these circumstances, Argyris argues, it is difficult for the participant to internalize whatever occurs as a consequence of the exercise. Assuming that the exercise achieves some resolution or catharsis of the previous dilemma, the likely consequence is that the participant thinks more highly of the leader who provides such a 'magic' solution to the dilemma. A group structure is enhanced wherein the leader becomes an esteemed, heroic figure.

The situation discussed by Argyris has changed in many ways in the ensuing decade. Whereas at that time the structured nonverbal exercise was indeed part of the expertise of the avant-garde leader, the books of Schutz and others have now ensured that such exercises are widely known. As often as not, in the late seventies, it will be group members who propose nonverbal exercises and it may be the leader who is more hesitant. Since the leader remains a powerful group member, it is nonetheless often the leader's stance which proves crucial to whether or not an exercise is carried out. Lieberman et al. present data which are supportive of Argyris' contention. In high-exercise groups, the leader was more favourably evaluated than in the low-exercise groups. This difference was still present eight months after the groups were over, and was reflected in the fact that members of high-exercise groups were more likely to actively persuade others to participate in groups than were members of low-exercise groups. Lieberman et al. suggest that the reason for the rapid diffusion of structured exercises over the past decade is that leaders like to be popular, and that they stand to benefit if former group members proselytize on their behalf.

While all of this may be true, the central question posed by Argyris remains unanswered. Does the utilization of structured exercises make the internalization of learning less probable? In so far as Lieberman et al.'s high-exercise groups did not do significantly worse than other groups, exercises clearly do not *prevent* learning, even if they fail to enhance it. It is rather likely that the simple opposition of structured exercise versus unstructured exercise is too crude to show up differences. One might expect that, as with other aspects of leader behaviour, the response will depend upon the manner in which an exercise is introduced. Where the leader communicates genuineness of concern, and provides the member with a truly open choice as to whether or not to undertake an exercise, the prospects for internalization will be enhanced. Where an exercise is imposed, it is much more likely that the exercise will be undertaken in a compliant manner, or if it is something congenial, in a manner which provides catharsis and identification with the trainer.

A central element in Schutz's description of his groups is that every member of the group is responsible for how he or she behaves. Thus, although transcripts in his books and films of his groups quite frequently show him instructing a member to behave in a certain way, he would argue that it is the member's responsibility to resist his suggestions if they are unacceptable. No evidence is available as to how frequently such resistance is either felt or expressed in open encounter. The assumption upon which such assertions rest, that all members of the group have equal power to determine what happens or does not happen, is not consistent with findings that leaders are very frequently the most powerful members of their groups. It might thus be that those who do internalize the benefits of open encounter are those who are able to experience the equality of responsiblity and freedom of action which Schutz assumes, while those who fail to internalize are those who experience the group as a more unequal place.

A somewhat similar conception of personal responsibility is also found among Gestalt therapists, whose approach will next be examined.

Gestalt therapy

The central procedures of Gestalt therapy were available as long ago as 1951 (Perls, Hefferline, and Goodman, 1951). The key figure in this approach, Perls, lost sympathy with the historical focus of psychoanalysis, and sought to create a therapy which derived from the theories of Gestalt psychologists, whose interest was mostly in the processes of perception. Our tendency to perceive the world as a *Gestalt* or whole, rather than as meaningless fragments applies, argued Perls, to ourselves as much as to other elements of the world we perceive. Very frequently we fail to experience this unity because we do not permit ourselves to experience aspects of ourself which are too painful or frightening. Perls' technique for alleviating this is often referred to as Gestalt therapy, but is in fact as much practised with normals as with those in therapy. The Gestalt approach involves an intensified awareness of one's immediate perceptions. As with all perceptions, these will be patterned into a central element or figure, and a context or ground. According to Perls, one plays a part in the creation of both figure and ground. Only if one accepts responsibility for these creations will one experience the unity of self and experience which is sought.

Perls' technique was employed both with individuals and groups. Where he worked with groups he would employ a 'hot-seat' procedure, whereby one member would volunteer to work with him while other members watched. The goal of the therapist in working with a client is to induce the client to take responsibility for his or her behaviour. The exercises which the therapist employs are flexibly and intuitively applied. The goal is to follow the present awareness of the client, rather than to impose new perceptions or interpretations. The client may be asked to describe current feelings or perceptions. Where there is some apparent contrast between figure and ground, the client may be asked to switch to exploration of what was previously the peripheral or ground aspect of the perception. For instance, they might be asked to express verbally feelings previously only apparent through nonverbal gestures or postures, or to express what was being ignored or avoided. The client who expresses a wish to avoid something will often be encouraged to express more fully that avoidance, for instance by imagining oneself as far away as possible from what is being avoided.

A favourite element in Gestalt technique is to have the client conduct a fantasy dialogue between two of the perceptual elements of which he or she is aware. These might be different elements in one's personality, such as a top dog and an underdog, different parts of one's body, different goals for oneself, or different elements in a dream or fantasy which one reports. In all these cases, the purpose of asking the client to speak for each element is to enhance the degree to which they accept responsibility for that aspect of their self. Perls devised a series of linguistic rules to encourage clients to accept such responsibility verbally. Thus they are discouraged from speaking of elements of themselves as 'he', 'she', 'it', or 'one', and encouraged to use 'I'. They are discouraged from using 'can't' and encouraged to use 'won't' and so forth.

The original form of Gestalt therapy devised by Perls most frequently used a 'hot-seat' procedure. However, he also provided methods of Gestalt awareness training which enabled a single leader to direct a group experience for a number of members at a time. This included exercises such as repeating many times over 'Now I am aware of . . .' in pairs or as a group. Both of these approaches have received increasing attention from the mid-sixties onwards.

In the Lieberman et al. study, three of the leaders made extensive use of the Gestalt approach, the two identified as Gestalt leaders, plus another referred to as an Esalen eclectic. These leaders all introduced between sixty and eighty exercises in their groups, and thus provided the highest degree of leader-initiated structure of any of the groups. These groups included one of the most highly successful and two groups towards the bottom of the range. How representative a sample this provides is unclear, since as Schutz (1975) indicates, one of these three leaders (the least successful) was 'one of the few leaders ever banned from giving groups at Esalen . . .'.

A number of studies have been reported of the effects of Gestalt therapy. The great majority of these have been made by Foulds and his colleagues in the counselling centre of Bowling Green State University, Ohio. These studies have all followed a closely similar design. The counselling centre has a waiting list for its programme of groups. Trainees and controls are selected from the waiting list in such a manner that the two groups are matched for age, sex, and initial scores on whichever test is to be employed. The sample within any one study is a single group of trainees and a similar size group of controls. Most of the groups are held as a marathon, meeting for up to twenty-four hours over a weekend. The measures employed include many of those utilized by other investigators and referred to in Chapter 3. All of the eighteen studies reported have found significant changes among the trainees, but not among controls. Some of the more recent studies have also tested to see whether the changes found among trainees persisted over the subsequent six months.

The specific findings of the Foulds group can now be examined. After Gestalt groups, members make significantly more positive ratings of themselves, whether these groups be held on a marathon basis (Foulds, Girona, and Guinan, 1970; Foulds and Guinan, 1973) or on a once-a-week basis (Foulds, 1973). Members become less dogmatic (Foulds, Guinan, and Warehime, 1974), and less neurotic (Foulds and Hannigan, 1976) after marathon groups. On the California Psychological Inventory, the scales which have shown changes in each of two groups (Foulds and Hannigan, 1974, 1978(a)) have been sense of well-being, tolerance, sociability, responsibility and conscientiousness, ability to create a good impression, achievement through conformity and through independence, personal and intellectual efficiency, and interest in the inner needs, motives, and responses of others.

In view of the emphasis on personal responsibility in Gestalt therapy, it is not surprising that Foulds has also used tests of perceived personal causality. Belief in the internal locus of control is found to increase, both after a marathon group (Foulds, Guinan and Warehime, 1974), and after two groups meeting weekly (Foulds, 1971). The inner-directedness measure of Shostrom's Personal Orientation Inventory is found to increase, both in weekly groups (Foulds, 1970, 1971), and in marathon groups (Guinan and Foulds, 1970; Foulds and Hannigan, 1976(a), (b); Foulds and Hannigan, 1978(b), (c)). Increases in inner-directedness found after two groups (Foulds and Hannigan, 1976(a)), were still present six months later.

Foulds' approach to groups is primarily described by him as 'experiential Gestalt', but he has also been influenced by Pesso's (1969) psychomotor group therapy. In separate studies concerning weekly groups using this method, he has found improved ratings of self (Foulds and Hannigan, 1974), increased internal locus of control, and a decreased wish to give socially desirable responses (Foulds and Hannigan, 1976).

These results make clear that the methods employed by Foulds and his colleagues do have consistently measurable effects. The measures employed in all studies have been psychometric self-report questionnaires, but the consistency of finding positive effects is impressive. The Lieberman et al. study indicated how wary one should be of accepting any one leader as representative of a particular approach. It is thus important to test whether or not the effects achieved by Foulds are also found by other investigators and other Gestalt therapists. Unfortunately, other studies are few and far between. Felton and Biggs (1972, 1973) also used Rotter's Locus of Control Scale to test the effects of Gestalt therapy. Increased belief in internal locus of control was found among each of two groups of college low-achievers. Finando et al. (1977) measured changes in ratings of self after two encounter groups and three Gestalt groups for counselling centre clients. Both types of group showed significant change of semantic differential ratings of oneself, whereas controls did not. Changes were greatest on items referring to self-esteem and potency. Each of these studies thus obtains findings very similar to some of those obtained by the Foulds group. Shapiro and Shiflett (1974) examined the effects of a series of Gestalt awareness exercises for teacher trainees. The total training time involving Gestalt awareness was over one hundred hours, but this was spread over nine months. A decrease was found for the degree to which trainees felt connected to one another, as measured by the Campbell Social Attitude Inventory. However this effect also occurred among controls, and the researchers concluded that it was attributable to the stresses of the impending end of the overall teacher training course.

Yalom (1977) made a study of the effects of a weekend Gestalt group on the behaviour of patients undergoing psychoanalytically oriented psychotherapy. At the same time controls attended a weekend of Tai Chi, a meditative approach. Ratings were made of excerpts from tapes of the psychotherapy sessions by judges who were unaware which patients had attended which type of weekend. Ratings were made both before and after the weekend. It was found that each of the two Gestalt groups had an immediate effect, whereas the Tai Chi group did not. However, after six weeks these effects were no longer visible. Yalom concludes that the effects of weekend Gestalt groups are likely to be only transitory. However, this does not agree with Foulds and Hannigan (1976(a)), who found effects of their weekend groups still present after six months. An equally plausible interpretation of Yalom's finding is that the effects of a weekend Gestalt group will not persist where members are concurrently undergoing a quite different form of therapy, based on quite different theories, and whose therapists may not have encouraged the persistence of those effects.

The Shapiro and Shiflett study is thus the only one of the twenty-one studies of Gestalt to be reviewed which failed to obtain any significant effect of training. It was also the only one to be concerned with Gestalt awareness rather than the more personally focussed Gestalt therapy proper.

The studies of Gestalt therapy have been too much focussed on the work of a single centre and a particular population to be entirely conclusive. They are also in some need of a broader range of instruments for the measurement of change. However, the results do so far appear highly promising. Perhaps the most striking thing about the results, is that the effects do appear to some degree different from the effects of other types of group. Since Gestalt employs methods which lay great stress on individuals' experiences of themselves as causal, the findings from the Shostrom POI and the Rotter Locus of Control Scale are notable. They contrast with the rather patchy results obtained with these measures in T-groups or open encounter. At the same time, there is clearly some overlap between the effects of Gestalt and of other approaches, as is illustrated by the only two studies (Lieberman et al., 1973; Finando et al., 1977) which have made direct comparisons between them.

Psychodrama

Although psychodrama now has a place among the range of structured approaches to encounter, it has a very much longer history than any of the other methods. As early as 1908, Moreno was experimenting with the use of role-playing for children in Vienna, while he himself was only sixteen. In subsequent years the procedure which he termed *psychodrama* gradually evolved. In his hands psychodrama became a fusion of psychotherapy and the theatre. The problems of the client, or protagonist as Moreno would have it, are role-played with a vividness and actuality which derives from casting the role play as a here-and-now event. For Moreno and his adherents, the construction of a psychodrama is nonetheless rather different than the rehearsal of a play. No one learns lines. The psychodrama is created by reference to the recollections of the protagonist with the assistance of the psychodrama director. At all times the protagonist, and others who may be assigned roles within the psychodrama, are encouraged to speak as though they are already in the role they are to portray. If this procedure leads events to work out in an unintended manner, the director may ask particular actors to reverse roles, so that each may better grasp the dilemmas of being in the other role, or so that the protagonist may demonstrate to others the type of response he or she would actually find most likely from others. There is thus no sharp differentiation between rehearsal and performance in psychodrama. A psychodrama most often involves a sequence of stages by which the director provides a warm-up for the group, locates an individual who wishes to work on a problem, creates a network of roles, facilitates the staging of the psychodrama, and then directs the event as its impact on the protagonist and others elicits feelings which may themselves modify or extend the psychodrama. The director's intention is to allow the psychodrama to unfold in such a manner as to create a catharsis for the protagonist.

Many of the elements of other approaches can be identified in these procedures. In essence the protagonist selects a problem or concern, either contemporary or drawn from earlier experience. He or she then takes responsibility for expressing feelings relating to that concern in a direct manner, but within a specially created safe setting. The resultant catharsis takes place before a concerned audience, who may themselves be next on stage, just as in Gestalt therapy.

For many years psychodrama developed in some isolation from other approaches (Greenberg, 1973). Its influence was not so much through adoption of the psychodramatic method as such, but through the increasing popularity of role-playing and through the diffusion of many of the warm-up exercises devised by Moreno. Moreno laid great stress on the importance of warm-up to the development of spontaneity in the psychodrama. Although later pioneers such as Schutz were unaware of the range of psychodrama warm-up exercises (Schutz, 1971), exercises very similar to Schutz's inventions turn out to have been devised by psychodramatists many years earlier. The originators of the T-group were also well aware of Moreno's work, and some of the early Bethel laboratories included substantial amounts of role-playing and of *sociodrama*, a further procedure devised by Moreno.

The groups studied by Lieberman et al. (1973) included two whose approach emphasized psychodrama, but neither of which followed closely the description of pure psychodrama outlined above. One of these groups was somewhat more successful than average, the other somewhat below average. The pure form of psychodrama has received only a little attention from researchers, most probably because Moreno himself presented his approach through assertion and through presentation of case studies.

Most of the studies which have control groups have concerned clients in psychiatric institutions, and are therefore not very closely comparable to studies of other types of group. Harrow (1951) evaluated psychodrama for hospitalized schizophrenics over a series of twenty-five sessions. No statistically significant differences were found between changes in trainees and controls on various tests, including the Rorschach projective test. Jones and Peters (1952) undertook a similar study and found improvement for the trained schizophrenics on ratings of behaviour in the ward by hospital staff. Various other test scores also improved, but since the tester was also the psychodrama director, the results are difficult to interpret. Haskell (1975) employed psychodrama among prison inmates preparing for release on parole. Trainees showed changes on a test of predicted role behaviours not found for controls. In this instance also, training lasted twenty-five hours. Pilkey et al. (1961) used psychodrama to attempt an increase in empathy among mentally retarded thirteen-year-olds. After eight hours of training there was some increase in the ability to predict how others in the class would rate themselves. In the only recent controlled study, Schönke (1975) provided twenty-four hours of psychodrama and counselling over a number of weeks to twelve German students. Self-ratings showed increases in aggression, desire for openness and extraversion, and decreases in composure, rigidity, and submissiveness. When changes for trainees and controls were compared, only the decrease in composure achieved significance. The effect of this programme appears to have been to enhance trainees' assertiveness.

These five studies do not provide a firm basis for conclusions about the effects of psychodrama. Since there is a considerable overlap between the procedures of psychodrama and more informal approaches to role-playing, further clues about its likely effects can be gleaned from some rather better designed studies of different types of role-playing. In these studies, researchers have found it useful to distinguish between those who actively participate in role-playing, those who observe others role-playing, and those not present at all. Active role-playing has been found to create attitude change relative to observers (Janis and King, 1954; Culbertson, 1957; Janis and Mann, 1965; Johnson, 1971), and relative to controls (Culbertson, 1957; Kelly et al., 1957; Jansen and Stolurow, 1962; Mann and Mann, 1958). Most of these role-playing sessions were fairly brief and did not involve any of the warm-up activities which psychodramatists see as important. The criterion measures were mostly rather specific attitude scales, rather than the more basic personality attributes in which a psychodramatist might seek to create change. In some studies (King and Janis, 1956), it has been found that where subjects were asked to improvize their role-playing, the attitude change was greater. However, more recent workers, influenced by the thinking of behaviour therapists, have shown a larger effect where the trainee is provided with an explicit model to copy (Jansen and Stolurow, 1962; Friedman, 1972).

The most sustained of the role-playing studies, that by Mann and Mann (1958), concerned students who had twelve hours of role-playing, while controls had an equivalent period of leaderless group discussion. The role-players showed a significantly greater increase on ratings of their own adjustment in relations with others. Role-playing studies do, therefore, offer some hope that psychodrama may have positive effects. Future studies would do well to differentiate those who participate as protagonists from those who do not. At present, so little is known as to the effects of psychodrama that it would be impossible to consider whether its effects are similar or different to those of other group approaches.

Of the studies mentioned, the one by Janis and Mann (1965) was the only one to assess whether the effects lasted. Janis and Mann set up an emotionally powerful role-play in which smokers were asked to role-play a series of interactions with a doctor who told them that they had lung cancer. Follow-up studies (Mann, 1967; Mann and Janis, 1968) showed that many of the smokers gave up smoking and did not resume. This effect was strongest where the role-playing was set up in such a way as to frighten the subject rather than more neutrally. It remains to be seen whether the durability of this effect is specific to the topic of the role-play. In so far as many enacted psychodramas have to do with heavily affect-laden aspects of people's lives, the effects found might be quite representative of changes to be found for protagonists.

This section is necessarily inconclusive. Psychodrama has a long history and a literature which abounds with case histories and accounts of new techniques. The empirical work is nonetheless scanty, and can provide no more than pointers and suggestions.

Programmes of exercises

If the leader's role in the group is conceived of as an introducer of structured exercises, it is clear that considerable economies may be achieved by dispensing with the leader, and utilizing instead written or tape recorded instructions for group members. Such a step involves the assumption that even in the case of leaders who employ numerous structured exercises, the timing and choice of particular exercises is not crucial to the success of a specific group. According to this assumption, a desirable sequence of exercises could be worked out through pilot testing and evaluation, and there would then be no reason why this sequence should not prove appropriate to a particular group.

The most sustained attempt to develop this approach has been that leading to the creation of Encountertapes, a set of ten tape recorded instructions, each designed to structure a two-hour meeting of a group. Although the ten tapes follow a preplanned sequence, it is not essential that they be used in that order, nor indeed that they all be used. Some idea of the orientation of the exercises may be gained from their titles: First Encounter Microlab, Ground Rules, Feedback, Progress Report, Secret Pooling, Break-Out, Descriptions (of one another in terms of metaphors), Strength Bombardment (telling each person what is good about them), Giving and Receiving (warmth and affection), Last Encounter Microlab. The sequence thus includes both verbal and nonverbal exercises, with emphasis on self-disclosure, feedback, and acceptance.

Lieberman et al. (1973) included in their study two groups who had no leader, but worked instead from the Encountertape programme. Interestingly enough, even though there were therefore absolutely no differences between the instructions received by each group, they nonetheless developed in rather different directions. Although both groups were somewhat resentful of not having been allocated a leader, one group tended to carry out the tape instructions as prescribed, whereas the other only did so when they felt the instructions were in accord with what they would have wanted to do anyway. The group which followed the instructions was about averagely successful, whereas the group which sometimes went its own way was the third most successful of all the groups studied by Lieberman et al. This evidence supports the position advanced in Chapter 6 as to the importance of group composition in determining group outcome.

Solomon, Berzon, and Weedman (1968) developed a forerunner of Encountertapes, known as the Vocational Improvement Program. They compared groups of vocational rehabilitation clients who worked from a booklet form of this programme, with other groups which were professionally led. Both treatments led to significant increases on semantic differential rating scales of 'the way I see myself', which were not found among controls. Ratings of the clients were also made by their counsellors. It was found that gains occurred on these scales also, but not for controls. Since no difference was found between professionally led groups and the groups using the structured programme, the researchers decided to concentrate on their programme and used no further professional leaders. Solomon, Berzon, and Davis (1970) studied further groups, now using an audio taped version of the instructions. After the groups they again found more favourable self-ratings, and also found an increased willingness to disclose oneself to others. Ratings made of interviews before and after the groups showed increased ratings on motivation to work and on self-understanding. A follow-up was undertaken six months later, and by this time the significant effects were no longer present, except that trainees were still judged to be more highly motivated to work.

Berzon, Reisel, and Davis (1969) report the first study of Encountertapes. They found enhanced ratings of self among various types of student groups. A rating of personal efficacy increased after some groups but the effect was gone three weeks later. Vail (1971) utilized Encountertapes with culturally disadvantaged girls, but found no difference afterwards between trainees and controls. His measure included the California Psychological Inventory. Vicino et al. (1973) utilized a different sequence of exercises which they developed, and which had a somewhat more cognitive emphasis. They too found a change in ratings of perceived self. They also computed the match between each individual's rating of actual self and rating of 'how I would like to be'. An increased match was found between the two sets of ratings after training.

Programmes of exercises clearly do have some potentiality for creating a worthwhile group experience. Five of the six studies reviewed have detected some effects. Whether these effects last seems more open to question. One of the Lieberman et al. groups clearly had a continuing impact, but the other follow-up studies were disappointing. Lieberman et al. argue that tape-led groups may be preferable to other approaches since at least members are protected from the potentially more hazardous approaches of some types of leaders. While there may be something to this in some circumstances, the hazards are not so great as to warrant such a cautious approach in general. The tape-led groups in their study felt deprived by the lack of a leader, and the presence of one in the group creates not only the small risk that the leader is less competent than those who constructed the tape, but also the far greater likelihood that the leader can tailor his or her interventions to the unique history of the group, in such a way as to enhance the prospects for internalized learning.

The evidence about programmed exercises is not wholly conclusive. They may have lasting effects, but the evidence does not yet require that conclusion. A live leader is much more able to fit interventions to what is happening in the group. Where live leaders are available, they are likely to remain more in demand than programmed exercises.

Summary

A range of methods has been described which seeks to structure learning opportunities more highly in groups. The fears expressed by Argyris and others that such structure takes away some of the preconditions for internalized learning do not appear well founded. Although the procedures of open encounter, Gestalt, psychodrama, and programmed exercises do appear to differ in substantial ways from one another and from less structured approaches, research data have not yet shown appreciable differences in the effects they create. Our knowledge of each one of these approaches is sketchy, but it is quite likely that where each works it does so, not because of its distinctiveness but because it is able to reproduce the conditions for internalized learning hypothesized in Chapter 4.

CHAPTER 9
SELF–HELP GROUPS

Most of the types of group experience examined in this book can be considered as instances of self-help groups, inasmuch as the emphasis is on a peer learning experience. The leader is seen as setting up the conditions for learning, but the actual process of learning occurs as often as not between different members of the group. In the types of group experience to be discussed in this chapter, this secularization is taken still further. Self-help groups necessarily have leadership functions, which may be distributed around the group or may be focussed on particular individuals. But even where there is a specific leader, that leader is not likely to be someone with a particular type of professional training. Most often leaders are those who have themselves benefitted from previous involvement in similar self-help groups.

Self-help groups constitute a rapidly growing element in contemporary society (Lieberman and Borman, 1979). This growth no doubt reflects a change in our conceptualization of the role of professionals in society. Whereas a decade or two ago a fair amount of idealism was invested in the ability of the welfare state to ameliorate social problems, we are now much more aware of the deficiencies as well as the strengths of welfare state provision. The incidence of many social problems does not fit well with the resources or skills which the welfare state has allocated to them, and those who find themselves unhelped by what is provided have started to ask whether they could not themselves achieve something more worthwhile by meeting others facing similar difficulties. Thus self-help groups have been created by alcoholics, drug addicts, gamblers, single parents, women, haemophiliacs, parents of children with various problem conditions, and so forth. Robinson and Henry (1977) list more than eighty such groups or organizations currently active in Britain. The potential of self-help groups clearly rests on the fact that the criterion around which each group is organized is highly motivating to all members. They all know what it is like to experience the particular problem with which the group is concerned. The support which flows from this sharing of adversity is likely to be a major element in their potential effectiveness. It may also be true that members of self-help groups are able to contribute more of their time and energy to them than are the leaders of professionally led groups.

The goals of some self-help groups are not particularly close to those of groups discussed in other chapters. However, many self-help groups do seek to create personal change through group experience, and it is these which will be discussed. Perhaps unsurprisingly there have been very few quantitatively based research studies of the effects of self-help groups (Emrick, Lassen, and Edwards, 1977), and still fewer which have also used control groups. This discussion will be based on available descriptions of some of the more widely known self-help groups and organizations, namely Alcoholics Anonymous, Synanon, co-counselling and the women's movement.

Alcoholics Anonymous

Alcoholics Anonymous (AA) originated in Ohio in 1934. Procedures employed in their meetings are organized and derive directly from a rationale laid down many years ago. The alcoholic joining a group is provided with a sequence of twelve steps through which to pass. Elements in this sequence include the use of first names only, the ritual assertion of 'I'm an alcoholic', the acknowledgement that the control of one's drinking has become impossible, prayer and awaiting the time when the 'higher power' will take away the compulsion to drink, confession of one's misdeeds to others in AA, and the spreading of AA's message to other alcoholics. The procedures thus derive more directly from a religious context than from the procedures of other types of group work. The work of AA is widely believed to have some effectiveness, but published quantitative evidence is not available.

Antze (1976) acknowledges that the social support given to one another by AA members in face of the stigma of alcoholism must be a major element in the impact of their programme. But he argues that simply to account for the effectiveness of AA or other types of self-help groups in terms of sharing of support, is to miss other more distinctive elements which are likely to be equally important. Antze suggests that the procedures of each type of self-help group add to the support which it provides to its members an ideology appropriate to the confrontation of the particular problem it is designed to solve. In the case of AA, this ideology is paradoxical. In order to control drinking, the alcoholic must acknowledge the *uncontrollability* of drinking and await the time when an external agency, the 'higher power', will grant such control. This conceptualization of the process of personal change makes interesting connections with the model advanced in Chapter 4. There also it was argued that personal change arises when the group member is confronted by paradoxical injunctions both to change and to stay the same. There would be a close equivalence between the two models if it could be shown that the standardized procedure adopted by AA is distinctively suitable for the creation of paradox within alcoholics. Antze reviews studies of the personality attributes of alcoholics, and concludes that they are characterized by an exaggerated conception of their sense of personal control. In other words, they frequently believe themselves to be able to control their behaviour when they cannot in fact do so. For an alcoholic then it would be more than usually difficult to 'touch bottom' in other words to acknowledge one's total lack of personal control. Only when alcoholics have achieved this, is it likely that they would be able to set more realistic goals for the personal control of their behaviour. In the latter stages of the AA programme, much provision is made for the alcoholic to seek the assistance of others if he or she feels in danger of slipping, i.e., drinking. Thus the alcoholic acknowledges the frailty of personal control and uses the support of others to sustain it.

The fixity of AA's approach can in this way be seen as tailored to the particular needs of alcoholics. The specific structure may intensify just that experience of paradox which is required for the creation of lasting change. In some other type of group this would be far less likely to occur, since it is much more likely that alcoholics would continue to succeed in fooling both themselves and others as to the degree to which they were just on the point of getting the problem under control.

Synanon

The Synanon game or encounter was devised by Chuck Dederich in California during the late fifties. Its prime use has been in residential communities of drug addicts. The central procedure is the expression of verbal abuse to those present. Any aspect of an individual's behaviour is seen as a legitimate target for others to attack. The Synanon game does not have the sequenced structure found with AA sessions, but the overall Synanon community is organized in a hierarchical manner. Those initially admitted to the community are allowed few privileges, and these may be increased as progress is made in contributing effectively to the community. In everyday living the community member is required to carry out assigned tasks and obey community rules. Reactions to the day's events or violations of rules are only to be expressed within the boundaries of scheduled game sessions. Many communities based on methods resembling Synanon also offer game clubs which are open to nonresidents and work within similar ground rules. The Synanon game does have leaders, in the sense that a community ensures that each game includes a number of those who are experienced in working within the rules of the game. But leaders are in no way immune from attack in the same manner as are all others who are present. In attacking others, members employ a maximum of inventiveness, reacting not simply to what the other may in fact have done, but also to what they might do, or what they might indirectly represent.

At first reading, the Synanon game sounds alarming and markedly different from other types of group. The emphasis on warmth, trust, and self-determination found elsewhere is not obviously present. There is some evidence that game participants also find it an alarming experience. De Leon and Biase (1975) measured heart rates among members of a Synanon community before and after game sessions and other community meetings. They found that with one group, heart rates were much enhanced prior to game sessions. With a second group no systematic differences were found.

The study by Lieberman et al. (1973) included some group members who attended sessions of a Synanon game club. The groups were differently composed for each of the weekly meetings. The researchers found these groups to be somewhat less than averagely successful. However, this overall conclusion does not show that they found a strong divergence in members' reaction to the experience. Some members were strongly positive, admiring the directness of speaking in the game sessions and seeing it as an antidote to the indirectness and evasiveness of everyday communication; others were strongly negative about the experience, and nearly half of the twenty-three members dropped out within the first four weeks of meeting. Two of the remaining members were judged by the researchers to have been harmed by the experience.

In evaluating Lieberman et al.'s findings, one must bear in mind that the prime function of the Synanon game is its use within the setting of a total community for addicts. Their evaluation of it is an evaluation of its use out of this context. Having said this, it is also true that Synanon methods are increasingly being used out of their original context. The high dropout rate should not in itself be seen as a negative quality of this approach, since it presumably indicates the belief of those dropping out that they are unlikely to learn from the Synanon game. The rate might be particularly high because, in the Lieberman et al. study, students were randomly assigned to groups rather than choosing the type of group from which they expected to benefit. The dropout rate was nonetheless higher than for other types of group under the same circumstances.

Antze (1976) suggests that Synanon procedures may be uniquely well suited to the treatment of heroin addicts. He reviews evidence suggesting that heroin addicts may be unusually prone to tension and stress, and that they may have learned that heroin provides the only way in which this stress can be reduced. In the Synanon community on the other hand, the routine procedures may serve to prohibit or at least reduce stress. At the same time the game provides a setting which first deliberately creates stress through deliberate and often unreasonable attack, and then permits a safe discharge of that stress through tears or anger. Thus addicts gradually learn to see stress not in terms of their need for a fix, but in terms of a feeling within themselves which has a social origin and can have a social discharge. From seeing their weakness as internally caused, they develop a new awareness that they have the strength to discharge these weak feelings through others.

One might argue that this analysis appears almost to suggest that addiction to heroin is replaced by addiction to the game. Addict communities both in Britain and the United States have indeed found that an unresolved problem is how to cope with successful graduates of their programmes. Extensive Synanon communites now exist in California, with some thousands of members and provision made for children's schooling and so forth (Simon, 1978).

The effectiveness of the Synanon game turns out to be rather firmly linked to the cohesive and sometimes playfully supportive framework with which Dederich originally imbued it. Within that framework it functions by providing emotional catharsis and consequent learning of personal control in relation to stress. Outside of that framework its effects are less foreseeable. The Lieberman et al. study suggests some of the hazards of its incautious use. Recent press reports concerning Synanon in California imply that the procedures in use there have now also become a good deal too incautious.

Co-counselling

Co-counselling is a procedure basically undertaken in pairs, which are often initially drawn from a larger group. The procedures employed were first devised by Jackins (1962), but they draw widely on other approaches to group work. In essence, a co-counselling pair take turns to listen to one another talk. The basic ground rule of co-counselling is that the talker has control of how the time at his or her disposal is to be used. The listener is required to give the other their active attention, but not to seek to control or impose their own reactions on the talker. The goal of co-counselling is to enable the talker to discharge hurts or feelings which they may have been unable to express previously. The listener is permitted to make occasional interventions with the goal of facilitating discharge, but these have the status of suggestions to the talker rather than instructions, and the talker is free to ignore them. The listener will be particularly on the look-out for cues from the talker as to unexpressed feelings. Such cues might be changes in voice tone or volume, hesitation, or facial expressions. Where such cues occur, the listener may suggest to the talker that he or she repeats what has just been said, or that what has just been said be stated in its opposite form. Another option would be to invite the speaker to express current thoughts or feelings where they are hesitating or have fallen silent. *Acting in* is a technique employed where the speaker is aware of some feelings but has difficulty in expressing them directly. Acting in involves beginning by acting as though the feeling *were* being expressed, for instance by raising one's voice, pounding a cushion, or accentuating gestures.

Co-counselling techniques are most typically learned in a group setting, working with a series of partners and with a structure provided by more experienced co-counsellors and the available manual. Jackins was initially concerned to maintain some control over the manner in which co-counselling was employed, but a variety of adaptations and modifications in his procedures have been made. The central element in all of these is the continuing diffusion of peer counselling techniques, whose method stresses catharsis and facilitates this with techniques reminiscent of structured encounter, particularly Gestalt therapy.

No studies are available of the effects of co-counselling. One would expect that its effectiveness should vary according to how well co-counsellors mastered the basic techniques. If they do o, there is a good prospect that they will succeed in creating the conditions for internalization of personal change. The experience of the other's attention, plus the successful expression of feeling, should facilitate the enhancement of the talker's sense of personal control over the expression of relevant feeling. Since the method does not focus primarily on here-and-now relationships, one might expect the experience of enhanced personal control to concern the discharge of feeling from prior events, rather than the initiation of changed ways of coping with ongoing situations.

Consciousness-raising groups

A variety of groups have become popular in recent years whose goal is to explore and often to seek to change the circumstance of a particular category of persons in society. Examples would be groups for those who are gay, or those who are black, or who are men, or who are women. Of the types of self-help group so far discussed, consciousness-raising groups are probably the ones which are most truly member-centred. Each of the preceding types has turned out to have some system of hierarchical structure, through which attempts are made to standardize procedures.

Because consciousness-raising groups often do not adhere to any such centralized structure, it is less easy to be certain how they typically take place. Procedures which are frequently employed include focussing on one particular topic for a session, having each member share their particular experience, or taking it in turns to structure a session. Lieberman and Bond (1976) report a survey intended to provide information about women's consciousness-raising groups in the United States. Responses were received from 1669 women. The data indicate that women attending groups tended to be somewhat more anxious and depressed than those who did not. Their motives in joining a women's group were primarily to share and compare the experiences and feelings of women. Further motives were seeking help from others and fulfilling needs to relate to others. The majority of groups spent their time sharing previous life experiences, noting in particular similarities between different people's experiences.

Lieberman and Bond, both of whom are men, argue that the women's movement does not fit Antze's proposition that each self-help group has an ideology which generates a structure uniquely adapted to its clients. In their view, this may be because the clientele of women's groups is far more diverse than those of AA or Synanon, or else it may be that women's groups are too recently evolved for there yet to be much consensus as to how they should be structured. It is not clear that Lieberman and Bond's data require such conclusions. One could equally well argue that the supportive sharing and comparing which characterize many consciousness-raising groups are indeed well adapted to the task of focussing attention on what members have in common. By avoiding here-and-now issues, and focussing on the commonality of women's experiences, the group encourages members to see previous adversities or problems not as caused by their own personal weakness, but as inherent in current social structures.

The effect of this could be to reduce anxiety and depression, and increase assertiveness or aggression. Depending on the culture of particular groups, these changes might be expressed more in terms of the personal relationships of each of those present, or in terms of more overtly political issues.

The potential effect of consciousness-raising groups thus lies in decreased self-blame for past and present failings. If the group is able, like AA, to convey to members that current adversities are attributable to circumstance, the way is opened for them to attempt to behave more as they wish, while drawing on the support of others.

The process of change hypothesized for women's groups may turn out to be characteristic of many of the types of self-help groups which are not highly centralized or highly structured. In each case, one might expect that pooling of experience by those who share some problem or circumstance should reduce the degree to which the difficulties or failings of that circumstance are blamed on oneself. Conversely, pooling of experience should increase the degree to which members feel able to assert their needs in relation to other groups.

Comparison with other types of group

The self-help groups which have been discussed fall into two patterns. The first, exemplified by co-counselling, is intended for a broad range of people but is structured in such a manner that it can be effectively used without direct professional assistance. The second, exemplified by Synanon, AA, and consciousness-raising groups is designed for specific homogeneous categories of people, and shows a range varying from the tightly structured to the decentralized network.

It was proposed in Chapter 4 that the creation of personal change required the simultaneous experience of both support and confrontation from others. These preconditions were shown to be necessary for the transfer of change from one specially created grouping to another. Self-help groups do not often emphasize the creation of this type of personal change. More frequently, the explicit goal is one of getting together in the face of a common goal or problem. It was shown in Chapter 6 that homogeneous groups are the ones in which support is likely to be strongest. Thus, it could be argued that self-help groups are likely to succeed in creating a strong identification between members, but less likely to create personal change which transcends the boundaries of the group. Such an analysis might well be correct where the meetings of a self-help group terminated, but so long as meetings of it continued there would be no reason why the member should not sustain personal change outside the group, by the help of continuing support from within the group.

This line of reasoning suggests why so many self-help groups have tended to become social movements, continuing to involve those who have already participated in them. Continuing involvement can provide continuing support which will sustain the changes achieved. Thus AA members continue to attend meetings and to seek new members, Synanon graduates remain within their communities, and members of women's consciousness-raising groups may seek further involvement in other aspects of the women's movement. Lieberman and Bond (1978) suggest that the manner in which membership of self-help groups tends to persist over a period of years, or to fluctuate according to the acuteness of one's difficulties, implies a need for different types of evaluation research procedures. Since involvement in self-help groups may have no clear beginning or end, it may be best to compare matched groups of those who are or are not involved in a particular type of group, rather than looking for changes in individuals over time.

Some self-help groups do of course provide confrontation in addition to support. Thus co-counselling provides not just an active listener, but someone who awaits moments when one experiences tension and then invites one to focus on these moments. Synanon also clearly involves a substantial element of confrontation. However, Enright (1971) suggests that game players rarely remember what is said to them when the game is on them. In his view, the therapeutic effects of Synanon are achieved not through receiving confrontation but through giving it. Antze's analysis would suggest that both giving and receiving confrontation might lead to catharsis. In either case, the absence of overt support precludes the likelihood of internalized personal change.

Summary

Self-help groups take their structure either from standardized procedures or from the affinity of those sharing a particular predicament. Their homogeneity ensures the predominance of support in many cases. Their distinctive procedures may also have particular appropriateness to the types of member whom each group attracts. Their effectiveness has been little studied, but it probably rests most frequently upon the experience of continuing support rather than the internalization of personal change.

CHAPTER 10
ORGANIZATIONAL DEVELOPMENT

A great deal of our behaviour in contemporary society is bounded by the context of this or that organization. The early view of sensitivity training as located on a cultural island, envisaged a process whereby what was learned during training would be transferred back for subsequent application in the context from which the trainee came. The findings reviewed in Chapter 3 indicate that such a conception is by no means useless. The effects detectable after training do, in many cases, persist after the trainee has returned home. With the passage of time however, many trainers have become dissatisfied with the amount of carryover which occurs. This has been particularly true for those forms of training in which the effects sought are primarily changes in work behaviour. The culture of the T-group composed of initial strangers, it is argued, is so different from that of a large hierarchical organization that it is scarcely surprising if the trainee finds some difficulty in sustaining changes stemming from the T-group. The earliest steps towards the creation of organizational development were taken by Blake, Shepard, and others within the Esso Company in the United States (Shepard and Blake, 1962).

During the past fifteen years, the arguments put forward by protagonists of organizational development have strengthened. It is pointed out that even the changes which do persist after training are necessarily changes in individual behaviour, where that which trainers might like to act upon is the overall effectiveness of an organization at a particular task. Some organizations (Winn, 1966) sought to change the culture of their organization by having as high a proportion as possible of their managers participate in sensitivity training. The results were felt to be disappointing in proportion to the enormous investment of time and money which this required. As Winn recounts, in the case of Alcan, this led to a rethinking of priorities and attempts to design training programmes instead, in which intact work teams were trained together rather than the previous groups drawn from all over a very large organization. Initial endeavours in organizational development, of which this was one, were thus T-groups conducted with intact teams.

Organizational development now comprises a rather broad range of methods for facilitating change in organizations (French and Bell, 1973). Such methods include various types of consultancy and training, in an attempt to match up the change target in a particular setting and an appropriate method of intervention. Group training methods comprise only a part of that range, although the more enthusiastic practitioners sometimes seem to imply that groups provide the only durable basis for the creation of change. This chapter will examine only the group-based methods, since it is these which are congruent with the theme of this book. The developing range of group methods will first be examined, followed by consideration of studies of their application within the various different types of organizations.

Training designs

As indicated already, the earliest use of groups within organizations involved the transposition of the stranger T-group into the organization. The goals of the experience remained those of personal learning, but the setting was organizational. With this type of design, the trainer's task continues to be the creation of a trusting setting within which feedback, self-disclosure, and the experience of personal control may be enhanced. The transposition of this training method into the organization makes the achievement of these goals considerably more difficult. It is not easy to ensure that those who attend have made a free choice to do so. It is likely that the level of self-disclosure in the group will be much constrained by past experience in the organization. If members are aware that, in the past, others who have spoken freely have been in any way penalized, they will not lightly do so in the group. They may also hesitate to give uncensored feedback to others with whom they must continue to work in the future, and who may be or could become in the future their organizational superiors.

These kinds of difficulty ensure that the simple transposition of the

T-group into an organization is rarely likely to be fruitful. Some adaptation of its purpose is also required. A frequently used adaptation is the team development design. Here an intact work group meets as before, but the agenda is limited to the improvement of working relations between those present. There is no longer an emphasis on the development of individual skills, but in its place the task is the development of a shared diagnosis of current work relationships, and the creation of changes where these are desired. This design still requires some trust and openness in order to be effective, but the limits are set more firmly, thereby making it a less risky endeavour. Very often this task is further delimited by having feedback between team members structured according to some format provided by the group leader. The risks of the team development approach are perhaps greatest for the organizational superior in such groups. Since resentment in work groups is rather frequently channelled towards authority figures, it is important that superiors work out in advance whether the potential benefits for the group as a whole seem likely to outweigh whatever personal discouragement may be in store for themselves.

A third mode of group-based organizational development is analogous to the intergroup exercise of the stranger T-group laboratory. Here the focus is on feedback between different segments of the organization whose tasks require some form of collaboration. Where the numbers involved might become excessively large, this may be based on key representatives of each section rather than the total population. While some projects have involved adversary organizations, such as unions and management, a more typical case would be drawn from within a single organization, such as different divisions or functions.

The final type of design to be described is the structured package. The best known of these is Blake and Mouton's (1978) *managerial grid*. In grid training, an organization works through a sequence of phases, using a modified T-group format. A simple diagnostic framework is provided, whereby the individual's behaviour is rated on two nine-point scales. The first of these indicates how much concern the individual has for others as people, while the second indicates the level of concern for the productivity of the organization. The purpose of grid training is to induce an organizational climate of 9,9, i.e., a climate where concern for both people and for productivity are maximally high. The first phase of the grid programme provides a structured T-group experience where trainees are drawn from the same organization, but do not work together. Most typically it is found that the majority of trainees already see their behaviour as 9,9, whereas feedback from others much less often confirms this. In phase two, team development meetings occur to consider the implications of what occurred during phase one. A series of further phases are then planned, involving first individual teams and later interteam relations. The premise of Blake and Mouton, that a 9,9 climate is in all circumstances most likely to lead to organizational effectiveness, is persuasively presented by them, but remains largely untested. It is unlikely to be true, in the light of the extensive research evidence showing different leadership styles and organizational climates to be appropriate in varying circumstances. It may of course, nonetheless, be the case that the organizations within which the grid method has been employed do stand to benefit from it.

In presenting aspects of group training for individuals in earlier chapters, it has been relatively simple to discuss training as an isolated event which is not necessarily confounded with other life experiences. Such isolation is of course an artefact of the research process. The creation of personal change is, for the individual concerned, intimately bound up with events both prior to and following the training experience. In presenting organizational development these linkages become much more directly apparent. None of the approaches which have now been briefly described is likely to be employed by an organization without a substantial amount of preparation and debate. This stage of preparation and debate may indeed turn out to be more important in determining the success or failure of the intervention, than what happens once the programme is under way. The role of the external consultant is thus a key one in organizational development. This individual brings to the client organization some knowledge of alternative possibilities which might be undertaken, together with some skills in facilitating the diagnosis of what may be required. It would be somewhat unusual for organizational development to comprise simply the application of one or other type of group experience. More often the consultant, in collaboration with those within the organization, employs a wider range of methods. These may include interviews and surveys, feedback from such data collection, training for individuals, consultancy with particular individuals, discussion of more structured types of innovation, and so forth. In some of the studies to be reviewed later in this chapter, a number of these other procedures were employed in addition to the use of groups. Often these other methods may be crucial to the establishment of sufficient trust between consultant and organization to permit the effective use of groups subsequently.

The complexity of the setting within which the organizational development consultant operates also makes it exceptionally difficult to obtain substantive data evaluating the effectiveness of an intervention. Armenakis et al. (1976) asked a large sample of American organizational development consultants what difficulties they had encountered in evaluating their work. The most frequently mentioned difficulties were the choice of appropriate criteria for measurement (22%), nonavailability of control groups (21%), effects of events extraneous to the project (20%), and administrative difficulties (19%). The lack of a control group is a particular problem, since if a project involves the whole of an organization, or the whole of one unique part, it is totally impossible to locate a control group. Even where there is another similar section of the organization which is unaffected by the intervention, it can scarcely comprise more than a comparison group, rather than a strictly defined control group, since there will be numerous differences in the history, culture, and circumstances of the two sections. These difficulties mean that, despite the fact that organizational development has been undertaken on a rather wide scale over the past fifteen years, there are only about twenty studies of its effects which meet the criteria for inclusion in this book. Some further reference to the broader range of studies of organizational development which lack control groups will be made in the final section of this chapter, which considers the circumstances under which organizational development is most likely to succeed.

Studies in industry and commerce

More studies have been reported from the industrial field than from any other, which is consistent with the fact that organizational development was first attempted in this field. One of the most impressive studies is that reported by Marrow et al. (1967) concerning the Harwood Manufacturing Company. Harwood's involvement in the use of groups to facilitate change goes right back to Coch and French's (1948) classic study of group decision methods. Marrow et al. report how, in 1962, Harwood took over a firm named Weldon which, like Harwood, was engaged in the manufacture of pyjamas. However, Harwood was being participatively managed with considerable economic success, whereas Weldon's autocratic management was incurring heavy losses. A decision was taken to attempt to transplant the climate of the Harwood plant to Weldon. In the next two years an extensive programme of change was undertaken, involving engineering consultants, operator training, in-plant T-groups at senior levels, group discussions at more junior levels, union recognition, and reorganization of work flow. This massive intervention led to dramatic changes in Weldon's performance. All changes were compared to the Harwood plant which served as a control.

Weldon's loss of 15% in 1962 became a profit of 17% by 1964. In the same period Harwood's profit rose from 17% to 21%. Operator turnover at Weldon fell from 10% per month to 4%, while Harwood was steady at less than 1%. Absence rates at Weldon fell from 6% to 3%, with Harwood ones unchanging at 3%. Attitude measures showed that the management at Harwood was perceived by employees as highly participative throughout. Weldon moved in that direction but did not reach the same level. Seashore and Bowers (1970) report that in subsequent years these changes were sustained, and in some cases extended, despite no further input of training. The researchers undertook a week-by-week analysis of productivity records in an attempt to determine which of the numerous interventions had had a notable effect. They concluded that four events were closely correlated with the productivity increases. These were individualized training for those with below average production records, T-groups for supervisors and staff, sacking of a small number of very low producers, and discussion groups with shop-floor operatives. This listing implies that the technological changes were not so important as the more interpersonally oriented interventions in creating the improvement. However, Marrow et al. make the point that the technological innovations may have helped to create a climate where the interpersonally focussed training was more acceptable.

Another large-scale programme is that reported by Kimberly and Nielsen (1975). They studied organizational development within a plant which used assembly line technology. The intervention comprised seven stages, of which the early part mainly comprised the collection and discussion of survey data. Stage six provided a two-day team building meeting for every team in the plant, while stage seven involved intergroup team building for groups whose tasks were linked. Comparison data were provided from figures for the industry as a whole over the several years which the project lasted. Ratings of various aspects of organizational climate and supervisor behaviour became much more positive during the period of the project. Quality ratings rose from 71% to 92% for the day shift, and from 69% to 92% for the night shift. However, there were no control data against which to compare these figures. Productivity was found to fall and then rise in a manner which closely paralleled data for the market as a whole. The profitability of the firm rose sharply and since this was less closely linked to the national average, the researchers attributed this to the effects of the project. They do not attempt to differentiate the effects of the different stages. The data here are somewhat less compelling than in the case of Harwood, but they do make clear that substantial change was achieved.

Not all organizational development programmes attempt such ambitious goals as did these two. Kegan and Rubinstein (1973) studied the effects of team building in two groups within a research and development laboratory. Neither group achieved greater goal satisfaction as measured by the Bonjean and Vance Measure of Self-Actualization. Increases were found in trust within the groups, but not in trust of other groups. The comparison groups showed no change. Friedlander (1967) also studied groups in research and development, this time in the military field. Six months after off-site team building meetings, the four trained groups showed significant increases on ratings of group effectiveness, mutual influence, and involvement, whereas eight untrained groups showed no change.

Margulies (1973) compared two types of training design for middle managers drawn from within one organization. In one group, a pure T-group approach was employed, while in three further groups half the time was spent working on personal and organizational problems which members currently faced. The measure of change employed was the Shostrom Personal Orientation Inventory which, as was seen in Chapter 3, does frequently detect changes after stranger T-groups. Margulies found increased self-actualization in all four groups, but not among controls. The groups which worked on real problems showed significantly more change than did the pure T-group. Unfortunately, since each group had different trainers, it is not possible to be sure that the differences found were due to the differing designs employed, rather than, for instance, the differing skills of the various leaders. The study does, nonetheless, provide some reassurance that the effects of groups as conducted with strangers can at least sometimes be reproduced within an organization. Margulies gives no detail of what type of organization was involved, nor of the specific purposes of the training.

De Michele (1967) reported the effect of an organizational development programme on twenty-one managers. Immediately after training, trainees showed decreased confidence in their own skills in human relations, less acceptance of others, and less initiation of action. However, they also rated themselves higher on self-understanding, the ability to listen to others, social sensitivity, expressing one's true feelings, trying out new methods, behavioural flexibility, and having a broad perception of problems. Many of these increases were also perceived by colleagues and supervisors. Further measures collected two months later showed that the decreases were no longer present, whereas the increases had been sustained. This study suggests that the initial impact of the project may have included a certain amount of confusion and disorientation, which then gave way to some more sustained benefits.

Initially adverse reactions were also detected in a large programme reported by Zand et al. (1969). Ninety middle managers attended five-day groups which were followed by two-day team development meetings with their superiors. Significant decreases were found on seven of the forty-two rating scales used. Most of the scales showing decreases referred to trust and openness within the organization. Zand et al. interpret these changes as indicating that trainees were now more ready to face up to problems which already existed within the organization. This is possible, but one must not exclude the possibility that the programme did have an adverse effect. One year later, trainees showed significant increases on two scales; the extent to which they saw people in the organization as facing up to conflicts, and their own willingness to ask for help from others. The adverse effects found earlier were no longer present. The detection of significant change on two scales out of forty-two can scarcely be seen as compelling evidence of change, since it barely exceeds the variability to be expected by chance. However, the authors do report further specific events, such as a reorganization of the company's structure, which arose rather directly from the impact of the training. These further changes were favourably evaluated both by trainees and by the comparison group, who were the subordinates of the trainees.

Both the study by De Michele and the one by Zand et al. provide further support for the idea, first introduced in Chapter 3, that the effects of groups may not be simply to induce change in behaviour but also to induce changes in the way in which behaviour is conceptualized, even where it does not change. Golembiewski et al. (1976) test this idea more directly. The project which they studied, the introduction of flexitime working, did not include the use of groups. However, even with such a straightforward innovation, they were able to show that the dimensions along which employees evaluated flexitime working did themselves change during the project. One might expect such effects to be stronger with group-based programmes, since they more directly challenge existing ways of thinking.

Harrison (1962) examined changes in ways that managers perceived others after team building meetings. He found that there was a decrease in the use of rational-technical categories to describe others, and a corresponding increase in the use of interpersonal categories. Of the two groups which Harrison studied, one did also show this change with regard to descriptions of those not present at the training, whereas the other did not. Controls showed no change. Where an organizational development programme encompasses only a part of an organization, it could well be that trainees seeking to apply changes arising from the project in other parts of the organization will encounter difficulties similar to those experienced by participants in stranger groups. Thus Harrison's sample found it easier to sustain their new perceptions of others in relation to those who had also participated in training together.

Smith and Honour (1969) also focussed on changes in perceptions, including both perceptions of individuals and of organizational norms. They studied fifty managers participating in phase one of managerial grid training in an English chemical plant. The changes found were contrasted with those among a comparison group in another similar plant. Trainees showed significant increases on three out of thirty-five scales used. These referred to involving subordinates in future planning, keeping subordinates in the picture, and aiding subordinates' learning on the job. Interviews revealed some tendency for changes to increase in magnitude over the months after training. Some subordinates were able to verify the changes in their superiors' behaviour while others were not. The management were somewhat lukewarm in their commitment to managerial grid training, and they decided not to proceed to the later phases. A number of other studies of the mangerial grid have been reported, some of them claiming much more positive effects than those reported by Smith and Honour. However, all of these studies have lacked control groups, so that the effects found cannot with certainty be attributed to grid training.

Beckhard and Lake (1971) conducted a team development programme within a bank. Training was initially within the mortgage production division. During the first year productivity rose, employee turnover fell by 20%, and absenteeism fell by 28%. Changes in comparison divisions were in the opposite, adverse direction. Four years later the mortgage production division was still performing better than the comparison division. Zenger (1968) compared the effects of team development with more conventional training and several comparison groups within a life insurance agency. The project extended over a year and a half and included team development initially with the supervisors, and later with each supervisor and his agents. Increases were found in the agents' income and the market ranking of the organization, as well as in perceptions of supervisors and one's peer group. Cooper and Oddie (1972) also compared two modes of intervention. One-week training programmes were provided for staffs of motorway cafeterias. Staff from two service areas participated in T-groups, while those from two others had social skill training. A further untrained sample was also studied. Both training programmes achieved a significant reduction in labour turnover. Ratings by customers twelve months after training was complete showed significant increases on four scales (friendly, welcoming, respectful, and tactful) after T-groups, but no change after the social skill training. After the T-groups, trainees also rated themselves higher on insight into the other's job, knowledge of the job, awareness of the problems of the job, understanding of job status, and thinking about the job, whereas social skill trainees again showed no change. This study is particularly interesting for its examination of the effects of organizational development at nonmanagerial levels. While some of the other projects reviewed (e.g., Kimberly and Nielsen) did extend to junior levels, none provide immediate data as to effects at these levels.

A very different type of study was that undertaken by Hellebrandt and Stinson (1971) with business school students. As part of their coursework, students participated in a business game simulation. After a number of decision periods were passed, some of the students were assigned to two-day task-oriented T-groups. While five five-man business game teams participated in the T-groups as intact groups, five further teams were recomposed for the training. The final five teams did not attend the training. After training, the business game was resumed, using the original teams. It was found that the teams which had trained intact became more cohesive than the other teams, but their performance in the game was significantly worse than the performance of either those who had training in recomposed groups or those who had no training at all. Presumably the skills required to do well in business games are not those enhanced by team development.

Bowers (1973) reports a broad survey of the results of organizational development in twenty-three organizations. Each of these had collaborated with the University of Michigan in some form of organizational development in the preceding decade. These projects encompassed a wide range of methods, of which team development was one of the more frequent. Bowers' data are based on repeated administrations of the Survey of Organizations Questionnaire developed at Michigan, which seeks to take a kind of audit of the state of interpersonal relations within an organization. The report does not make it clear among how many of the twenty-three organizations team development was conducted, but 116 trainees were involved. The data indicate that while relationships after some treatments, notably survey feedback, tended to improve, after team development there was a deterioration. Although group process was seen as more adequate, peer support declined as did various aspects of the organizations' climate, in particular the value placed on the importance of human relationships. Bowers discusses why such negative outcomes should have been obtained, in the light of the much more positive results reported in other studies. He concludes that the organizations in the sample who undertook team development were already in a state of declining morale, which training failed to arrest. Some of the other approaches were adopted by organizations who were becoming more successful. Bowers attempts to eliminate this source of noncomparability in his data through statistical procedures, and concludes that team development did in fact have some positive effects, in particular the facilitation of closer and more cooperative working relationships. It appears, nonetheless, that these positive effects failed to outweigh the decline already in progress at the time of training. In this paper Bowers offers no information as to the possible sources of this decline. Bowers and Hausser (1977) examined the data further to see whether particular training methods may have distinctive usefulness for work groups with a particular type of culture. However, they found that within their sample, team development was unhelpful for almost all types of groups.

The last two studies contrast with the preceding ten in that they indicate some limitation on the effectiveness of team development. All of the preceding studies reported some success in achieving the goals of training, albeit of widely varying magnitude. Failures often provide a more potent source of learning than do successes, and these two studies provide hypotheses as to limits on the usefulness of team development. These will be taken up when the nonindustrial studies have been examined.

Studies in schools and higher education

The earliest study of organizational development within a school (Benedict et al., 1967) found virtually no effects. A four-day workshop was conducted for members of a New Jersey school system. Extensive measures were employed but the only significant change was that after the training, trainees rated their relationships as less close and personal than did controls. Bailey (1968) studied the effect of a three-day workshop on the teaching faculty of a secondary school, through the perceptions of their students. A significant increase was found in ratings of teachers' ability to explain clearly. At a subsequent follow-up measurement, this change was no longer apparent. On this project also, therefore, the effects appear somewhat meagre. However, in this instance, the setting in which changes might have been most expected, namely relationships among the teaching faculty, was not studied.

In both the Benedict et al. and the Bailey studies, the training input was a good deal briefer than in many of the industrial studies reviewed. A more extensive intervention was that by Schmuck, Runkel, and Langmeyer (1969). They initiated a project with the entire staff of a junior high school in Oregon. An initial period of five days of training was divided between a range of structured exercises early in the week and consideration of three problems which the school faced later in the week. This led to the establishment of three continuing project groups, as well as two $1\frac{1}{2}$-day follow-up meetings some months later. A questionnaire concerning the behaviour of the school principal showed that the staff saw him as improved on eighteen out of twenty-four scales, with none of the remainder changing. Data from six control schools showed no such improvements. A second questionnaire referred to staff meetings. Here significant improvements were reported on twenty-one of the thirty-seven items. Data on this measure were only available for three control schools, but none of these showed similar change.

Bigelow (1971) studied an attempt to induce changes in the classroom behaviour of fifteen teachers in a junior high school. The majority of training time occurred during school hours with, in addition, a series of one-hour meetings after school each day. Training concluded with a full one-day meeting at a weekend. The focus of these meetings was on analysis of communication difficulties and ways of solving problems within the school. Analysis of tape recordings of teachers' classroom behaviour before and after training showed increased use of praise, greater use of students' ideas, and more initiating by students. Control teachers from another school showed increases in giving directions, criticizing and justifying, and there was more confusion and silence. Questionnaire data showed improved student attitudes towards one another. Various other changes occurred both for trainees and controls.

Keutzer et al. (1971) were able to study a situation also in Oregon, in which two new high schools opened concurrently. One of the schools engaged in two weeks of preparatory group work, while the other did not. The first week of training was made up of T-group meetings and structured exercises, while the second concentrated on impending organizational questions, such as decision making and organizational participation. Questionnaire measures from the staff were collected before and after training, and again at the end of the school year. The trained school showed significant rises in candour and in acceptance of conflict after training, and these differences persisted through the year. Students also made ratings on thirty-six scales indicating how things were at present and how they would like them to be. During the year, movements on all thirty-six scales were in the desired direction at the trained school. At the control school there was consensus on the desired direction of change on only twenty items, and positive change occurred on only five of these.

Smith and Willson (1975) report on the use of organizational development to work on problems in multiracial schools in England. A weekend workshop was held for white teachers and black parents drawn from three schools in a large city. The design employed was an intergroup one, with some of the time spent working in separate groups, and the remainder spent sharing images of each group and making plans for future actions. Ratings based on interviews showed some changes after the weekend among both parents and teachers. Teachers became more favourable to the West Indian way of life, saw West Indian parents as more concerned about their children, and became more aware of the problems facing black children. Compared to controls, black parents increased their attendance at PTA and similar meetings, and showed decreased approval of teachers' disciplinary methods. They also saw teachers as less concerned about black children than they had previously assumed.

Controlled studies of organizational development in higher education are scarce. McConnell (1971) examined the use of four-day groups in a business school setting. His sample was 120 incoming master's degree students. Two comparison groups comprised doctoral degree students and an introductory undergraduate psychology course. After training, participants rated themselves as significantly more at ease with their new environment, more satisfied with their peers, and more aware of themselves, both interpersonally and intrapersonally. The comparison groups showed no such changes. McConnell repeated the use of his questionnaire two months later, and found that only one of the changes, comfort with new environment, had persisted. Meanwhile, various other changes had occurred including a more negative view of others, and a more positive view of one's own contributions. McConnell sees these latter changes as caused not by the group experience but by the culture of the master's degree programme. More closely matched comparison groups would have made it possible to judge whether this were so.

As with the industrial studies, organizational development within educational institutions does appear to produce measurable effects with some frequency. A somewhat higher proportion of projects appear to be either unsuccessful or to have only slight effects. Whether this is due to some quality inherent in educational organizations or to the lesser level of resources invested in many of these projects, remains to be discussed.

Studies in the social services and other organizations

Shapiro and Ross (1971) evaluated a group for supervisors in an institution for delinquent girls in Canada. Controls were other supervisors within the same institution. The group met twice weekly over a period of three months. After training, group members selected significantly more positive adjectives from a checklist when describing themselves than previously. Over the same period controls moved in the reverse direction, choosing more negative adjectives to describe themselves. Follow-up measures showed these differences to be still present one year later. The girls residing in the institution were also asked to select adjectives describing their supervisors. This measure showed the same pattern as the other one – more favourable descriptions of trainees and less favourable descriptions of controls. The improved descriptions of the trained supervisors were also still obtained one year later, even though by that time all the girls in the institution were ones who had not been present initially.

In one way the Shapiro and Ross study provides impressive evidence for the durability of change arising from a relatively simple and straightforward intervention. The difficulty in accepting this conclusion lies with the findings not for the trainees, but for the controls. It is of course quite possible that some factor extraneous to the training programme caused the lasting decline in the self-image of the controls. Shapiro and Ross consider this possibility, but are unable to suggest any plausible extraneous causes. The alternative possibility is that the decline is caused by the control group's jealousy or resentment at exclusion from the training. The authors speak of supervisors being assigned to experimental or control status, which implies that they had no personal choice in the matter. There is no way of testing whether this was in fact the case, but it does appear possible that the enhanced morale of half the supervisors was purchased at the expense of the depressed morale of the other half.

This hazard of group work within organizations has been encountered in a number of other projects which are not included in this chapter, for lack of systematic measurement. The most typical pattern within such projects is where one subgroup's fervent advocacy of group-based approaches to change in the organization mobilizes a reaction among those who feel threatened by the first subgroup, thus polarizing the organization. A slightly different instance of this is provided by Teahan's (1975) study of training within the Detroit police department. Training was provided for new recruits which was primarily based on role-playing, but also included some T-groups. The training included considerable emphasis on relationships between blacks and whites. Evaluation measures showed that, after training, white officers became more racially prejudiced, while black officers became less prejudiced. Teahan suggests that this occurred because trainees saw the multiracial basis of training as evidence that senior police were pro-black, thus confirming the worst fears of the whites and the best hopes of the blacks.

Lacks et al. (1970) studied the effects of two organizational development workshops which between them encompassed all of the staff of the children's services unit of a mental health centre. Comparison data were obtained from the staff of a day hospital on the same site. No changes were found on a scale of attitudes towards mental illness or on ratings of other disciplines. However, there were changes towards more frequent and better quality communication between those members of the unit who had not previously been in contact. The effect of the workshops was thus team building, as might be anticipated, rather than personal change. These changes were found to be still present five months later.

The scarcity of studies of organizational development within the social services and allied fields no doubt reflects the relative infrequency with which these approaches have been used in these areas. One final area of which even fewer systematic studies are currently available is the use of group methods with couples and families. While a family is clearly not an organization in the same sense as a large corporation is, it does share some qualities which might lead one to expect that group work with families would have something in common with group work in organizations. These qualities include long duration, high interdependence, and role differentiation. The recent development of training programmes for 'normal' families achieves a differentiation between training and therapy, which makes easier the application of approaches such as organizational development, which began in fields where training rather than therapy was the norm. Team development for families has thus far tended to be rather highly structured, and quite often includes only the parents. For instance, Benson et al. (1975) employed role-playing with parents for a series of seven evenings. The trained parents showed significant increases on ratings of confidence in one's role as a parent, perception of oneself as causal with regard to one's child's behaviour, acceptance of the child's behaviour, and mutual trust and sharing with one's child. Controls showed no changes.

Burns (1972) examined the effect of basic encounter with ten married student couples. After the groups participants became more open and less defensive, and saw themselves more favourably on six of nine self-concept scales. Perception of one's spouse showed a significantly increased match with the spouse's self-concept on two of the nine scales. Control couples showed none of these changes.

Gurman and Kniskern (1977) review twenty-three further studies of marital enrichment which included control groups in their design. About two-thirds of these studies showed positive effects, but Gurman and Kniskern point out that many of the studies used very crude types of measurement, and only four of them obtained follow-up measures. Results from this area appear to show some promise, but more substantial research studies are required.

Success and failure in organizational development

The range of interventions which have been classified as organizational development in this chapter is rather diverse. Even within a particular occupational field, there are likely to be numerous factors working for or against success. While the successful application of learning from the stranger group may depend primarily on attributes of the training programme and the individual participant, the success of organizational development is inevitably bound up also with the culture of the organization in which it occurs. If one were to judge only from the studies reported in this chapter, it would appear that organizational development is very frequently successful. Almost all of the studies mentioned did show some positive effects, although their magnitude varied greatly. It is very likely however that interventions upon which research is undertaken, particularly research which is itself well designed, represent only the more successful end of the spectrum.

A number of attempts have been made to see what distinguishes successes from failures in this field. Greiner (1967) presents a case study of the company in which the first substantial application of managerial grid training took place. He suggests that the organization's history over many years was crucial in determining the framework within which the intervention was interpreted. In this case, the end of an era of stability and certainty in the firm ensured that there was widespread concern within it to explore new ways of coping with changed circumstances. Drawing on a wider range of cases, Greiner proposed that successful changes are often associated with some degree of external pressure on the organization, some degree of internal tension or conflict, and the use of external as well as internal change agents. Both external pressure and internal conflict would most likely encourage the organization to seek solutions to its current problems. The use of external change agents should, if they are well chosen, provide access to appropriate skills in confronting these problems.

Friedlander (1968) analysed the basis of the success of a programme in research and development groups, which was described earlier. He found that of the four group interventions, the most successful was the one for which the consultant spent more time in the organization before and after training. This included the gathering and feeding back of data on the effectiveness of current working relationships, and the use of an internal planning group to decide the next steps in the programme at each stage. Thus, the relative impact of these four groups was determined not by what happened during training at all, but by events before and after this.

Of the organizational development projects reviewed in this chapter, the most obvious failures were Benedict et al. (1967), Hellebrandt and Stinson (1971), Bowers (1973), and Teahan (1975). Relevant detail is not available from all these studies, but it is clear that there was relatively little contact between trainers and clients before and after training in the first two of these. The detail given by Bowers is so sparse as to preclude speculation. Furthermore, his data are attitudinal, as contrasted with the behavioural data available from a number of the successful projects. The Teahan project may have failed because an inappropriate training design was employed, and this was most likely an element in the Hellebrandt and Stinson findings also.

The difficulty of delineating what is or is not crucial to the success of organizational development no doubt derives from the way in which successful intervention comprises a whole sequence of actions, any one of which could turn out to be crucial in a particular circumstance. Greiner's and Friedlander's findings do provide parts of the picture, but more systematic study is required if elements are not to be overlooked. A step in this direction is reported by Franklin (1976). Franklin reviewed the data reported earlier on the impact of various types of organizational development undertaken by the University of Michigan. Since the range of types of intervention encompassed was rather broad, it is not surprising that no single dimension was found which invariably distinguished successes from failures. However, it was found that successes were more probable in organizations that were already relatively successful and therefore able to adjust to changes more adequately. Their organizational development projects were more specifically focussed and had firmer support from top management. Their internal change agents were more carefully selected, and they worked collaboratively with the external change agents. This study did not include detail of the actual activities which comprised the intervention, and so inevitably its conclusions emphasize the context rather than the substance of the projects. The conclusions do nonetheless provide more systematic support for the importance of the variables first delineated by Greiner and by Friedlander. A still larger sample of successful and unsuccessful projects was surveyed by Dunn and Swierczek (1977), who tested eleven hypotheses drawn from the literature on organizational development. Only three of these received much support. The successful projects were found to involve higher levels of participation by those in the organization, to be based on collaborative types of intervention, and to use participative types of change agent. Thus the three successful hypotheses all stressed participation. It is possible that the contrast between these and Franklin's findings arises from the fact that Dunn and Swierczek's sample was much more diverse. Since Franklin's data all derive from projects undertaken by Michigan, who are committed to participative approaches, it would be unlikely that any of the projects in his sample were nonparticipative.

While Dunn and Swierczek's study was based on published case studies, Fullan, Miles, and Taylor (1980) made a survey of ongoing organizational development projects in North American schools. Seventy-six projects were located. It was found that three separate criteria of rated success were not very closely correlated with one another. These were the immediate impact on the school, the development of favourable attitudes towards organizational development, and the institutionalization of a continuing programme within the school district. The variables most strongly associated with favourable impact were the provision of adequate resources, including funds, materials, time, and number of consultants, and a focus on system or task variables rather than personal learning goals. Positive attitudes were also linked to many of these variables, but relevance to educational matters within the school was also important. Institutionalization of further organizational development work was most likely when the project was not too big or expensive, but was focussed on system or task variables.

The surveys reported by Franklin, by Dunn and Swierczek, and by Fullan et al. included all forms of organizational development, not just those using group-based interventions. Their findings might at first seem to contradict the emphasis of earlier chapters. The success of organizational development turns out to depend only partly on qualities inherent in the actual training and just as much on the quality of its environment. In previous chapters, the argument has been that it is the nature of the individual's experience in the group which facilitates subsequent change. Such a contradiction is more apparent than real. The organizational development consultant takes some pride in tailoring any intervention to the outcome of prior diagnosis and data collection. Particularly in the case of large-scale projects, such diagnoses are made with a good deal of skill and expertise, and groups are most likely to be employed if there is a clear rationale for them, and suitable resources and skills are available. By contrast, individuals who attend training may do so for a variety of less well-informed reasons, although some will, of course, have a clear conception of the appropriateness of what is offered to what they are seeking. Thus, for individuals there should be wide variability in the degree to which the groups are or are not able to provide what is sought. For organizations, on the other hand, there should be less variability in the appropriateness of the groups; the programme has been tailored to ensure its appropriateness. If it does not work, this is much more likely to be due to factors beyond the control of trainers, such as market changes, changes in the attitude of top management, or previously unforeseen intergroup problems. The case studies provided by Mirvis and Berg (1977) provide some vivid illustrations of the ways in which just such difficulties do all too frequently arise.

If the central element in the stranger group is the experience of enhanced personal control over one's behaviour, one might look to organizational groups for a similar effect. Since the focus of organizational groups is not so much on oneself as an individual but on the problems of the group or organization as a whole, the effect should be different. Sustained attention to the problems the group faces could induce several types of changes. Increased pooling of data is likely to enhance perceptions that problems in the group are shared, and therefore worth working on. Where the problems concern those present, the group provides a setting for the experience of success in working on those problems. Where the problems concern those not present, the sharing of perceptions is likely to enhance the wish to confront the other party. If the design is an intergroup design, this will then be possible. The achievement of each of these successes is dependent on the group's ability to define the problems raised as soluble or worth working on. Where this is not a likely outcome, the time is most likely not ripe for this type of intervention.

One test of this line of reasoning is provided by Porras and Berg (1978), who examined the types of change reported in published organizational development projects. They found that the variables most frequently showing improvement ranged from individual variables such as enhanced awareness or self-actualization, through group performance variables such as involvement and trust, to organizational ones, particularly leadership and decision making. The size of the Porras and Berg sample did not permit them to test whether this range of effects was systematically related to the types of training design used or other environmental variables.

The variability of these effects suggests why it is that diagnosis and preparation prove to be such crucial elements in organizational groups. If the relevant persons within the organization have already participated in decisions about the nature of current problems, and whether or not groups might be a good way to work on them, they have already sampled personal control in relation to those problems. Such experience provides a basis around which some confidence and further commitment may be built. However, even this does not guarantee success. It still remains necessary for the trainers to bring to the programme the skills and resources which will sustain that initial confidence and commitment. Gross et al. (1971) provide a classic case study of how this was not done in one instance. An attempt was made to introduce discovery-orientated methods into a ghetto school. Despite high initial staff enthusiasm, the project was a total failure because no provision was made for the technical resources or training the teachers required.

The use of groups within organizations thus provides opportunities for a much more precise tailoring of training method to training goal. While this may mean less utilization of groups than some would wish, it provides a much more certain way of ensuring that enhanced control rather than alienation is the outcome. Where the circumstances are right, substantial changes may be created. Where they are not, a range of alternative modes of intervention is evolving, some of which create changes which may lead the way towards the later use of groups.

Research into the use of groups in organizational development is, at least in some occupational fields, much more adequate than it was a few years ago. We can be sure that organizational development does quite frequently create changes which would not occur spontaneously. Some data and suggestions have been advanced as to why this occurs, but our knowledge is still meagre. Many years ago, the well-known Hawthorne experiment was said to have established that radical change in productivity might be achieved simply through changing employees' expectations about decisions in which they might participate. While this particular study is no longer seen as conclusive, more recent demonstrations have shown even more striking effects. King (1974) studied a firm in which management informed some of the managers who were introducing schemes for job enlargement and job rotation, that productivity *would* be likely to rise as a result, while other managers involved in the schemes were informed that it *would not* rise. Productivity did rise where it was said to be likely to do so, but not in the other plants. While there may be all sorts of specific explanations for the results obtained in this study, it does argue for a certain amount of caution in explaining why changes do or do not occur in organizations. At least in some circumstances it appears that people's beliefs can be self-fulfilling. It could be that organizational development achieves its effect by leading people to believe that particular organizational problems are soluble. The art of the organizational development consultant may be to only do this where the prospects are sufficiently good that the belief will prove true when people take the risk of testing it out.

Summary

Organizational development has arisen directly from attempts to make learning from sensitivity training more relevant to behaviour in organizations. It no longer encompasses only group-based methods. There is good evidence of its effectiveness in industry and education, and scattered evidence from elsewhere. Group-based organizational development is most effective when embedded in a context of organizational support. It may achieve its effect through inducing beliefs that particular problems *are* soluble, and through the conjunction of individual and collective effort.

Section 4

The Social Context of Group Work

CHAPTER 11
SOME CONTINUING ISSUES

It has been seen in the preceding chapters that varying kinds of group experience can have measurable benefits and that in some circumstances these may be sustained. Not all commentators see the field in such a positive manner, and this chapter will seek to explore and learn from some of the doubts and difficulties which are frequently voiced. These range from concerns about the hazards to group members and the practical and ethical dilemmas which leaders face, to the prospects for continuing utilization of group learning methods.

The hazards of group work

The studies of group outcome which have been examined in earlier chapters have almost all relied upon the application of some test or other before and after group experience, leading to the calculation of an overall score for mean change. This procedure certainly represents the best single method of summarizing whether change has occurred or not. However, it tells us very little about the distribution between different people of the changes which have been detected. For instance, an overall positive change might be made up of a large number of small positive changes, or of some very large positive changes coupled with some smaller negative changes.

It is thus possible that, despite the various reports of positive change outlined earlier, there may be a minority of trainees who are adversely effected. Suggestions that this might be the case were strengthened by publications from psychiatrists giving case studies of people who were distressed during or after group experience (Gottschalk and Pattison, 1969; Crawshaw, 1969; Jaffé and Scherl, 1969). These case studies pose two questions. Firstly we need to know whether such adverse effects are any more frequent after groups than after various other types of life experience. If they are, then we need to know more about the types of adverse effect to be found and how they may be minimized.

Once again the major contributor to this debate has been the study by Lieberman et al. (1973). These authors defined a *casualty* as someone who 'as a direct result of his experience . . . became more psychologically distressed or employed more maladaptive mechanisms of defence, or both; furthermore this negative change was not a transient but an enduring one, as judged eight months after the group experience'. Using this criterion, Lieberman et al. concluded that their sample contained sixteen casualties, which was 7.5% of the total. This finding has had an enormous impact on the subsequent development of the field. As Yalom (1975) recounts, thousands of requests for reprints of the original report on casualties (Yalom and Lieberman, 1971) were received, whereas very much less interest was shown in other aspects of the project. Subsequent discussions frequently allude to this study as having established that encounter groups in particular are highly dangerous. Even Yalom (1975, p. 482), who was the investigator with principal responsibility for the casualty study, believes that the dangers of groups have been exaggerated as a result of it. Let us consider what was actually found.

Lieberman et al. examined their various sources of data for signs of possible adverse effects. Of the 210 students who attended groups, they designated 104 as casualty suspects. Eight months after the groups were finished, they attempted to make contact with these suspects. Seventy-nine suspects were successfully contacted. Of these, forty-nine appeared after a telephone interview to require further investigation. These were interviewed personally and a clinical judgment was made as to whether they were or were not casualties. The sixteen casualties identified ranged from a manic psychotic to those who were more depressed or mistrustful of others. Further members of the sample suffered adverse effects, including one who committed suicide, but these were judged by the researchers not to be casualties within the meaning of their definition, because the balance of evidence indicated that these effects were *not* due to the groups.

These findings indicate that there undoubtedly were a substantial number of adverse effects following the groups studied by Lieberman et al. The study is on much less firm ground in asserting which of these effects were caused by group experience, and which would have happened anyway.

Essentially, in this part of the study, one is asked to accept that it is possible for the researchers to make valid judgements about which event causes a given adverse effect. It is much more plausible to expect that adverse effects have multiple causes, which indicates that the judgements made by the researchers must have been extraordinarily difficult to make and certainly fallible. A safer procedure would have been to apply a similar casualty detection procedure to their control subjects and see what level of adverse effects was found among them. Unfortunately this was not done. This study therefore leaves us unable to choose validly between two possible explanations of its findings. Either certain types of encounter group induce a substantial rate of casualties among their members, or there is a high rate of casualties among students at university, which certain of the groups did little to prevent.

One way of testing which of these explanations may be the more plausible is to examine other studies which have attempted to estimate the frequency of adverse effects after groups. Ross et al. (1971) made a questionnaire survey of all psychiatrists in the Cincinnatti area. They were asked to state whether they were or had been seeing patients who had become psychotic or acutely disorganized as a result of group training. Nineteen patients were identified. It was estimated that these patients derived from a population of approximately 2,900 participants in groups over the preceding five years. Five of the patients had been among 1,750 participants in managerial grid seminars (Blake and Mouton, 1978), which represents an adverse effect rate of 0.3%. The remaining fourteen patients derived from a population of 1,150 in T-groups, which gives an adverse effect rate of 1.2%. Six of the patients had been hospitalized, but only one was still there four months later. A somewhat larger number of casualties was found in another survey by Kane et al. (1971), but in this study no attempt appears to have been made to check whether any of the patients had been seen by more than one of the psychiatrists, thus possibly inflating the figures. The authors also did not try to estimate the size of the sample within which their casualties were found.

Other less thorough surveys are in general agreement with the frequencies obtained by Ross et al. NTL Institute (1969) reports that thirty-three out of 14,200 group members in their programmes left before the end. Since Ross et al. found that about half the adverse reactions appear before the end of the group, this implies an adverse effect rate of no more than 0.5%. Batchelder and Hardy (1968) found only three instances of severe negative experiences among 1,200 participants in YMCA groups, although their search procedure does not appear sufficiently thorough.

Studies based on group members' own assessments of their experiences have found very few casualties. Posthuma and Posthuma (1973) compared samples attending encounter groups, structured classes in human relations, and no training at all. Ratings made after training and again six months later showed no differences between the groups in the rate of negatively evaluated changes. Smith (1975(b)) attempted to identify casualties after one-week groups, using the procedure found most effective by Lieberman et al. This involved asking group members to identify who had been most hurt by the group. Eleven casualty suspects were identified among a population of ninety-four participants, but examination of their own and others' responses at the close of the groups and five months later indicated that none could be considered to be casualties.

A study by Cooper (1974) illustrates the manner in which different criteria of whether or not someone is adversely affected may conflict with one another. He found that after one-week groups, a population of social workers scored higher on the Neuroticism Scale of the Eysenck Personality Inventory. However, the same trainees were rated by themselves and by their families and friends as better able to cope with problems, happier, and better able to communicate with others. There were no significant relationships between changes on the personality questionnaire and scores on the various rating scales. One should be cautious, therefore, about concluding that the personality test does indeed detect an adverse effect. An equally plausible interpretation would be that after the group, members were somewhat more willing to admit their anxieties in response to the questionnaire items.

The same possibility arises in regard to two other studies which have used personality tests. Reddy (1970) found that two student groups showed an increase in their number of deviant signs score on the Tennessee Self-Concept Scale. Cooper and Bowles (1975) used the Cattell 16PF Test as an index of psychological disturbance, and found slightly more negative changes than positive ones among groups of managers. Neither of these studies examines whether the changes found on the tests were reflected in any particular kind of behaviour.

This survey of studies of adverse effects of groups provides a broader context within which to evaluate the striking findings obtained by Lieberman et al. It has been seen that most other studies have reported much lower casualty rates, or else rest upon the use of personality tests whose usefulness as indices of adverse effects is unproven. Of these other studies, none was so thorough as that of Lieberman et al., but equally none involved such a wide range of leadership styles, and none (except Reddy, 1970) were concerned with students.

One other study is available which provides some basis for evaluating whether or not Lieberman et al.'s findings may have been aberrant because they derived from student groups. While Lieberman et al. were undertaking their study at Stanford University, Bebout and Gordon (1972, 1974) were investigating the effects of groups at the nearby Berkeley campus. Comments from participants which were judged to be seriously negative were received from nineteen participants, which is 2.9% of the 680 respondents. The authors apparently regarded none of these as a bona fide clinical casualty, and indicated that four cases of serious psychotic or uncontrollable behaviour all preceded the group meetings. One wonders whether the casualty rates detected in the Stanford and Berkeley projects rested more on differences between the two projects, or on the judgement criteria employed by the respective clinicians within them. We shall most likely never know. However, if we take these data at face value, they provide little support for the proposition that casualty rates in student groups are a reflection of an overall higher rate of stress among students. Alternative explanations must be considered.

· One major difference between the Stanford and Berkeley projects was that at Stanford, paid professional leaders representing a wide range of orientations were used, whereas at Berkeley the groups were led by relatively untrained leaders who had attended previous groups as members. Herein lies a rather more promising line of explanation for the Lieberman et al. findings. Their results indicate that although the overall casualty rate was 7.5%, there were marked variations in the outcomes of groups with different types of leader. Almost half the casualties occurred in groups whose leaders were categorized as energizers, and most of the remainder occurred where the leaders were impersonals and laissez-faire. It would thus be possible to reconcile the various findings reviewed, if it could be established that the Lieberman et al. sample had within it many more leaders of these types than did the other studies. Some of the defenders of encounter groups have certainly not been timid about criticizing the representativeness of the leaders used by Lieberman et al. (Schutz, 1975; Rowan, 1975; Russell, 1978). It appears that of the five groups whose leaders were designated as energizers, one had been banned from leading groups at Esalen Institute, while another had been excluded for some months. Two more of these groups were those using the Synanon approach, in which there is no formally designated leader. Apart from the groups led by energizers, the only other group yielding more than one casualty was that led by an experienced clinician with a laissez-faire style. He had never before led a group outside a clinical setting. The selection of leaders does, therefore, seem to have been somewhat at odds with what one might expect from Lieberman et al.'s assertion that 'all were highly experienced group leaders, and were uniformly esteemed by their colleagues as representing the best of their approach'. It may nonetheless be the case that the leaders they selected *were* representative of the range of types of group experience available in California in the late sixties.

Argument will no doubt continue about the validity of these aspects of Lieberman et al.'s findings. In one way it need be no surprise that some people get worse after groups, while others get better. Similar findings have been shown to be obtained concerning the outcome of both group and individual psychotherapy. The difference between the critics of the newer types of group work and their defenders, is that the critics see psychotherapy as a somewhat safer undertaking than are the new groups, whereas the defenders see the new groups as a good deal safer than more traditional forms of therapy. For the present, the last word should perhaps go to Yalom (1975), around whose judgements the controversy has raged. He writes:

> I believe that if the leader is well-trained (both clinically and in group dynamics), is responsible, screens his members either before or during the group, provides sufficient information for applicants to deselect themselves, and permits members to proceed at their own pace, the group experience is quite likely to be a safe and rewarding one.

Some of these proposals require further discussion.

Reducing the risks

In earlier chapters the viewpoint was advanced that leaders who provided their groups with an optimal mix of support and confrontation, would be those who generated greatest learning. This conclusion should be reexamined in the light of concern about the possible harmful effects of groups. Is the same prescription required in order to minimize the hazards as is required to maximize learning? Among the Lieberman et al. leader types, the energizers were most strongly linked to the occurrence of adverse effects. Their style laid high stress on emotional stimulation, and the case studies of casualties provided by Lieberman et al. indicate that excessive confrontation was a key element in several instances. This confrontation sometimes came directly from the leader, but in other instances it came from group members who were following the style of interaction initiated by the leader. The other types of leader most strongly linked to the occurrence of adverse effects were the impersonals and laissez-faire leaders. Casualties in these groups were more a function of lack of supportiveness than of excessive confrontation. The most typical instances were those of members making some kind of self-disclosure, which was then either ignored or treated without any element of caring by the group. Since the leaders of these groups were essentially passive, they did not repair these omissions by group members.

These two mechanisms for achieving casualty status are seen by Lieberman et al. as most frequent in their sample. There is thus some reassurance to the leader that use of the support plus confrontation model will serve to minimize the risks. Lieberman et al. identify three other ways in which casualties arose. These were through failure to achieve unrealistically high goals, through the experience of coercive demands from the group, and through input overload or excessive stimulation. These findings clearly underlie Yalom's recommendations, cited earlier, for providing maximal information, allowing people to go at their own pace, and screening group members. The only one of these which is at all contentious is the proposal to screen potential members of groups.

It was seen in Chapter 3 that those who volunteer to attend groups may include a disproportionate number of people who are somewhat disturbed. This will not always be so, depending on such factors as the sponsorship and reputation of a particular programme of groups. Even where this is so, it need be no particular disadvantage so long as the programme is tailored to the needs of those who come. The dilemma facing leaders is whether to rely solely on the diffusion of information about one's group programmes as a self-selection device, or whether to exclude certain people from groups for which they appear unsuited. The most extensive information as to who it is who tends to come to groups is that provided by Epps and Sikes (1977). They obtained demographic data on 392 people who had attended groups in the Kansas City area in the preceding two years. These were compared with the known demographic data for the population as a whole in that area. Those attending groups were found to be disproportionately likely to be aged 35–54, female, middle class, rich, highly educated, religious, and either divorced or separated.

The only published account of an attempt to screen group members in advance is that by Stone and Tieger (1971), who screened 105 applicants for a week-long church group training programme. Seventeen applicants were screened out, and an additional six withdrew after the screening procedure. This included an application form, a personality test, and a small group discussion. Despite this elaborate procedure, one group member was judged to be a casualty among those who ultimately attended. This contrasts with four out of forty-one who experienced difficulties in a similar unscreened population. This type of procedure has been only rarely employed, and there cannot be many populations which could require such a substantial rejection rate. The reluctance of group leaders to use such procedures is no doubt partly because it implies that what is to follow is particularly hazardous, and partly because screening procedures place the leaders in a powerful controlling role, which may not mesh easily with their subsequent intended behaviour once the groups are started.

One much simpler alternative to such procedures is the provision of full information to prospective group members as to what is entailed. In some circumstances, brief sample sessions of the approach to be employed may be worthwhile. Where such information is freely available, the great majority of intending group members are well able to make appropriate choices. McCanne (1977) compared students attending groups in a university counselling centre, students attending a group process course, and students enrolling in a one-day introductory sensitivity training workshop. She found that each population had distinctively different goals, which were well matched to the orientation of each type of experience.

As often as not, the problem of inadequate match between a group's procedures and the member's expectations derives not from inadequate screening of members, but from insufficiently skilled or responsible behaviour from the leader. The evidence from the Lieberman et al. study indicates that the most effective way to reduce casualties would be either to screen leaders, or to devote more attention to their training.

The training of leaders

Many of the skills most strongly required of a group leader are those which group experience is itself intended to foster. It follows that, before anything else, an intending group leader must have had extensive experience of groups as a participant. This experience must not simply be a matter of having 'done time' in groups. There must be evidence that, both in the eyes of oneself and of others, one can where appropriate give and receive feedback, self-disclose, be aware of one's own and others' needs, and carry through a variety of initiating behaviours in group settings. While this bald statement describes in outline most of what an effective group leader requires, it will not provide the main basis of this section. Most attempts to train group leaders start from the assumption or requirement that such skills are already present. They further assume that being a group leader is not simply a matter of being a more than averagely effective group member. Additional types of skill are required, and it is these which will be discussed here.

Massarik (1972) proposes that effective leaders require four qualities: conceptual knowledge, training experience, technical skill, and humanness. Conceptual knowledge includes awareness of the theories and empirical data which underlie current training practice. Its usefulness can be both as a basis for one's personal thinking about what to do or not do as a leader in a group, and as a resource for more direct kinds of teaching or meaning attribution, as Lieberman et al. termed it, where these are appropriate. By training experience, Massarik implies not only participating in groups as a member, but also working in an apprentice role with more established leaders. Technical skill refers primarily to the development of suitable ways of contributing to groups in which one is the leader, but includes also the design skills explored in Chapter 6. Humanness, as Massarik puts it, is ineffable. His meaning is perhaps close to the concept of genuineness, which the Rogerians use, but Massarik adds that the 'human' leader will be sufficiently self-aware not to give his or her needs priority over those of group members, particularly the more vulnerable ones.

Lakin (1972) provides a more practically oriented set of suggestions as to how such goals may be approached. He proposes that the intending group leader shall:

(1) Participate as a member in two groups.
(2) Observe five further groups, discussing with the leader what occurred after each session.
(3) Co-lead another five groups with experienced leaders.
(4) Lead five groups, with observers watching who later discuss what occurred.

(5) Participate in psychotherapy or some other sustained form of experiential self-study.

(6) Review with care comments and evaluations received from experienced and well-qualified group leaders.

(7) Participate in seminars and discussions concerning issues such as the leader role and function.

(pp. 170–171, somewhat amended.)

These guidelines are more practical for some than for others. They rest, for instance, on the availability of substantial numbers of groups who are willing to be watched by observers. However, the guidelines certainly provide useful pointers as to desirable elements in the process of becoming a leader. Some assistance in following such a sequence can be obtained through programmes specifically designed to facilitate leader development. Programmes of this kind are provided in North America by National Training Laboratories. In Britain, some elements in this sequence may be encompassed through the activities of the Group Relations Training Association.

The principal difficulty in the path of becoming a group leader is the enormous diversity of current applications of group work. It may perhaps be ideal that a group leader's flexibility could encompass everything from a Tavistock role to encounter and Gestalt, taking in also the middle ground of T-groups. But even among experienced leaders, there are few indeed who can claim such wide-ranging expertise. Most leaders find some styles more congenial than others, and focus their expertise within that range. The dilemma is that the more leaders opt for what they find personally congenial, the less flexibility they leave themselves to adapt to the expressed needs of group members.

Harrison (1970) has made a perceptive analysis of these issues, particularly with regard to the use of group methods in organizational settings. He proposes that most group leaders have a preference for deep, personally intense types of intervention. Such interventions most probably feel more important than interventions at other levels, but Harrison points out that working at deep levels also enhances the group's dependence on the leader's expertise to ensure a favourable outcome, which the leader may find gratifying. In order to arrest this seemingly inexorable slide towards emotionally intense modes of intervention, Harrison proposes two criteria to decide how to intervene. Interventions should be at a level no deeper than that required to produce enduring solutions to the problems at hand. They should also be at a level no deeper than that at which the energy and resources of the client can be committed to change. Where these criteria conflict, one should favour the second. In practice this is likely to mean that in organizational settings, the client's statement as to the nature of the problem is taken at face value, rather than being redefined as an instance of a much more basic problem which has been so far overlooked. In nonorganizational settings, this problem is best coped with by group leaders stating in advance the type of group work which is being offered on a particular programme, and then sticking to this contract.

The development of expertise as a leader, then, should include experience of at least a range of different types of group work, even if not the entire range. A broad experience of groups makes it more likely that novice leaders will find those approaches which enable them to express their particular type of humanness. It will also make it more likely that they are able to respond adaptively to unexpected events within their groups.

Most novice leaders find the experience of being a group leader initially strange and unsettling. Most typically, the responses one receives from group members differ somewhat from those received when one has been in groups as a member. Group leaders in the interpretive tradition look for and indeed anticipate such changes or distortions in perception. To them, these distortions are expressions of a transference relationship, and the leader's nongratifying role in interpretive groups ensures that these reactions frequently have a substantial element of hostility to them. They provide the raw material for the group's learning. Leaders in other traditions of group work are more prone to overlook the effect, since their more gratifying approach to the group tends to be rewarded with approval and encouragement. I do not seek to argue that all approval and encouragement from group members to leaders is somehow suspect, only that leaders quite often find themselves receiving praise which is quite disproportionate to what they have in fact done.

Seldman et al. (1974) attempted to investigate this phenomenon in fifteen-hour marathon groups for students. Ratings of the group leaders by members were compared with ratings on the same scales by experts, who observed the groups from behind an observation mirror. The leaders were seen as much more sensitive, open, and genuine by members than they were by the experts. This was particularly true in the case of members who had high dependency needs, as measured by personality tests. Shapiro and Klein (1975) compared leaders' self-percepts and members' perceptions of them in a group of mental health professionals. On virtually every scale, group members rated the leaders more favourably than did the leaders. Both of these studies leave a good deal to be desired methodologically. They do not, for instance, test whether similar effects are obtained when one compares members' self-ratings with ratings by others. However, it most probably is the case that leaders are subject to a positive 'halo' response from group members. Whether one chooses to discuss this effect in terms of transference or in terms of the assumptions that group members make about someone who occupies the designated role of leader, is not of great importance. What is much more crucial is to consider ways in which the novice leader can learn to cope with this effect.

Lieberman et al. (1973) found that among the leaders they studied, the ones who received the most extravagant praise were those who employed the greatest number of structured exercises. We have seen that high-exercise groups in their sample became more cohesive, but were ultimately no more successful than low-exercise groups. Lieberman et al. suggest that the very wide and rapid diffusion of structured exercises in the groups of the early seventies occurred precisely because of the degree to which group leaders felt gratified and encouraged by their groups' enthusiasm, both for the exercises and for themselves.

One way to conceptualize these aspects of leader-group relationships is in terms of the processes of support and confrontation. It appears that in the early stages of many types of group, there are strong pressures towards the splitting of support and confrontation. Where the leaders are initially inactive, they are experienced as unhelpful and a climate of increasing confrontation arises. Where the leaders are high initiators, particularly of the types of structured exercise which encourage personal closeness, they are rewarded by the support and approval of the group. In either case a climate of emotional splitting has been established. Whether this stage can be passed, leading into a group climate where the processes of support and confrontation are intermingled, will depend on the needs of members, the setting of the group, and not least the behaviour of the leaders. A key element in the leader's developing expertise will be the ability to discern when opportunities arise in the group for this to occur. The transition will most likely not be a single event, but a series of them. In the case of interpretive groups, the key events may be those actions by leaders or others which reveal that the leader's inactivity need not inhibit the development of supportive relationships. In the case of supportive groups, the events might be those which showed that the supportive atmosphere of the group need not be destroyed by the process of confrontation.

If the skill of group leadership includes not only the enhancement of learning opportunities, but also the prevention of harm, then the training of group leaders requires some attention to this issue. It is particularly easy for a group leader, to whom experiential group work has become a familiar setting, to forget the confusion and stress which a group may create for some of those who come to one for the first time. Just how stressful people find groups has been the subject of a good deal of debate. Lubin and Zuckerman (1969) investigated how much anxiety, depression, and hostility was experienced during a one-week residential group training programme for managers. Stress, as measured by levels of anxiety, depression, and hostility, was found to peak at the sixth meeting of the groups on the programme. At this time it was found that none of the scores of the forty-three participants passed the level usually regarded as deviant on this test. Comparison of these scores with those of others undergoing perceptual isolation experiments, showed that the experiments caused much more stress than the groups did. In a further study, Lubin and Lubin (1971) showed that the stress of attending a group was also less than that experienced by students taking examinations. These studies may be criticized on the grounds that those attending the groups were not the same people as those who took the examinations or experiments. However, Johnson et al. (1973) compared students taking exams with the same students attending groups. They also found that the exams caused more anxiety than the groups.

These studies indicate at least that groups need not be highly stressful. Some vigilance is nonetheless required by the leader to ensure that stress in a particular group is not excessive. It is much more likely that one or two individuals will be particularly ill at ease, than that the whole group will be. Lieberman et al.'s findings give little cause for complacency on this score. Of the casualties they detected, the substantial majority were not reported by the leaders as having been harmed in any way. A useful device for leaders seeking to be as aware as possible of group members' responses is to review between sessions not only what has occurred, but also to try to answer questions such as 'Who am I ignoring?', 'Who am I taking for granted?', and so forth. The study by Smith (1976) found that group members who felt hurt by the group were quite likely to seek out leaders of other groups. It can therefore often be useful for staff members of a programme to review together programme members about whom they feel some anxiety. Such meetings can of course also provide needed support for leaders in their attempts to work out how best to respond to members who are particularly stressed.

Among the elements required for the development of effective group leaders, one of the most frequently overlooked is the importance of providing adequate support for leaders. It needs to be established that it is not only legitimate but also desirable for leaders to spend substantial time together before a programme. Some of this time is required for design and planning, but some of it should also be invested in the strengthening of relationships within the leader group. A group of leaders who are not actively engaged in exploring their own relationships are not likely to be much help to their groups in the same task. Such supportive contact can with benefit be sustained throughout a programme, at appropriate times.

Perhaps the most fundamental issue which must be faced by someone becoming a group leader is what one might term the loss of spontaneity. Someone attending a group for the first time can, if they wish, accept the leader's invitation to try new ways of behaving and do so without too much certainty as to what will subsequently happen. Leaders, whether by dint of participating in many groups or of reading books such as this one, will inevitably lose some of this spontaneity. They may know that their contributions to a group will be more effective if they are fresh and spontaneous rather than mannered or routine. But inexorably they will develop a certain wisdom as to how this or that course of action in a group tends to work out. As Farson (1978) has argued, when this point is reached the leader is in danger of transforming a method which is rooted in humanistic values into a form of applied technology. The leader's task becomes one of ensuring in a controlled and unspontaneous way, that the appropriate conditions for learning are present. This dilemma has two aspects, one practical and one ethical. The practical dilemma is that if we, as leaders, start to feel that setting up an effective learning climate in a group is solely a matter of technique and not something in which we feel a sense of personal commitment and caring, we may very well lose our ability to provide the conditions which our intellectual knowledge tells us are required. The ethical dilemma is that if group members are advised that group experience establishes a setting in which one can explore and learn for oneself, whilst the leader construes his or her task in terms of predetermined technique, there must be some deception going on somewhere.

These are paradoxes with which any group leader – and many others in the helping professions – must contend. One cannot ask that those who wish to become leaders can resolve them, since established leaders are, if anything, even more firmly in their grip. What one can ask is that those becoming leaders be aware of the dilemmas and inconsistencies of the leader's role as most often practised, and be willing to debate these issues with group members when they arise.

The regulation of group work

The bewildering variety of modes of group work which has evolved in the past decade, combined with rumours and beliefs about harmful effects, have led some to the conclusion that some type of regulation is required as to who shall be empowered to lead groups. Similar arguments have been rather more pressingly made with regard to psychotherapy. To date, much more experience of these issues is available in the United States than in Britain. Many states now require that in order to practise, a psychologist must be certificated, i.e., must have satisfied various conditions and examinations specified by the state. A certification system does not prevent others from undertaking activities identical to those done by psychologists, but it does prevent them from calling themselves psychologists. One or two lawsuits, in which NTL were sued by former members of groups, have been settled out of court, while NTL have not admitted any liability in these cases. Such events have triggered some discussion of whether a certification procedure has much to recommend it. A thorough analysis of the arguments is provided by Hogan (1974). He argues that it is extraordinarily difficult to regulate a process legally, unless one can say precisely what it is. One also needs to be able to say precisely what the leader must and must not do in order to be effective. Although we may be somewhat better able to do this than a decade or two ago, there is still little certainty and low consensus as to how best to run groups. The experience gained in states with certificated psychologists offers little hope that such a system could be beneficial. In these states it is often the case that, in order to practice psychotherapy as a certificated psychologist, a person must have passed a variety of formal examinations whose relevance to the effective conduct of therapy is, at the very least, unclear.

Rather than awaiting legislation of doubtful utility, one alternative is to seek some form of voluntary regulation. This was attempted in 1972 through the establishment of the International Association of Applied

Social Scientists (IAASS). This organization proposed to accredit leaders in one or more of four fields: organizational development, community development, laboratory education (i.e., T-groups), and personal growth groups (i.e., encounter). Hogan (1977) recounts some of the difficulties which IAASS has also come up against. These have to do both with how to define each of these fields without also including some of the others, and how to assess whether or not someone is competent within a given field. IAASS decided in 1976 to discontinue accrediting personal growth group leaders, but has instituted a further category for Tavistock group leaders. They also plan to reevaluate their members' skills every five years. Accreditation decisions have so far mostly been based on written materials submitted by the applicant, and on testimonials provided by those who trained one, others with whom one has worked and, in some of the fields, clients. As Hogan (1977) points out, whether or not these procedures differentiate the competent from the incompetent depends very much on the competence of those who provide the testimonials. IAASS has recently added the possibility of interviews to its assessment system. Despite its name, this organization has almost all its members in the United States.

There are at present no attempts to regulate the practice of group work in Britain, although discussions are underway concerning a certification scheme for psychotherapists. A regulatory scheme was operated in Holland for a number of years in the 1960s, whereby the only persons permitted to conduct T-groups were those who had been trained by the Netherlands Association of Trainers in Social Relations (TSR). The system was enforced through the threat that any TSR member who collaborated in running groups with non-TSR members would be expelled. The system broke down under the pressure of the increasing diversification of styles of group work in the late sixties.

It appears that no self-evidently viable systems have yet been devised for the regulation of group work, although the IAASS scheme has some promise. The danger of all such systems is that they will adopt as criteria those skills or attributes of group leaders which are easiest to measure, such as how long was their training. An effective system would be one which validly assesses how far a leader could provide to a group a requisite balance of behaviours such as support, confrontation, and meaning attribution, which have been shown to have a more direct link to group outcome.

Research and theory

This book has differed from most others concerning groups, in the emphasis it lays on research data as a basis for the development of theory and practice in group training. In most areas of the social sciences there is a somewhat uneasy relationship between researchers and practitioners. Researchers have often been vulnerable to the view that only what can be measured is real, while practitioners have fallen victim to the belief that anything which views their actions from a stance of scepticism or questioning can have little good in it.

A more ideal relationship between research, theory, and practice would be one in which each informs and draws from the other. Where such a relationship can be established, research can enhance practice by highlighting the key issues which practitioners face. Practice can enhance research by clear expression of how those key issues are experienced. Debate between researchers and practitioners may then serve as an additional form of regulation of the quality of work done in the field. This regulation would rest not on the form of controls explored in the previous section, but on the voluntary enhancement of practice by trainers and researchers through discussion and debate.

A number of the issues explored in this book could provide the basis for such discussions. Two particular issues stand out as crucial ones at the present time; how one assesses change after a group, and how precisely one can specify the effective leader role.

The problem of how to measure change has been touched on at various points. The difficulties arise basically from the fact that many of the effects of groups concern how people feel and how they perceive themselves and others. Changes detectable after a group may be visible to oneself but not others, or to others but not oneself. One cannot simply opt for measurement of changes in behaviour observable by others, since that implicitly concedes that changes in a person's feelings are not real, a concession which few in this field would be willing to make. The difficulties which arise from the fact that some of the most important changes after groups are changes in feelings and cognitions, have been most fully explored by Golembiewski (Golembiewski et al., 1976; Golembiewski, 1980). He proposes that the very yardsticks against which we judge whether or not change has occurred, are themselves modified by the experience. Thus, an aspect of ourselves which we dislike before a group may remain unchanged, but may now be acceptable to us. Or our perception of ourselves as being a particular kind of person may change, as a result of comparison with others' self-percepts. The consequence of all this is that it is often hard to judge whether changes obtained on some scale or other do represent a change in actual behaviour, or a change in how one thinks about oneself. Furthermore, detected changes may be only a fragment of those which are not detected, since undetected change may be based not on change along some given dimension, but on the creation of new dimensions for thinking about oneself or others.

These difficulties do not make the researcher's task any easier, but if researchers are able to face up to them they may find themselves measuring more closely the types of change which practitioners contend with. The most obvious ways in which researchers can move in such directions are through the use of more diversified types of measuring instrument. The use of standardized personality tests has served some function in delineating changes which *do* occur, but future research should lean more on instruments which can detect cognitive change, on data analysis which shows the variability of effects, and on measurements derived from persons other than the trainee. Of the outcome studies reviewed in this book, the huge majority employed only one or two outcome measures. The richness of the data arising from those studies such as Lieberman et al. (1973) which used many more, shows what can be achieved. Not every study requires such elaboration, but some movement in this direction should repay itself.

The second crucial issue in the field at this time is that of effective leader behaviour. This issue is closely linked with the adequacy of current models of learning in groups. The two-factor model of change presented in Chapter 4 has provided one of the main themes for this book. It appears that there is some empirical validity to its predictions, and that it may prove useful in debating both appropriate leader behaviour and the likely impact of particular designs. The major novelty of the model is its requirement that internalized learning requires both support *and* confrontation to be experienced. Few would argue with the proposition that the experience of support is a crucial element in group learning, and most would also agree that support by itself is insufficient to assure lasting effects. Thus the contentious element in the model is the requirement for confrontation. The difficulty in evaluating this aspect of the model is to know what behaviours a particular group member will, in fact, find confronting. Of the various leader behaviours found to be linked to learning, meaning attribution, emotional stimulation, and genuineness might all lead to a member being confronted. However, each of these concepts, like that of confrontation, is diffuse. Meaning attribution, for instance, presumably encompasses anything from a group-oriented psychoanalytic interpretation to a supportive attempt to clarify a misunderstanding between two group members, or a self-disclosure by the leader as to why he or she was acting in a particular way. Thus it *may* be true that confrontation is what is required for learning in addition to support, but more rigorous tests of the proposition require greater clarity as to which of the leader's behaviours do in fact have confronting effects. One particularly promising development in this direction is Bunker's (1980) study of group leaders' theories of practice. This study should shed more light on how group leaders choose which of a range of interventions to make. Once support is established, the leader's choice to confront or not confront, and selections among the range of possible ways of confronting, may turn out to be a vital element in leader effectiveness. The current diversity of findings gives us few clues as to which of the types of confrontation, which others have termed meaning attribution, emotional stimulation, and genuineness, might be most frequently effective.

Group work: past, present, and future

Opinions differ rather sharply as to the role and usefulness of group experiences in society. Among the optimists is Rogers (1968), who asserts that 'the intensive group experience (is) perhaps the most significant social invention of the century. . .'. In this paper, which is entitled *Interpersonal Relationships: USA 2000*, he stresses that his goal is not prediction but the exploration of alternative future paths. He sees small group experiences as having great potential in aiding society to cope with an ever-increasing rate of social change. By such means we may be able to better adapt to relationships which are at once intimate and transitory. We may also be able to structure organizations such as schools, industry, and the church in ways which give more direct expression to the needs of those who participate in them. He acknowledges that little of this may be achieved, and that we may instead be headed for a period of much more overt social conflict, but he firmly asserts that we do have the choice to direct the future in the manner which he proposes.

Rogers writes as someone with a lifetime's experience in psychotherapy, and a continuing involvement in his own particular orientation towards encounter. He shares very little common ground with Back (1972), a sociologist who has analysed what he sees as the rise and fall of the encounter movement. Within Back's perspective, sensitivity training and encounter constitute a particular social movement, whose occurrence at a given point in history can be analysed. The contemporary encounter movement can be seen as having something in common with earlier, ostensibly different, phenomena such as mediaeval pilgrimages. Both generate at times a somewhat fervent feeling of liberation and release. Both look rather different from the viewpoint of the observer and of the participant. Back proposes that the encounter movement has arisen because of the mobility, affluence, education, and secularization of advanced industrial societies. In the circumstances created by these trends, many people experience a loss of personal closeness to others and of certainty as to how they wish to live. In Back's view, intensive groups are well tailored to provide, at the least, a sort of instant intimacy and to some extent a renewed sense of meaning and purpose. But he is sceptical that these effects last, and dismissive of the research data which he examines. In a later analysis (Back, 1978), he and others attribute the decline in the encounter movement during the seventies to an increasing awareness that although the movement is tailored to the current social concerns of many, it cannot deliver what it promises.

Back's analysis has considerable cogency. The more extended examination of research data undertaken in this book suggests that while he may be wrong to assert that little change persists after groups, he is certainly right in his claim that the effects do tend to fade over time. This author would, however, take issue with Back over two points. It is not at present clear whether it is true to say that the small group movement is in decline, nor is it self-evident that the fade-out of training effects is inexorable or unavoidable. A number of studies have been reviewed which showed sustained persistence of effects.

It is very likely true that fewer people are attending groups than did so eight or ten years ago, both in North America and in Western Europe. The fashionableness of groups at that time has clearly passed, and nowadays the groups which do occur have a rather more routine and workaday air to them. There are fewer encounter and growth centres than there used to be in the big cities, and fewer spontaneous groups run by students for students. On the other hand, there appears to be substantial growth in the utilization of organizational development approaches and in the diffusion and size of self-help groups. Furthermore, more people have attended the summer programmes of National Training Laboratories during 1978 and 1979 than in any year since 1970. Back's epilogue for the small group movement may be somewhat premature. There does certainly appear to be a continuing change in the types of group work gaining most emphasis, as there was also between the fifties and sixties, but there is no certainty that the movement is in decline.

The changes in the types of group approach emphasized as these methods have developed, are no doubt explicable in terms of broader social trends as well as developments within the field. Within the field, two publications stand out as landmarks on the route to changed emphases. The first of these, Campbell and Dunnette (1968), reviewed the then available evaluation studies of T-groups. It is very frequently cited by advocates of organizational development as having established that the results of training individuals in T-groups were of no benefit to their employing organizations. What Campbell and Dunnette actually concluded was that while the studies showed that individuals did show change after groups, there was very little evidence as to whether the changes achieved benefitted the trainee's employing organization or not. This conclusion is worded with a lot more appropriate caution than many readers have made of it. Most probably those whose increasing commitment was to organizational development were already rather sure that changes in individual behaviour might be more reliably linked to organizational change by organizational interventions. The role of Campbell and Dunnette's review was thus not to inform a debate about training design, but to be used as supporting evidence by those who were already set upon devising different forms of group-based intervention.

The second landmark publication in the field has been that by Lieberman et al. (1973). The range of aspects of group experience illuminated by these authors, and the degree to which this book has drawn support from their study, will by now be self-evident. However, its citation by other writers has again involved some degree of distortion. An overwhelming emphasis is apparent upon the incidence of casualties. This is most marked in the writings of those in the clinical field. The book has become ammunition in a continuing conflict over which modes of therapy are the safest and most effective. More conservative clinicians have drawn from it some reassurance for their suspicion of the new quasi-therapies. To a greater extent than was so with Campbell and Dunnette, it does appear that the authors intended this conclusion to be drawn from their study, albeit only as one among a number of others which are less frequently referred to by others. Lieberman et al. do provide a brief comparison of success rates in their study of encounter groups, and in nine studies of individual psychotherapy previously published by others. They conclude that encounter groups show less positive change and more harmful effects than does individual psychotherapy. Russell (1978) points out that such a comparison is scarcely valid, since types of client, measures used, duration, amount of therapist time per client, and many other variables all differ between the groups and the individual therapy studies.

The Lieberman et al. study has been used to provide a rationale for a return to more conservative methods of therapy, and has most likely also stimulated the move away from using the term encounter to describe particular kinds of group work. The influence of the publications by Campbell and Dunnette and by Lieberman et al. on the field cannot be simply categorized as, for instance, helpful or harmful. In each instance they appear to have been used to accentuate a trend away from one type of group work and towards another. In each case it is not wholly clear that the effect was quite what the authors intended, but the role of research findings in the social sciences has rarely been to inform, more often to provide a basis for argument.

The implication of this line of reasoning is that explanations of the continuing evolutionary trends in group work practice must be sought not so much within the field of group work itself, but within the broader field of social change in which group work practitioners and clients alike are immersed. Two separate kinds of analyses of this kind have been advanced, one profoundly pessimistic, the other less so. The first possibility is an essentially Marxist analysis (e.g., Rosenthal, 1971). In this view, the small group movement is a middleclass phenomenon of capitalist societies. During the sixties the types of group experience which were devised served to sustain the status quo of existing organizations by providing opportunities for managers and administrators to attend groups unrelated to the context of their jobs. A manager attending a group might have been previously frustrated or fighting to initiate particular kinds of change. After a cathartic group experience in which he expressed all kinds of feelings usually suppressed, the manager returns feeling less frustrated and more willing to go along with the status quo. The effect is much like that of a good holiday, and organizations can use it as a reward for good performance or as a promise of future promotion. The experience of the sixties showed, according to this view, that while this pattern worked well enough with some employees, it backfired with others. Either they returned with visions of different ways of structuring organizations, or they returned saying that they now realized that their job was insufficiently fulfilling, and resigned. Clearly there was a need for organizations to maintain a closer control over the ways in which group training was linked to the priorities of the organization, and this led to the creation of organizational development programmes. In a similar manner, the cathartic benefits of encounter group experience could serve to reduce the frustrations of other middleclass groups such as students and housewives. When the encounter movement became so large as to provide a serious threat of competition for clients with more established mental health professionals, particularly those in private practice, conflict was inevitable. The claim that encounter groups were dangerous, an accusation that has been made against almost every social innovation, proved to have sufficient basis in truth to weaken its appeal substantially.

I have designated this analysis as pessimistic in so far as it offers little hope that the various forms of group work, present or future, offer much prospect of change in the social structure of organizations or of society. At one level the analysis is certainly correct. Most residential group training programmes reflect the society in which they occur. Participants and leaders are middleclass and spend their time sitting around and talking about their relationships to one another. Meanwhile others, who are mostly working class, prepare their meals and housing. The interface between these two classes comprising a residential group training programme is rarely explored, or seen as relevant to the task of learning about interpersonal relations. Only in a tiny minority of training designs is the allocation of money or the preparation of food treated as having any importance for learning.

The difficulty in taking further a Marxist-type analysis of the role of group work in society is that such analysis asks of group work a type of social change that many of its practitioners would not expect it to achieve. Little enough is known of the circumstances which might permit a major restructuring of society, but they must certainly include events a lot more compelling than the practice of group work. It aids no one's case to confuse one's understandings of the circumstances which can create personal, organizational, and societal changes. If one can successfully maintain a separation between conceptions of change on these different levels, some new possibilities become apparent. For instance, group methods may have some usefulness in resolving the personal or organizational difficulties experienced by radical groups. Work of this kind has certainly been undertaken both in Britain and the United States, but no published descriptions of outcome are available.

The second possible approach to the analysis of social changes impinging on group work is well exemplified by Farson (1978). Farson argues that the approaches fostered by humanistic psychologists may cause us to see as problems events which were not previously seen as such. By establishing and disseminating widely a variety of methods of group work, we assert to ourselves and others that interpersonal relationships and relationships in groups may vary in quality and are amenable to improvement. Prior to the development of such approaches, one imagines, it would have been a great deal easier to accept that however one's relationship with someone else was, that was the only way it could be. This effect, if Farson is correct in asserting that it has occurred, could easily be seen as a part of the rather broader changes during the present century, reviewed by Back (1972). These trends have encouraged and increased the belief that the problems of oneself or of society are not fixed or preordained, but are amenable to effort from oneself or others towards some kind of improvement.

This changing pattern of belief about agency or the causation of events can have either positive or negative effects. As argued in Chapter 4, where a person comes to see themself as able to cause a particular behaviour, they are much more likely to try out that new behaviour. Many of the positive effects of groups are likely to occur in just such a way. However, a group may also lead one to develop unrealistic expectations about the likely response of others to one's initiatives. Where one's initiatives with others lead not to enhanced relationships, but to crisis and misunderstanding, one is somewhat worse off than if no initiative for change had been made.

Farson cites the soaring divorce statistics of most countries as evidence that people in recent years are asking rather more of their relationships than they used to. Of course, divorce laws have also become more liberal in many countries, but he quotes survey data indicating that an increasing proportion of couples separate not for traditional reasons such as brutality, desertion, or adultery, but on account of difficulties in communication, child rearing, and sexual fulfilment.

The relevance of these arguments to the development of the small group movement seems clear. The creation of these methods has no doubt played a part in the growth of beliefs that relationship problems, like technical problems, are amenable to improvement. Advocates of group work, and especially of encounter, have often failed to make a clear distinction between the manner in which a group can, with some reliability, help to create change in one's own behaviour and the fact that that group can make no valid promises as to how others outside the group will react to that change. The overselling of what groups can achieve leads inexorably to the pattern where this year's newest form of group work is next year's discredited fad. Even where there is no overselling of the group, change may occur, but its positive evaluation is outdistanced by rather larger changes in what group members now aspire towards. Some of the outcome studies reviewed earlier illustrated this point.

The cultural context delineated by Farson will most likely be with us for some time, whether we like it or not. He points out that those who are most vulnerable to the ebb and flow of experiential fashions are those who are most marginal and insecure. There may nonetheless be advantages as well as disadvantages to the recurring cycle of innovation and disillusion. The disillusion which one experiences with a particular type of group work can be something less than total. For instance, in the case of sensitivity training, which achieved its peak popularity in the sixties, experience in its use did not simply give rise to later variants such as encounter and organizational development, but also told us more than we initially knew about the circumstances under which it still makes sense to employ it. Thus there *is* some cumulative effect of experience and expertise as different methods evolve. Furthermore, although each approach may very sensibly be tailored to a somewhat different need, conceptual frameworks and empirical findings from one method may help to predict the effectiveness of others. A case in point is the use of the support and confrontation model in this book.

The impact of Farson's analysis is rather different from the Marxist one. While both suggest that the broader context of group work has elements which we might rather do without, Farson's offers some possibility that we can design improved forms of group work. If our very emphasis on striving to improve relationships with others has within it the seeds of further dissatisfaction, new approaches may be those which lay less stress on striving for improvement. Both Farson himself and Lieberman et al. suggest that perhaps our emphasis is wrong, maybe we should not ask of groups 'do they work?' or 'do they lead to improvement?', but 'do they lead to moments which compare with our most cherished aesthetic experiences?'.

Clearly there is fuller scope than many have allowed for looking at groups in just such ways. However, it is not at all certain how many opportunities future society will find for types of group work which are not more immediately focussed on experienced problems. The most direct attempt to foresee the future of group work is that by Levine and Cooper (1976). They review economic and demographic forecasts for the coming twenty years, and argue that the scope for group work will diminish unless methods can be devised which connect with coming crises. These include economic recession, an ageing population, reduced social mobility, and increasing internationalization of social science. The cutting edge of several of these changes, namely increasing unemployment and the fear of it, has already achieved marked effects among students and many others. These changes are likely to mean that the group work of the future will need to be structured in ways which provide direct assistance to those facing specific problems. Where society fails to provide the resources to confront these problems, there will no doubt be a continuing growth of self-help groups. Where resources are forthcoming, there will be a role for group work in clinical, educational, and organizational contexts. Back (1972) quotes a sentence from a speech by Adolf Hitler, who clearly had a different type of future in mind: 'I'm not saying there will be improvements, but there must be changes.' (1933).

This book has sought to present the view that whichever forms of group work, present or future, are employed, their use is best guided by systematic research and by refinement of models of change. The continuing diversification of methods means that we now have some approaches which operate primarily through the creation of support for individuals or groups in a given setting; we have other approaches which seek to facilitate personal change in one setting and its transfer to other settings; we have approaches whose main goal is system development and its maintenance; and finally we have approaches whose goal is person-centred and whose rationale is aesthetic or hedonistic. In each of these cases, we know more than we used to do about how to set up and sustain such experiences. Unfortunately, the malaise which Farson so elegantly analyses afflicts group leaders and researchers just as much as anyone else. The cult of perfectability and improvement leads us to be dissatisfied with training designs and research findings which impressed us a decade ago. Hartman (1979), in discussing various reviews of studies of group work, expresses puzzlement at the relatively optimistic conclusions of this author's 1975(a) review. Our search for perfection breeds a spirit of scepticism and critique, which certainly has its constructive side, but which should not be allowed to blind us to what has already been achieved.

REFERENCES

Adams, P. L. 'Experiential group counselling with intern teachers'. *Dissertation Abstracts International*, 1970, *31A*, 605–606.

Adelson, J. P. 'Feedback and group development'. *Small Group Behavior*, 1975, *6*, 389–401.

Alperson, B. L., Alperson, E. D., and Levine, R. 'Growth effects of high-school marathons'. *Experimental Publication System*, American Psychological Association, 1971, *10*, MS. no. 369 – 56.

Andrews, J. D. W. 'Interpersonal challenge: a source of growth in laboratory training'. *Journal of Applied Behavioral Science*, 1973, *9*, 514–533.

Andrews, J. D. W. 'Interpersonal challenge workshop: a way to enhance laboratory experiences'. *Interpersonal Development*, 1975, *5*, 26–36.

Antze, P. 'The role of ideologies in peer psychotherapy organizations: some theoretical considerations and three case studies'. *Journal of Applied Behavioral Science*, 1976, *12*, 323–346.

Archer, D. 'Power in groups: self-concept changes of powerful and powerless group members'. *Journal of Applied Behavioral Science*, 1974, *10*, 208–220.

Argyris, C. 'Explorations in interpersonal competence – 11'. *Journal of Applied Behavioral Science*, 1965, *1*, 255–269.

Argyris, C. 'On the future of laboratory education'. *Journal of Applied Behavioral Science*, 1967, *3*, 153–183.

Aries, E. 'Interaction patterns and themes of male, female, and mixed groups'. *Small Group Behavior*, 1976, *7*, 7–18.

Armenakis, A. A., Feild, H. S., and Holley, W. H. 'Guidelines for overcoming empirically identified evaluation problems of OD change agents'. *Human Relations*, 1976, *29*, 1147–1161.

Aron, A. *Interaction effects of neuroticism and trainer style on T-group induced change*. Unpublished MA thesis, University of California, Berkeley, 1968.

Asch, S. 'Studies of independence and conformity: a minority of one against a unanimous majority'. *Psychological Monographs*, 1956, *70*, Whole no. 416.

Assagioli, R. *Psychosynthesis*. New York, Psychosynthesis Research Foundation, 1965.

Babad, E. Y. and Amir, L. 'Trainers' liking, Bion's emotional modalities, and T-group effect'. *Journal of Applied Behavioral Science*, 1978, *14*, 511–522. (a)

Babad, E. Y. and Amir, L. 'Bennis and Shepard's theory of group development: an empirical examination'. *Small Group Behavior*, 1978, *9*, 477–492. (b)

Babad, E. Y. and Melnick, I. 'Effects of a T-group as a function of trainers' liking and members' participation, involvement, quantity, and quality of received feedback'. *Journal of Applied Behavioral Science*, 1976, *12*, 543–562.

Back, K.W. *Beyond Words: The story of sensitivity training and the encounter movement*. New York, Russell Sage, 1972.

Back, K. W. (ed.) *In Search of Community: Encounter groups and social change*. Boulder, Colorado, Westview Press, 1978.

Batchelder, R. L. and Hardy, J. M. *Using Sensitivity Training and the Laboratory Method: An organisational case study in the development of human resources*. New York, Association Press, 1968.

Bailey, W. J. 'Student perceived behavioral changes occurring in a secondary school faculty as a result of a human relations in-service workshop'. *Dissertation Abstracts*, 1968, *28A*, 3398–3399.

Bandura, A. *Social Learning Theory*. Englewood Cliffs, New Jersey, Prentice-Hall, 1977.

Bare, C. E. and Mitchell, R. R. 'Experimental evaluation of sensitivity training'. *Journal of Applied Behavioral Science*, 1972, *8*, 263–276.

Bebout, J. and Gordon, B. 'The value of encounter'. *New Perspectives on Encounter Groups*, L.N. Solomon and B. Berzon (eds.), San Francisco, Jossey-Bass, 1972. (a)

Bebout, J. and Gordon B. 'The use of encounter groups for interpersonal growth: initial results of the TIE project'. *Interpersonal Development*, 1972, *2*, 91–104. (b)

Becker, J. L. 'The effects of instructional audiotape in self-directed encounter groups'. *Dissertation Abstracts International*, 1971, *31B*, 4325–4326.

Beckhard, R. and Lake, D. 'Short- and long-range effects of a team development effort'. *Social Intervention: A behavioral science approach*, H. A. Hornstein, B. B. Bunker, W.W. Burke, M. Gindes, and R. J. Lewicki (eds.), New York, Free Press, 1971.

Bednar, R. L. and Battersby, C. P. 'The effects of specific cognitive structure on early group development'. *Journal of Applied Behavioral Science*, 1976, *12*, 513–522.

Bellanti, J. 'The effects of an encounter group experience on empathy, respect, congruence and self-actualisation'. *Dissertation Abstracts International*, 1972, *32B*, 6668–6669.

Benedict, B. A., Calder, P. H., Callahan, D. M., Hornstein, H. A., and Miles, M. B. 'The clinical-experimental approach to assessing organisational change efforts'. *Journal of Applied Behavioral Science*, 1967, *3*, 347–380.

Benne, K. D. 'History of the T-group in the laboratory setting'. *T-Group Theory and Laboratory Method: Innovation in re-education*, L. P. Bradford, K. D. Benne., and J. R. Gibb, (eds.), New York, Wiley, 1964.

Bennis, W. G. and Shepard, H. A. 'A theory of group development'. *Human Relations*, 1956, *9*, 415–437.

Benson, L., Berger, M., and Mease, W. 'Family communication systems'. *Small Group Behavior*, 1975, *6*, 91–105.

Berne, E. *Transactional Analysis in Psychotherapy*. New York, Grove Press, 1961.

Berne, E. *Games People Play*. New York, Grove Press, 1964.

Berzon, B., Reisel, J., and Davis, D. P. 'An audiotape program for self-directed small groups'. *Journal of Humanistic Psychology*, 1969, *9*, 71–92.

Biberman, G. *Trainer Behavior in a T-Group Setting: A survey of current practice.* Unpublished Ph.D. thesis, Temple University, Philadelphia, Pennsylvania, 1977.

Bierman, R. 'Dimensions of interpersonal facilitation in psychotherapy and child development'. *Psychological Bulletin*, 1969, *72*, 338–352.

Bloom, S. 'A study of the impact of sensitivity training on the elderly'. *Interpersonal Development*, 1976, *6*, 150–152.

Bigelow, R. C. 'Changing classroom interaction through organization development'. *Organization Development in Schools*, R.A. Schmuck and M. B. Miles (eds.), Palo Alto, California, National Press, 1971.

Bion, W. R. *Experiences in Groups*. London, Tavistock, 1961.

Blake, R. R. and Mouton, J. S. 'The intergroup dynamics of win-lose conflict and problem-solving collaboration in union-management relations'. *Intergroup Relations and Leadership: Approaches and research in industrial, ethnic, cultural and political areas*, M. Sherif (ed.), New York, Wiley, 1962.

Blake, R. R. and Mouton, J. S. 'The union-management intergroup laboratory'. *Journal of Applied Behavioral Science*, 1965, *1*, 25–57.

Blake, R. R. and Mouton, J. S. *The New Managerial Grid*. Houston, Texas, Gulf, 1978.

Boderman, A., Freed, D. W., and Kinnucan, M. T. 'Touch me, like me': testing an encounter group assumption'. *Journal of Applied Behavioral Science*, 1972, *8*, 527–533.

Bolman, L. 'Laboratory versus lecture in training executives'. *Journal of Applied Behavioral Science*, 1970, *6*, 323–335.

Bolman, L. 'Some effects of trainers on their T-groups'. *Journal of Applied Behavioral Science*, 1971, *7*, 309-325.

Bolman, L. 'Some effects of trainers on their T-groups: a partial replication'. *Journal of Applied Behavioral Science*, 1973, *9*, 534-539.

Bolman, L. 'Group leader effectiveness'. *Developing Social Skills in Managers*, C. L. Cooper (ed.), London, MacMillan, 1976.

Boehringer, G., Zeruolis, V., Bayley, J., and Boehringer, K. 'Stirling: the destructive application of group techniques to a conflict'. *Journal of Conflict Resolution*, 1974, *18*, 257–275.

Bowers, D. G. 'OD techniques and their results in 23 organizations: the Michigan ICL study'. *Journal of Applied Behavioral Science*, 1973, *9*, 21–43.

Bowers, D. G. and Hausser, D. L. 'Work group types and intervention in OD'. *Administrative Science Quarterly*, 1977, *22*, 76–94.

Boyd, J. D. and Elliss, J. *Findings of Research into Senior Management Seminars.* Toronto, Hydroelectric Power Commission of Ontario, 1962.

Bradford, D. L. and Eoyang, C. 'The use and misuse of structured exercises'.

Developing Social Skills in Managers, C. L. Cooper (ed.), London, MacMillan, 1976.

Bradford, L. P., Benne, K. D., and Gibb, J. R. (eds.) *T-Group Theory and Laboratory Method: Innovation in re-education*. New York, Wiley, 1964.

Brook, R. C. 'Self-concept changes as a function of participation in sensitivity training as measured by the Tennessee Self-Concept Scale'. *Dissertation Abstracts*, 1968, *29A*, 1700.

Bugen, L. 'Composition and orientation effects on group cohesion'. *Psychological Reports*, 1977, *40*, 175–181.

Bugen, L. 'Expectation profiles: members expect more than they get while leaders give more than they expect'. *Small Group Behavior*, 1978, *9*, 115–123.

Bunker, B. B. 'Developing a theory of practice of experiential learning'. *Advances in Experiential Social Processes*, C. P. Alderfer and C. L. Cooper (eds.), 1980, *2*, 189–219.

Bunker, D. R. 'Individual applications of laboratory training'. *Journal of Applied Behavioral Science*, 1965, *1*, 131–147.

Bunker, D. R. and Knowles, E. S. 'Comparison of behavioral changes resulting from human relations training laboratories of different lengths'. *Journal of Applied Behavioral Science*, 1967, *3*, 505–523.

Burns, C. W. 'Effectiveness of the basic encounter group in marriage counselling'. *Dissertation Abstracts International*, 1972, *33B*, 1281.

Buss, A. R. 'Causes and reasons in attribution theory: a conceptual critique'. *Journal of Personality and Social Psychology*, 1978, *36*, 1311–1321.

Butkovich, P., Carlisle, J., Duncan, R., and Moss, M. 'Social systems and psychoanalytic approaches to group dynamics: complementary or contradictory?'. *International Journal of Group Psychotherapy*, 1975, *25*, 3–31.

Campbell, J. P. and Dunnette, M. D. 'Effectiveness of T-group experiences in managerial training and development'. *Psychological Bulletin*, 1968, *70*, 73–104.

Carron, T. J. 'Human relations training and attitude change: a vector analysis'. *Personnel Psychology*, 1964, *17*, 403–424.

Chambers, W. M. and Ficek, D. E. 'An evaluation of marathon counseling'. *International Journal of Group Psychotherapy*, 1970, *20*, 372–379.

Cicatti, S. M. 'Comparison of three methods of facilitating encounter groups in a college environment'. *Dissertation Abstracts International*, 1970, *31B*, 2954.

Cirigliano, R. J. 'Group encounter effects upon the self-concepts of high school students'. *Dissertation Abstracts International*, 1972, *33A*, 2760–2761.

Coch, L. and French, J. R. P. Jr. 'Overcoming resistance to change'. *Human Relations*, 1948, *1*, 512–532.

Cohen, B. M. and Keller, G. 'The relationship between laboratory training and human relations growth in varying organizational climates'. *Catalog of Selected Documents in Psychology*, 1973, *3*, MS. no. 442.

Cooper, C. L. 'The influence of the trainer on participant change in T-groups'. *Human Relations*, 1969, *22*, 515–530.

Cooper, C. L. 'An attempt to assess the psychologically disturbing effects of T-group training'. *British Journal of Social and Clinical Psychology*, 1972, *11*, 342–345.

Cooper, C. L. 'Coping with life stress after sensitivity training'. *Psychological Reports*, 1972, *31*, 602.

Cooper, C. L. 'Psychological disturbance following T-groups: relationship between the Eysenck personality inventory and family/friends judgments'. *British Journal of Social Work*, 1974, *4*, 39–49.

Cooper, C. L. 'Adverse and growthful effects of experiential learning groups: the role of the trainer, participant, and group characteristics'. *Human Relations*, 1977, *30*, 1103–1129.

Cooper, C. L. and Bowles, D. 'Physical encounter and self-disclosure'. *Psychological Reports*, 1973, *33*, 451–454.

Cooper, C. L. and Bowles, D. 'Structured exercise-based groups and the psychological conditions of learning'. *Interpersonal Development*, 1975, *5*, 203–212.

Cooper, C. L. and Oddie, H. *An Evaluation of Two Approaches to Social Skill Training in the Catering Industry*. London, Hotel and Catering Industry Training Board, 1972.

Crawshaw, R. 'How sensitive is sensitivity training?'. *American Journal of Psychiatry*, 1969, *126*, 868–873.

Crews, C. Y. and Melnick, J. 'Use of initial and delayed structure in facilitating group development'. *Journal of Counseling Psychology*, 1976, *23*, 92–98.

Culbert, S. 'Trainer self-disclosure and member growth in two T-groups'. *Journal of Applied Behavioral Science*, 1968, *4*, 47–73.

Culbertson, F. 'Modification of an emotionally held attitude through role-playing'. *Journal of Abnormal and Social Psychology*, 1957, *54*, 230–233.

Cureton, L. *T-Groups and Intergroups in Teacher Training*. Unpublished M.Phil. thesis, University of Sussex, 1968.

Danish, S. J. 'The influence of leader empathy (affective sensitivity), participant motivation to change and leader-participant relationship on changes in affective sensitivity of T-group participants'. *Dissertation Abstracts International*, 1970, *30A*, 5229–5330.

Danish, S. J. and Kagan, N. 'Measurement of affective sensitivity: toward a valid measure of interpersonal perception'. *Journal of Counseling Psychology*, 1971, *18*, 51–54.

D'Augelli, A. R. and Chinsky, J. M. 'Interpersonal skills and pretraining: implications for the use of group procedures for interpersonal learning and for the selection of non-professional mental health workers'. *Journal of Consulting and Clinical Psychology*, 1974, *42*, 65–72.

Davis, D. and Brock, T. C. 'Use of first person pronouns as a function of increased objective self-awareness and performance feedback'. *Journal of Experimental Social Psychology*, 1975, *11*, 381–388.

Davis, T. B., Frye, R. L., and Joure, S. 'Perceptions and behaviors of dogmatic subjects in a T-group setting'. *Perceptual and Motor Skills*, 1975, *41*, 375–381.

De Charms, R. *Personal Causation: The internal affective determinants of behavior*. New York, Academic Press, 1968.

De Leon, G. and Biase, D. V. 'Encounter group: measurement of systolic blood pressure'. *Psychological Reports*, 1975, *37*, 439–445.

De Julio, S. S., Lambert, M. J., and Bentley, J. 'Personal satisfaction as a criterion for evaluating group success'. *Psychological Reports*, 1977, *40*, 409–410.

De Michele, J. H. 'The measurement of rated training changes resulting from a sensitivity training laboratory in an overall program of organization development'. *Dissertation Abstracts*, 1967, *27A*, 3578–3579.

Desmond, R. E. and Seligman, M. 'A review of research on leaderless groups'. *Small Group Behavior*, 1977, *8*, 3–24.

Diamond, M. J. 'From Skinner to Satori? Toward a social learning analysis of encounter group behavior change'. *Journal of Applied Behavioral Science*, 1974, *10*, 133–148.

Diamond, M. J. and Shapiro, J. L. 'Changes in locus of control as a function of encounter group experiences: a study and a replication'. *Journal of Abnormal Psychology*, 1973, *82*, 514–518.

Dies, R. R. and Greenberg, B. 'Effects of physical contact in an encounter group context'. *Journal of Consulting and Clinical Psychology*, 1976, *44*, 400–405.

Doob, L. W. and Foltz, W. J. 'The impact of a workshop upon grass-roots leaders in Belfast'. *Journal of Conflict Resolution*, 1974, *18*, 237–256.

Dua, P. S. 'Effects of laboratory training on anxiety'. *Journal of Counseling Psychology*, 1972, *19*, 171–172.

Dunn, W. N. and Swierczek, F. W. 'Planned organizational change: toward grounded theory'. *Journal of Applied Behavioral Science*, 1977, *13*, 135–158.

Dunphy, D. 'Phases, roles and myths in self-analytic groups'. *Journal of Applied Behavioral Science*, 1968, *4*, 195–225.

Duval, S. and Hensley, V. 'Extensions of objective self-awareness theory: the focus of attention-causal attribution hypothesis'. *New Directions in Attribution Research*, J. H. Harvey, W. J. Ickes, and R. F. Kidd (eds.), Hillsdale, New Jersey, Erlbaum, 1976.

Duval, S. and Wicklund, R. A. *A Theory of Objective Self-Awareness*. New York, Academic Press, 1972.

Elliott, G. R. 'Effects of T-group training on the communication skills of counselor trainees'. *Small Group Behavior*, 1978, *9*, 49–58.

Emrick, C. D., Lassen, C. L., and Edwards, M. T. 'Non-professional peers as therapeutic agents'. *Effective Psychotherapy: A Handbook of Research*, A. S. Gurman and A. M. Razin (eds.), Oxford, Pergamon, 1977.

Enright, J. B. 'On the playing fields of Synanon'. *Confrontation: Encounters in self and interpersonal awareness*, L. Blank, G. B. Gottsegen, and M. G. Gottsegen (eds.), New York, Macmillan, 1971.

Epps, J. D. and Sikes, W. W. 'Personal growth groups: who joins and who benefits?'. *Group and Organization Studies*, 1977, *2*, 88–100.

Esposito, R. P., McAdoo, H., and Scher, L. 'The Johari window as an evaluative instrument for group process'. *Interpersonal Development*, 1976, *6*, 25–37.

Farrell, M. P. 'Patterns in the development of self-analytic groups'. *Journal of Applied Behavioral Science*, 1976, *12*, 523–542.

Farson, R. 'The technology of humanism'. *Journal of Humanistic Psychology*, 1978, *18*, 5–36.

Felton, G. S. and Biggs, B. E. 'Teaching internalization behavior to collegiate low achievers in group psychotherapy'. *Psychotherapy: Theory, Research and Practice*, 1972, *9*, 281–283.

Felton, G. S. and Biggs, B. E. 'Psychotherapy and responsibility: teaching internalisation behavior to black low achievers through group therapy'. *Small Group Behavior*, 1973, *4*, 147–155.

Finando, S. J., Croteau, J. M., Sanz, D., and Woodson, R. 'The effects of group type on changes of self-concept'. *Small Group Behavior*, 1977, *8*, 123–134.

Flannigan, M. W. 'A study of attitude changes through group processes'. *Dissertation Abstracts International*, 1971, *31A*, 2102.

Foulds, M. L. 'Effects of a personal growth group on a measure of self-actualisation'. *Journal of Humanistic Psychology*, 1970, *10*, 33–38.

Foulds, M. L. 'Measured changes in self-actualisation as a result of a growth group experience'. *Psychotherapy: Theory, Research and Practice*, 1971, *8*, 338–341. (a)

Foulds, M. L. 'Changes in locus of internal-external control: a growth group experience'. *Comparative Group Studies*, 1971, *2*, 293–300. (b)

Foulds, M. L. 'The effects of a personal growth group on ratings of self and others'. *Small Group Behavior*, 1973, *4*, 508–512.

Foulds, M. L., Girona, R., and Guinan, J. F. 'Changes in ratings of self and others as a result of a marathon group'. *Comparative Group Studies*, 1970, *1*, 349–356.

Foulds, M. L. and Guinan, J. F. 'Marathon group: changes in ratings of self and others'. *Psychotherapy: Theory, Research and Practice*, 1973, *10*, 30–32.

Foulds, M. L., Guinan, J. F., and Warehime, R. F. 'Marathon group: changes in a measure of dogmatism'. *Small Group Behavior*, 1974, *5*, 387–392.

Foulds, M. L., Guinan, J. F., and Warehime, R. G. 'Marathon group: changes in perceived locus of control'. *Journal of College Student Personnel*, 1974, *15*, 8–11.

Foulds, M. L. and Hannigan, P. S. 'Marathon group: changes in scores on the California Psychological Inventory'. *Journal of College Student Personnel*, 1974, *15*, 474–479. (a)

Foulds, M. L. and Hannigan, P. S. 'Effects of psychomotor group therapy on ratings of self and others'. *Psychotherapy: Theory, Research and Practice*, 1974, *11*, 351–354. (b)

Foulds, M. L. and Hannigan, P. S. 'Effects of psychomotor group therapy on locus of control and social desirability'. *Journal of Humanistic Psychology*, 1976, *16*, 81–88. (a)

Foulds, M. L. and Hannigan, P. S. 'Gestalt marathon group: does it increase reported self-actualisation?' *Psychotherapy: Theory, Research and Practice*, 1976, *13*, 378–383. (b)

Foulds, M. L. and Hannigan, P. S. 'Effects of a gestalt marathon workshop on a measure of extraversion and neuroticism'. *Journal of College Student Personnel*, 1976, *17*, 50–54. (c)

Foulds, M. L. and Hannigan, P. S. 'Effects of gestalt marathon workshops on measured self-actualisation'. *Journal of Counseling Psychology*, 1976, *23*, 60–65. (d)

Foulds, M. L. and Hannigan, P. S. 'Gestalt marathon group: changes on a measure of personal and social functioning'. *Journal of Humanistic Psychology*, 1978, *18*, 57–67.

Frankiel, H. H. 'Mutually perceived relationships in T-groups: the cotrainer puzzle'. *Journal of Applied Behavioral Science*, 1971, 7, 449–465.

Frankl, V. *The Will to Meaning: Foundations and applications of logotherapy*. London, Souvenir Press, 1971.

Franklin, J. L. 'Characteristics of successful and unsuccessful organization development'. *Journal of Applied Behavioral Science*, 1976, *12*, 471–492.

French, J. R. P. Jr., Sherwood, J. J., and Bradford, D. L. 'Change in self-identity in a mangement training conference'. *Journal of Applied Behavioral Science*, 1966, *2*, 210–218.

French, W. L. and Bell, C. H. *Organization Development*. Englewood Cliffs, New Jersey, Prentice-Hall, 1973.

Friedlander, F. 'The impact of organizational training laboratories on the effectiveness and interaction of work groups'. *Personnel Psychology*, 1967, *20*, 289–309.

Friedlander, F. 'A comparative study of consulting processes and group development'. *Journal of Applied Behavioral Science*, 1968, *4*, 377–400.

Friedlander, F. 'The primacy of trust as a facilitator of further group accomplishment'. *Journal of Applied Behavioral Science*, 1970, *6*, 387–400.

Friedman, P. H. 'Effects of modeling, role-playing and participation on behavior change'. *Progress in Experimental Personality Research*, B. A. Maher (ed.), 1972, *6*, 41–81.

Friedman, S. B., Ellenhorn, L. J., and Snortum, J. R. 'A comparison of four warm-up techniques for initiating encounter groups'. *Journal of Counseling Psychology*, 1976, *23*, 514–519.

Fullan, M., Miles, M. B., and Taylor, G. 'Organisational development in schools: the state of art'. *Review of Educational Research*, 1980, (at press).

Garber, J. et al. 'A psychoeducational therapy program for delinquent boys: an evaluation report'. *Journal of Drug Education*, 1976, *6*, 331–342.

Gassner, S. M., Gold, J., and Snadowsky, A. M. 'Changes in the phenomenal field as a result of human relations training'. *Journal of Psychology*, 1964, *58*, 33–41.

Geitgey, D. A. 'A study of some effects of sensitivity training on the performance of students in associated degree programs of nursing education'. *Dissertation Abstracts*, 1966, *27B*, 2000–2001.

Gibbard, G. S. and Hartman, J. 'The oedipal paradigm in group development'. *Small Group Behavior*, 1973, *4*, 305–354.

Gibbard, G. S., Hartman, J., and Mann, R. D. (eds.) *Analysis of Groups*. San Francisco, Jossey-Bass, 1974.

Gilligan, J. F. 'Personality characteristics of selectors and non-selectors of sensitivity training'. *Journal of Counseling Psychology*, 1973, *20*, 265–268.

Gilligan, J. F. 'Sensitivity training and self-actualisation'. *Psychological Reports*, 1974, *34*, 319–325.

Goffman, E. *The Presentation of Self in Everyday Life*. New York, Anchor, 1959.

Gold, J. S. 'An evaluation of a laboratory human relations training program for college undergraduates'. *Dissertation Abstracts*, 1968, *28A*, 3262–3263.

Golembiewski, R. T. *The Small Group: An analysis of research concepts and operations*. Chicago, University of Chicago Press, 1962.

Golembiewski, R. T. 'Organisation development in industry: perspectives on Progress/Stuckness'. *Small Groups and Personal Change*, P. B. Smith (ed.), London, Methuen, 1980.

Golembiewski, R. T., Billingsley, K., and Yeager, S. 'Measuring change and persistence in 'human affairs: types of change generated by OD designs'. *Journal of Applied Behavioral Science*, 1976, *12*, 133–157.

Golembiewski, R. T. and McConkie, M. 'The centrality of interpersonal trust in group processes'. *Theories of Group Processes*, C. L. Cooper (ed.), London, Wiley, 1975.

Goodstein, L. D., Goldstein, J. J., D'Orta, C. V., and Goodman, M. A. 'Measurement of self-disclosure in encounter groups: a methodological study'. *Journal of Counseling Psychology*, 1976, *23*, 142–146.

Gottschalk, L. A. and Pattison, E. M. 'Psychiatric perspectives on T-groups and the laboratory movement'. *American Journal of Psychiatry*, 1969, *126*, 823–839.

Greenberg, I. A. (ed.) *Psychodrama: Theory and therapy*. New York, Behavioral Publications, 1974.

Greiner, L. 'Antecedents of planned organization change'. *Journal of Applied Behavioral Science*, 1967, *3*, 51–85.

Gross, N., Giacquinta, J. B., and Bernstein, M. *Implementing Organizational Innovations: A sociological analysis of planned educational change*. New York, Basic Books, 1971.

Guinan, J. F. and Foulds, M. L. 'Marathon group: facilitator of personal growth?'. *Journal of Counseling Psychology*, 1970, *17*, 145–149.

Gurman, A. S. 'The patient's perception of the therapeutic relationship'. *Effective Psychotherapy: A handbook of research*, A. S. Gurman and A. M. Razin (eds.), Oxford, Pergamon, 1977.

Gurman, A. S. and Kniskern, D. P. 'Enriching research on marital enrichment programs'. *Journal of Marriage and Family Counseling*, 1977, *3*, 3–11.

Haase, R. K. and Kelly, F. D. 'Characteristics of those who seek, those who complete, and those who drop out of sensitivity groups'. *Counseling Center Research Reports*, University of Massachusetts, 1971, no. 26.

Haiman, F. S. 'The effects of training in group processes on openmindedness'. *Journal of Communication*, 1963, *13*, 236–245.

Haley, J. W. *Problem-Solving Therapy: New strategies for effective family therapy*. San Francisco, Jossey-Bass, 1978.

Hall, J. 'Observations on the invalid scoring algorithm of 'NASA' and similar consensus tasks: a response'. *Group and Organization Studies*, 1979, *4*, 116–118.

Handlin, V., Breed, G., Noll, G., and Watkins, J. 'Encounter group process as a function of group length'. *Small Group Behavior*, 1974, *5*, 259–273.

Harrison, R. 'The impact of the laboratory on perceptions of others by the experimental group'. *Interpersonal Competence and Organizational Effectiveness*, C. Argyris (ed.), Homewood, Illinois, Irwin-Dorsey, 1962.

Harrison, R. *Cognitive Models for Interpersonal and Group Behaviour: A theoretical framework for research*. Washington, D.C., National Training Laboratories 1965. (a)

Harrison, R. 'Personal style, group composition, and learning: Part II'. *Journal of Applied Behavioral Science*, 1965, *1*, 294–301. (b)

Harrison, R. 'Group composition models for laboratory design'. *Journal of Applied Behavioral Science*, 1965, *1*, 409–432. (c)

Harrison, R. 'Choosing the depth of an organizational intervention'. *Journal of Applied Behavioral Science*, 1970, *6*, 181–202.

Harrison, R. and Lubin, B. 'Personal style, group composition, and learning: Part I'. *Journal of Applied Behavioral Science*, 1965, *1*, 286–293.

Harrow, G. 'The effects of psychodrama group therapy on role behavior of schizophrenic patients'. *Group Psychotherapy*, 1951, *3*, 316–320.

Harrow, M., Astrachan, B., Tucker, G., Klein, E. G., and Miller, J. 'The T-group and study group laboratory experiences'. *Journal of Social Psychology*, 1971, *85*, 225–237.

Hartman, J. 'Small group methods of personal change'. *Annual Review of Psychology*, M. Rosenzweig and L. Porter (eds.), 1979, *30*, 454–476.

Heck, E. J. 'A training and research model for investigating the effects of sensitivity training for teachers'. *Journal of Teacher Education*, 1971, *22*, 501–507.

Hellebrandt, E. T. and Stinson, J. E. 'The effects of T-group training on business game results'. *Journal of Psychology*, 1971, *77*, 271–272.

Henry, J. *Pathways to Madness*. New York, Random House, 1972.

Hewitt, J. and Kraft, M. 'Effects of an encounter group experience on self-perception and interpersonal relations'. *Journal of Consulting and Clinical Psychology*, 1973, *40*, 162.

Higgin, G. W. and Bridger, H. 'The psychodynamics of an intergroup experience'. *Human Relations*, 1964, *17*, 391–446.

Hipple, J. L. 'Effects of differential human relations laboratory designs on personal growth'. *Small Group Behavior*, 1976, *7*, 407–422.

Hoerl, R. T. 'Encounter groups: their effect on rigidity'. *Human Relations*, 1974, *27*, 431–438.

Hogan, D. B. 'Encounter groups and human relations training: the case against applying traditional forms of statutory regulation'. *Harvard Journal on Legislation*, 1974, *11*, 659–701.

Hogan, D. B. 'Competence as a facilitator of personal growth groups'. *Journal of Humanistic Psychology*, 1977, *17*, 33–54.

Hollander, E. P. and Willis, R. H. 'Current issues in the study of conformity and non-conformity'. *Psychological Bulletin*, 1967, *68*, 62–75.

Homans, G. C. *The Human Group*. New York, Harcourt, Brace, and World, 1950.

Hull, W. F. 'Changes in world-mindedness after a cross-cultural sensitivity group experience'. *Journal of Applied Behavioral Science*, 1972, *8*, 115–121.

Hurley, J. R. 'Two prepotent interpersonal dimensions and the effects of trainers on T-groups'. *Small Group Behavior*, 1976, *7*, 77–98.

Hurley, J. R. and Force, E. J. 'T-group gains in acceptance-rejection of self and others'. *International Journal of Group Psychotherapy*, 1973, *23*, 166–176.

Hurley, J. R. and Hurley, S. J. 'Toward authenticity in measuring self-disclosure'. *Journal of Counseling Psychology*, 1969, *16*, 271–274.

Hurley, J. R. and Pinches, S. K. 'Interpersonal behavior and effectiveness of T-group leaders'. *Small Group Behavior*, 1978, *9*, 529–539.

Innis, M. N. N. 'An analysis of sensitivity training and laboratory method in effecting changes in attitudes and concepts'. *Dissertation Abstracts International*, 1971, *31A*, 6404.

Insel, P. and Moos, R. 'An experimental investigation of process and outcome in an encounter group'. *Human Relations*, 1972, *25*, 441–447.

Jackins, H. *Fundamentals of Cocounseling Manual*. Seattle, Washington, Rational Island Publishers, 1962.

Jacobs, A., Jacobs, M., Cavior, N., and Burke, J. 'Anonymous feedback: credibility and desirability of structured emotional and behavioral feedback delivered in groups'. *Journal of Counseling Psychology*, 1974, *21*, 106–111.

Jacobs, M. 'A comparison of publicly delivered and anonymously delivered verbal feedback in brief personal growth groups'. *Journal of Consulting and Clinical Psychology*, 1977, *45*, 385–390.

Jacobs, M., Jacobs, A., Feldman, G., and Cavior, N. 'Feedback 11 – the 'credibility gap': delivery of positive and negative and emotional and behavioral feedback in groups'. *Journal of Consulting and Clinical Psychology*, 1973, *41*, 215–223.

Jacobs, M., Jacobs, A., Gatz, M., and Schaible, T. 'Credibility and desirability of positive and negative structured feedback in groups'. *Journal of Consulting and Clinical Psychology*, 1973, *40*, 244–252.

Jacobson, E. A. and Smith, S. J. 'The effect of weekend encounter group experience upon interpersonal orientations'. *Journal of Consulting and Clinical Psychology*, 1972, *38*, 403–410.

Jaffe, S. L. and Scherl, D. J. 'Acute psychosis precipitated by T-group experiences'. *Archives of General Psychiatry*, 1969, *21*, 443–448.

Janis, I. L. and King, B. T. 'The influence of role-playing on opinion change'. *Journal of Abnormal and Social Psychology*, 1954, *49*, 211–218.

Janis, I. L. and Mann, L. 'Effectiveness of emotional role-playing in modifying smoking habits and attitudes'. *Journal of Experimental Research in Personality*, 1965, *1*, 84–90.

Jansen, M. J. and Stolurow, L. M. 'An experimental study of role-playing'. *Psychological Monographs*, 1962, *76*, Whole no. 550.

Jeffers, J. J. L. 'Effects of marathon encounter groups on personality characteristics of group members and group facilitators'. *Dissertation Abstracts International*, 1972, *32A*, 4153.

Jesness, C. F. 'Comparative effectiveness of behavior modification and transactional analysis programs for delinquents'. *Journal of Consulting and Clinical Psychology*, 1975, *43*, 759–779.

Johnson, D. W. 'Effectiveness of role reversal: actor or listener'. *Psychological Reports*, 1971, *28*, 275–282.

Johnson, D. W., Kavanagh, J. A., and Lubin, B. 'T-groups, tests and tension'. *Small Group Behavior*, 1973, *4*, 81–88.

Johnson, D. W. and Lewicki, R. J. 'The initiation of superordinate goals'. *Journal of Applied Behavioral Science*, 1969, *5*, 9–24.

Jones, E. E. and Nisbett, R. E. *The Actor and Observer: Divergent perceptions of the causes of behavior*. Morristown, New Jersey, General Learning Press, 1971.

Jones, F. D. and Peters, H. N. 'Experimental evaluation of group psychotherapy'. *Journal of Abnormal and Social Psychology*, 1952, *47*, 345–353.

Jourard, S. *The Transparent Self*. Princeton, Van Nostrand, 1964.

Kane, F. J. Jr., Wallace, C. D., and Lipton, M. A. 'Emotional disturbance related to T-group experience'. *American Journal of Psychiatry*, 1971, *127*, 954–957.

Kassarjian, H. H. 'Social character and sensitivity training'. *Journal of Applied Behavioral Science*, 1965, *1*, 433–440.

Katz, S. I. and Schwebel, A. I. 'The transfer of laboratory training'. *Small Group Behavior*, 1976, *7*, 271–286.

Kaye, J. D. 'Group interaction and interpersonal learning'. *Small Group Behavior*, 1973, *4*, 424–448.

Kegan, D. L. and Rubinstein, A. H. 'Trust, effectiveness and organization development: a field study in R and D'. *Journal of Applied Behavioral Science*, 1973, *9*, 498–513.

Kelman, H. C. 'Compliance, identification and internalisation'. *Journal of Conflict Resolution*, 1958, *2*, 51–60.

Kernan, J. P. 'Laboratory human relations training: its effect on the 'personality' of supervisory engineers'. *Dissertation Abstracts*, 1964, *25*, 665–666.

Keutzer, C. S., Fosmire, F. R., Diller, R., and Smith, M. D. 'Laboratory training in a new social system: evaluation of a consulting relationship with a high school faculty'. *Journal of Applied Behavioral Science*, 1971, *7*, 493–501.

Khanna, J. L. *Training of Educators for Hard Core Areas – A Success?* Paper presented at the 17th Congress, International Association for Applied Psychology, Liege, 1971.

Kimball, R. and Gelso, C. J. 'Self-actualisation in a marathon group: do the strong get stronger?'. *Journal of Counseling Psychology*, 1974, *21*, 38–42.

Kimberly, J. R. and Nielsen, W. R. 'Organizational development and change in organizational performance'. *Administrative Science Quarterly*, 1975, *20*, 191–206.

Kinder, B. N. and Kilmann, P. R. 'The impact of differential shifts in leader structure on the outcome of internal and external group participants'. *Journal of Clinical Psychology*, 1976, *32*, 857–863.

King, A. S. 'Expectation effects in organizational change'. *Administrative Science Quarterly*, 1974, *19*, 221–230.

King, B. T. and Janis, I. L. 'Improvised versus non-improvised role-playing in producing opinion change'. *Human Relations*, 1956, *9*, 177–186.

King, M. 'Changes in self-acceptance of college students associated with the encounter model class'. *Small Group Behavior*, 1976, *7*, 379–384.

King, M., Payne, D. C., and McIntire, W. G. 'The impact of marathon and prolonged sensitivity training on self-acceptance'. *Small Group Behavior*, 1973, *4*, 414–423.

Kleeman, J. L. 'The Kendall College human potential seminar model: research'. *Journal of College Student Personnel*, 1974, *15*, 89–95.

Klein, E. B. 'An overview of recent Tavistock work in the United States'. *Advances in Experiential Social Processes*, C. L. Cooper and C. P. Alderfer (eds.), 1978, *1*, 181–202.

Klein, E. B. and Astrachan, B. M. 'Learning in groups: a comparison of study groups and T-groups'. *Journal of Applied Behavioral Science*, 1971, *7*, 659–693.

Klein, M. 'Our adult world and its roots in infancy'. *Human Relations*, 1959, *12*, 291–303.

Klein, R. S. 'The effects of differential treatments on encounter groups'. *Dissertation Abstracts International*, 1973, *34B*, 415–416.

Klingberg, H. E. 'An evaluation of sensitivity training effects on self-actualisation, purpose in life and religious attitudes of theological students'. *Journal of Psychology and Theology*, 1973, *1*, 31–39.

Kohler, A. T., Miller, J. R., and Klein, E. B. 'Some effects of intergroup experiences on study group phenomena'. *Human Relations*, 1973, *26*, 293–305.

Kolb, D. A. and Fry, R. 'Towards an applied theory of experiential learning'. *Theories of Group Processes*, C. L. Cooper (ed.), London, Wiley, 1975.

Kolb, D. A., Winter, S. K., and Berlew, D. E. 'Self-directed change: two studies'. *Journal of Applied Behavioral Science*, 1968, *4*, 453–472.

Korn, R. P. 'Self as agent and self as object: a theory of interpersonal incompetence and human intervention'. *Group Psychotherapy and Psychodrama*, 1975, *28*, 184–210.

Krear, M. L. 'The influence of sensitivity training on the social attitudes of educational leaders of racially-imbalanced schools'. *Dissertation Abstracts*, 1968, *29A*, 1954–1955.

Kuch, K., Harrower, M., and Renick, J. 'Observations on a time-extended group with campus volunteers'. *International Journal of Group Psychotherapy*, 1972, *22*, 471–487.

Kuiken, D., Rasmussen, R. V., and Cullen, D. 'Some predictors of volunteer participation in human relations training groups'. *Psychological Reports*, 1974, *35*, 499–504.

Lacks, P. B., Landsbaum, J. B., and Stern, M. R. 'Workshop in communication for members of a psychiatric team'. *Psychological Reports*, 1970, *26*, 423–430.

Laing, R. D. and Esterson, A. *Sanity, Madness and the Family*. London, Tavistock, 1964.

Lakin, M. *Interpersonal Encounter: Theory and practice in sensitivity training*. New York, McGraw Hill, 1972.

Lakin, M. and Carson, R. C. 'Participant perception of group process in group sensitivity training'. *International Journal of Group Psychotherapy*, 1964, *14*, 116–122.

Langer, E. J. 'Rethinking the role of thought in social interaction'. *New Directions in Attribution Research Volume II*, J. H. Harvey, W. Ickes, and R. F. Kidd (eds.), Hillsdale, New Jersey, Erlbaum, 1978.

Larson, J. L. 'The effects of a human relations workshop on personal and interpersonal perceptions in a military setting'. *Dissertation Abstracts International*, 1972, *33A*, 2716.

Lavoie, D. 'The phenomenological transformation of the self-concept towards self-actualisation through the sensitivity training laboratory'. *Interpersonal Development*, 1971, *2*, 201–212.

Lee, R. E. 'Relationship between basic encounter group and change in self-concepts and interpersonal relationships of college low achievers'. *Dissertation Abstracts International*, 1969, *30A*, 2336–2337.

Lee, W. S. 'Human relations training for teachers: the effectiveness of sensitivity training'. *California Journal of Educational Research*, 1970, *21*, 28–34.

Lennung, S. A. *Metalearning, Laboratory Training and Individually Different Change*. Stockholm, Swedish Council for Personnel Administration, 1974.

Levenberg, S. B. and Spakes, J. W. 'Locus of control of reinforcement and attraction in sensitivity group settings'. *Psychological Reports*, 1975, *37*, 719–723.

Levin, E. M. and Kurtz, R. R. 'Structured and non-structured human relations training'. *Journal of Counseling Psychology*, 1974, *21*, 526–531.

Levine, N. R. 'Emotional factors in group development'. *Human Relations*, 1971, *24*, 65–90.

Levine, N. and Cooper, C. L. 'T-groups – twenty years on: a prophecy'. *Human Relations*, 1976, *29*, 1–24.

Lieberman, M. A. 'The influence of group composition on changes in affective approach'. *Emotional Dynamics and Group Culture*, D. Stock and H. A. Thelen (eds.), Washington, D.C., National Training Laboratories, 1958.

Lieberman, M. A. and Bond, G. R. 'The problem of being a woman: a survey of 1700 women in consciousness-raising groups'. *Journal of Applied Behavioral Science*, 1976, *12*, 363–379.

Lieberman, M. A. and Bond, G. R. 'Self-help groups: problems of measuring outcome'. *Small Group Behavior*, 1978, *9*, 221–241.

Lieberman, M. A. and Borman, L. D. *Self-Help Groups*. San Francisco, Jossey-Bass, 1979.

Lieberman, M. A. and Gardner, J. 'Institutional alternatives to psychotherapy: a study of growth center users'. *Archives of General Psychiatry*, 1976, *33*, 157–162.

Lieberman, M. A., Yalom, I. D., and Miles, M. B. *Encounter Groups: First Facts*. New York, Basic Books, 1973.

Livingston, L. B. 'Self-concept change of black college males as a result of a weekend black experience encounter workshop'. *Dissertation Abstracts International*, 1971, *32B*, 2423.

Lohmann, K., Zenger, J. H., and Weschler, I. R. 'Some perceptual changes during sensitivity training'. *Journal of Educational Research*, 1959, *53*, 28–31.

Lomranz, J., Lakin, M., and Schiffman, H. 'Variants of sensitivity training and encounter: diversity or fragmentation?' *Journal of Applied Behavioral Science*, 1972, *8*, 399–420.

Long, T. J. and Bosshart, D. A. 'The facilitator behavior index'. *Psychological Reports*, 1974, *34*, 1059–1068.

Long, T. J., Schuerger, J. M., Bosshart, D. A., and Menges, R. J. 'Fluctuation in psychological state during two encounter group weekends'. *Psychological Reports*, 1971, *29*, 267–274.

Long, T. J. and Schulz, E. W. 'Empathy: a quality of an effective leader'. *Psychological Reports*, 1973, *32*, 699–705.

Lowen, A. *The Language of the Body*. New York, MacMillan, 1971.

Lubin, B. and Lubin, A. 'Laboratory training stress compared with college examination stress'. *Journal of Applied Behavioral Science*, 1971, *7*, 502–507.

Lubin, B. and Zuckerman, M. 'Affective and perceptual cognitive patterns in sensitivity training groups'. *Psychological Reports*, 1967, *21*, 365–376.

Lubin, B. and Zuckerman, M. 'Level of emotional arousal in laboratory training'. *Journal of Applied Behavioral Science*, 1969, 5, 483–490.

Luft, J. *Group Processes*. Palo Alto, California, National Press, 1963.

Luke, R. A. 'The internal normative structure of sensitivity training groups'. *Journal of Applied Behavioral Science*, 1972, 8, 421–437.

Lundgren, D. C. 'Trainer style and patterns of group development'. *Journal of Applied Behavioral Science*, 1971, 7, 689–708.

Lundgren, D. C. 'Trainer-member influence in T-groups: one-way or two-way?'. *Human Relations*, 1974, 27, 755–766.

Lundgren, D. C. 'Interpersonal needs and member attitudes toward trainer and group'. *Small Group Behavior*, 1975, 6, 371–388.

Lundgren, D. C. 'Member attitudes towards the leaders and interpersonal attraction in short-term training groups'. *Group Process*, 1976, 6, 141–148.

Lundgren, D. C. 'Developmental trends in the emergence of interpersonal issues in T-groups'. *Small Group Behavior*, 1977, 8, 179–200.

Lundgren, D. C. and Knight, D. 'Trainer style and member attitudes toward trainer and group in T-groups'. *Small Group Behavior*, 1977, 8, 47–64.

Lundgren, D. C. and Knight, D. 'Sequential stages of development in sensitivity training groups'. *Journal of Applied Behavioral Science*, 1978, 14, 204–222.

Lundgren, D. C. and Schaeffer, C. 'Feedback processes in sensitivity traing groups'. *Human Relations*, 1976, 29, 763–782.

Malan, D. H., Balfour, F. H. G., Hood, V. G., and Shooter, A. M. N. 'Group psychotherapy: a long-term follow-up study'. *Archives of General Psychiatry*, 1976, 33, 1303–1315.

Mann, J. *Encounter: A weekend with intimate strangers*. New York, Pocket Books, 1970.

Mann, J. H. and Mann, C. 'The effect of role-playing experiences on self-ratings of personal adjustment'. *Group Psychotherapy*, 1958, 11, 27–32.

Mann, L. and Janis, I. L. 'A follow-up on the long-term effects of emotional role-playing'. *Journal of Personality and Social Psychology*, 1968, 8, 339–342.

Mann, L. 'The effects of emotional role-playing on desire to modify smoking habits'. *Journal of Experimental Social Psychology*, 1967, 3, 334–348.

Mann, R. D. 'The development of the member-trainer relationship in self-analytic groups'. *Human Relations*, 1966, 19, 85–115.

Mann, R. D. 'Winners, losers and the search for equality in groups'. *Theories of Group Processes*, C. L. Cooper (ed.), London, Wiley, 1975.

Marks, C. *The Meaning of Encounter Group Process: A research analysis*. Paper presented at Association for Humanistic Psychology Convention, Squaw Valley, California, 1972.

Margulies, N. 'The effects of an organizational sensivitity training program on a measure of self-actualisation'. *Studies in Personnel Psychology*, 1973, 5, 67–74.

Marrow, A. J., Bowers, D. G., and Seashore, S. E. *Management by Participation*. New York, Harper & Row, 1967.

Martin, R. D. and Fischer, D. G. 'Encounter group experience and personality change'. *Psychological Reports*, 1974, 35, 91–96.

Massarik, F. 'Standards for group leadership'. *New Perspectives on Encounter*

Groups, L. N. Solomon and B. Berzon (eds.), San Francisco, Jossey-Bass, 1972.

May, R. J. and Tierney, D. E. 'Personality changes as a function of group transactional analysis'. *Journal of College Student Personnel*, 1976, *17*, 485–488.

McCanne, L. P. 'Dimensions of participant goals, expectations and perceptions of small group experiences'. *Journal of Applied Behavioral Science*, 1977, *13*, 533–541.

McConnell, H. K. 'Individual differences as mediators of participant behaviour and self-descriptive change in two human relations training programs'. *Organizational Behavior and Human Performance*, 1971, *6*, 550–572.

McFarland, G. N. 'Effects of sensitivity training utilised as in-service education'. *Dissertation Abstracts International*, 1971, *31A*, 4013.

McFarland, H. B. N. 'An analysis of the effect of interpersonal communication group work on dogmatism and self-concept of student teachers'. *Dissertation Abstracts International*, 1971, *31A*, 6456.

Mead, G. H. *Mind, Self and Society*. Chicago, University of Chicago Press, 1934.

Melnick, J. and Woods, M. 'Analysis of group composition research and theory for psychotherapeutic and growth-oriented groups'. *Journal of Applied Behavioral Science*, 1976, *12*, 493–512.

Miles, M. B. 'Human relations training: processes and outcomes'. *Journal of Counseling Psychology*, 1960, 7, 301–306.

Miles, M. B. 'On temporary systems'. *Innovation in Education*, M. B. Miles (ed.), New York, Teachers College, Columbia University, 1964.

Miles, M. B. 'Changes during and following laboratory training: a clinical experimental study'. *Journal of Applied Behavioral Science*, 1965, *1*, 215–242.

Miller, G. M. 'The effects of sensitivity training design and personality factors upon the attitude of group participants'. *Dissertation Abstracts International*, 1970, *30A*, 3836–3837.

Mills, T. M. *Group Transformation: An analysis of a learning group*. Englewood Cliffs, New Jersey, Prentice-Hall, 1964.

Mirvis, P. and Berg, D. *Failures in Organizational Development and Change*. New York, Wiley, 1977.

Mitchell, P., Reid, W., and Sanders, N. 'The human potential seminar at Muskegon community college'. *Michigan Personnel and Guidance Journal*, 1973, *4*, 31–37.

Morrison, T. C. and Thomas, M. D. 'Participants' perception of themselves and leaders in two kinds of group experience'. *Journal of Social Psychology*, 1976, *98*, 103–110.

Moscovici, S. and Faucheux, C. 'Social influence, conformity bias, and the study of active minorities'. *Advances in Experimental Social Psychology*, L. Berkowitz (ed.), 1972, *6*, 150–202.

Moscow, D. 'The transfer of training from T-groups to the job situation'. *Proceedings of the 16th International Congress of Applied Psychology*, Amsterdam, Swets and Zeitlinger, 1969.

Moscow, D. 'T-group training in the Netherlands: an evaluation and a cross-cultural comparison'. *Journal of Applied Behavioral Science*, 1971, 7, 427–448.

Moss, C. J. and Harren, V. A. 'Member disclosure in personal growth groups:

effects of leader disclosure'. *Small Group Behavior*, 1978, *9*, 64–79.

Murphy, A. J. 'Effects of body contact on performance of a simple cognitive task'. *British Journal of Social and Clinical Psychology*, 1972, *11*, 402–403.

Myers, G. E., Myers, M. T., Goldberg, A., and Welch, C. E. 'Effect of feedback on interpersonal sensitivity in laboratory training groups'. *Journal of Applied Behavioral Science*, 1969, *5*, 175–186.

Noll, G. A. and Watkins, J. T. 'Differences between persons seeking encounter group experience and others on the Personal Orientation Inventory'. *Journal of Counseling Psychology*, 1974, *21*, 206–209.

Norton, B. E. 'The effects of human relations training upon teacher trainees' level of facilitative communication, self-concept and creativity'. *Dissertation Abstracts International*, 1973, *33A*, 4094–4095.

NTL Institute 'Commonly asked questions about sensitivity training'. *News and Reports*, 1969, *3*, 4.

Oatley, K. 'Theories of personal learning in groups'. *Small Groups and Personal Change*, P. B. Smith (ed.), London, Methuen, 1980.

O'Connor, G. and Alderson, J. 'Human relations groups for human services practitioners'. *Small Group Behavior*, 1974, *5*, 495–505.

O'Day, R. 'Training style: a content-analytic assessment'. *Human Relations*, 1973, *26*, 599–637.

O'Day, R. 'Individual training styles: an empirically derived typology'. *Small Group Behavior*, 1976, *7*, 147–182.

Olch, D. and Snow, D. L. 'Personality characteristics of sensitivity group volunteers'. *Personnel and Guidance Journal*, 1970, *48*, 848–850.

Pacoe, L. V., Naar, R., Guyett, I. P., and Wells, R. 'Training medical students in interpersonal relationship skills'. *Journal of Medical Education*, 1976, *51*, 743–750.

Pagès, M. 'Bethel culture, 1969: impressions of an immigrant'. *Journal of Applied Behavioral Science*, 1971, *7*, 267–284.

Pagès, M. *The Laboratory Method of Changing and Learning*, K. D. Benne, L. P. Bradford, J. R. Gibb, and R. O. Lippitt (eds.), Palo Alto, California, Science and Behavior Books, 1975.

Parker, C. C. and Huff, V. E. 'The effects of group counseling on rigidity'. *Small Group Behavior*, 1975, *6*, 402–413.

Perls, F. S., Hefferline, R. and Goodman, P. *Gestalt Therapy*. New York, Julian Press, 1951.

Pesso, A. *Experience in Action*. New York, New York University Press, 1973.

Peters, D. R. 'Self-ideal congruence as a function of human relations training'. *Journal of Psychology*, 1970, *76*, 199–207.

Peters, D. R. 'Identification and personal learning in groups'. *Human Relations*, 1973, *26*, 1–22.

Pfister, G. 'Outcomes of laboratory training for police officers'. *Journal of Social Issues*, 1975, *31*, 115–121.

Pino, C. J. and Cohen, H. 'Trainer style and trainee self-disclosure'. *International Journal of Group Psychotherapy*, 1971, *21*, 202–213.

Poe, B. J. 'The effect of sensitivity training on the relations between risk-taking and other selected behavior factors'. *Dissertation Abstracts International*, 1972, *32B*, 6037–6038.

Pollack, D. and Stanley, G. 'Coping and marathon sensitivity training'. *Psychological Reports*, 1971, *29*, 379–385.

Pollack, H. B. 'Change in homogeneous and heterogeneous sensitivity training groups'. *Journal of Consulting and Clinical Psychology*, 1971, *37*, 60–66.

Poppen, P. J. 'Who gives and who receives in T-groups: some personality characteristics of benefitors and contributors'. *Cornell Journal of Social Relations*, 1972, *7*, 101–115.

Porras, J. and Berg, P. O. 'The impact of organization development'. *Academy of Management Review*, 1978, *3*, 249–266.

Posthuma, A. B. and Posthuma, B. W. 'Some observations of encounter group casualties'. *Journal of Applied Behavioral Science*, 1973, *9*, 595–608.

Powell, T. A. 'An investigation of the T-group and its effect on decision-making skills'. *Dissertation Abstracts International*, 1972, *32A*, 6084–6085.

Psathas, G. and Hardert, R. 'Trainer interventions and normative patterns in the T-group'. *Journal of Applied Behavioral Science*, 1966, *2*, 149–169.

Reader, D. H. and Von Mayer, B. 'T-groups and a process-oriented model of their development'. *Psychologia Africana*, 1966, *11*, 74–89.

Reddy, W. B. 'Sensitivity training or group psychotherapy: the need for adequate screening'. *International Journal of Group Psychotherapy*, 1970, *20*, 366–371.

Reddy, W. B. 'Interpersonal compatibility and self-actualisation in sensitivity training'. *Journal of Applied Behavioral Science*, 1972, *8*, 237–240. (a)

Reddy, W. B. 'On affection, group composition, and self-actualisation in sensitivity training'. *Journal of Consulting and Clinical Psychology*, 1972, *38*, 211–214. (b)

Reddy, W. B. 'Interpersonal affection and change in sensitivity training: a composition model'. *Theories of Group Processes*, C. L. Cooper (ed.), London, Wiley, 1975.

Reisel, J. 'Observations on the trainer role: a case study'. *Leadership and Organisation: A behavioral science approach*, R. Tannenbaum, I. R. Weschler, and F. Massarik (eds.), New York, McGraw Hill, 1961.

Reisel, J. 'Phases of group development'. *Leadership and Organisation: A behavioral science approach*, R. Tannenbaum, I. R. Weschler, and F. Massarik (eds.), New York, McGraw Hill, 1961.

Rettig, S. 'Active and reactive states of being'. *Small Group Behavior*, 1978, *9*, 7–13.

Rice, A. K. *Learning for Leadership*. London, Tavistock, 1965.

Robinson, S. and Henry, S. *Self-Help and Health: Mutual aid for modern problems*. London, Martin Robertson, 1977.

Rogers, C. R. *Client-Centered Therapy*. Boston, Houghton Mifflin, 1951.

Rogers, C. R. 'Interpersonal relationships: USA 2000'. *Journal of Applied Behavioral Science*, 1968, *4*, 265–280.

Rogers, C. R. *Encounter Groups*. New York, Harper & Row, 1970.

Rohrbaugh, M. 'Patterns and correlates of emotional arousal in laboratory training'. *Journal of Applied Behavioral Science*, 1975, *11*, 220–240.

Rohrbaugh, M. and Bartels, B. D. 'Participants' perceptions of 'curative factors' in therapy and growth groups'. *Small Group Behavior*, 1975, *6*, 430–456.

Rosenthal, B. G. 'The nature and development of the encounter group movement'. *Confrontation: Encounters in self and interpersonal awareness*, L. Blank, G. B. Gottsegen, and M. G. Gottsegen (eds.), New York, MacMillan, 1971.

Ross, W. D., Kligfeld, M., and Whitman, R. W. 'Psychiatrists, patients and sensitivity groups'. *Archives of General Psychiatry*, 1971, *25*, 178–180.

Rotter, J. B. 'Generalised expectancies for internal versus external control of reinforcement'. *Psychological Monographs*, 1966, *80*, Whole no. 609.

Rowan, J. 'Encounter group research? No joy'. *Journal of Humanistic Psychology*, 1975, *15*, 19–28.

Rubin, I. M. 'Increased self-acceptance: a new means of reducing prejudice'. *Journal of Personality and Social Psychology*, 1967, *5*, 233–238.

Rubin, I. M. 'The reduction of prejudice through laboratory training'. *Journal of Applied Behavioral Science*, 1967, *3*, 29–50.

Russell, E. W. 'The facts about 'Encounter Groups: First Facts' '. *Journal of Clinical Psychology*, 1978, *34*, 130–137.

Sampson, E. E. 'Leader orientation and T-group effectiveness'. *Journal of Applied Behavioral Science*, 1972, *8*, 564–576.

Satir, V. *Conjoint Family Therapy*. Palo Alto, California, Science and Behavior Books, 1964.

Schaefer, C. E. 'The development of a transactional analysis scale for the Adjective Checklist'. *Journal of Psychology*, 1976, *94*, 59–63.

Schaible, T. D. and Jacobs. A. 'Feedback III: sequence effects: enhancement of feedback acceptance and group attractiveness by manipulation of the sequence and valence of feedback'. *Small Group Behavior*, 1975, *6*, 151–173.

Schein, E. H. and Bennis, W. G. *Personal and Organisational Change Through Group Methods*. New York, Wiley, 1965.

Scherz, M. E. 'Changes in self-esteem following experimental manipulation of self-disclosure and feedback conditions in a sensitivity training laboratory'. *Dissertation Abstracts International*, 1972, *33B*, 1805–1806.

Schmuck, R. A. 'Helping teachers improve classroom group processes'. *Journal of Applied Behavioral Science*, 1968, *4*, 401–435.

Schmuck, R. A., Runkel, P. J., and Langmeyer, D. 'Improving organisational problem-solving in a school faculty'. *Journal of Applied Behavioral Science*, 1969, *5*, 455–482.

Schönke, M. 'Psychodrama in school and college'. *Group Psychotherapy and Psychodrama*, 1975, *28*, 168–179.

Schutz, W. C. *FIRO: A 3-dimensional theory of interpersonal behavior*. New York, Rinehart, 1958.

Schutz, W. C. *Joy: Expanding human awareness*. New York, Grove Press, 1967.

Schutz, W. C. *Here Comes Everybody*. New York, Harper & Row, 1971.

Schutz, W. C. 'Not encounter and certainly not facts'. *Journal of Humanistic Psychology*, 1975, *15*, 7–18.

Schutz, W. C. and Allen, V. 'The effects of a T-group laboratory on interpersonal behavior'. *Journal of Applied Behavioral Science*, 1966, *2*, 265–286.

Seashore, S. E. and Bowers, D. G. 'Durability of organizational change'. *American Psychologist*, 1970, *25*, 227–233.

Seldman, M. L., McBrearty, J. F., and Seldman, S. L. 'Deification of marathon encounter group leaders'. *Small Group Behavior*, 1974, *5*, 80–92.

Seldman, M. L. and McBrearty, J. F. 'Characteristics of marathon volunteers'. *Psychological Reports*, 1975, *36*, 555–560.

Shapiro, J. L. and Diamond, M. J. 'Increases in hypnotisability as a function of encounter group training'. *Journal of Abnormal Psychology*, 1972, *79*, 112–115.

Shapiro, J. L. and Gust, T. 'Counselor training for facilitating human relationships'. *Counselor Education and Supervision*, 1974, *13*, 198–206.

Shapiro, J. L. and Ross, R. L. 'Sensitivity training for staff in an institution for adolescent offenders'. *Journal of Applied Behavioral Science*, 1971, *7*, 710–723.

Shapiro, R. J. and Klein, R. H. 'Perceptions of the leaders in an encounter group'. *Small Group Behavior*, 1975, *6*, 238–248.

Shapiro, S. B. and Shiflett, J. M. 'Loss of connectedness during an elementary teacher training program'. *Journal of Educational Research*, 1974, *68*, 144–148.

Shepard, H. A. and Blake, R. R. 'Changing behaviour through cognitive change'. *Human Organisation*, 1962, *21*, 88–96.

Sheridan, K. and Shack, J. R. 'Personality correlates of the undergraduate volunteer subject'. *Journal of Psychology*, 1970, *76*, 23–26.

Sherrill, J. D. 'The effects of group experience on the personal-vocational development of vocationally-undecided college students'. *Dissertation Abstracts International*, 1973, *34A*, 573.

Sherry, P. and Hurley, J. R. 'Curative factors in psychotherapeutic and growth groups'. *Journal of Clinical Psychology*, 1976, *32*, 835–837.

Sherwood, M. 'Bion's *Experiences in Groups*: a critical evaluation'. *Human Relations*, 1964, *17*, 113–130.

Sigal, J., Braverman, S., Pilon, R., and Baker, P. 'Effects of teacher-led curriculum-integrated sensitivity training in a large high school'. *Journal of Educational Research*, 1976, *70*, 3–9.

Silver, R. J. and Conyne, R. K. 'Effects of direct experience and vicarious experience on group therapeutic attraction'. *Small Group Behavior*, 1977, *8*, 83–92.

Simon, S. 'Synanon: toward building a humanistic organisation'. *Journal of Humanistic Psychology*, 1978, *18*, 3–20.

Singer, J. L. *Imagery and Daydream Methods in Psychotherapy and Behaviour Modification*. New York, Academic Press, 1974.

Slevin, D. 'Observations on the invalid scoring algorithm of 'NASA' and similar consensus tasks'. *Group and Organisation Studies*, 1978, *3*, 497–507.

Smith, P. B. 'Attitude changes associated with training in human relations'. *British Journal of Social and Clinical Psychology*, 1964, *3*, 104–112.

Smith, P. B. 'Correlations between some tests of T-group learning'. *Journal of Applied Behavioral Science*, 1971, *7*, 508–511.

Smith, P. B. 'Group composition as a determinant of Kelman's social influence modes'. *European Journal of Social Psychology*, 1974, *4*, 261–277.

Smith, P. B. 'Controlled studies of the outcome of sensitivity training'. *Psychological Bulletin*, 1975, *82*, 597–622. (a)

Smith, P. B. 'Are there adverse effects of sensitivity training?' *Journal of Humanistic Psychology*, 1975, *15*, 29–48. (b)

Smith, P. B. 'Social influence processes and the outcome of sensitivity training'. *Journal of Personality and Social Psychology*, 1976, *34*, 1087–1094. (a)

Smith, P. B. 'Sources of influence in the sensitivity training laboratory'. *Small Group Behavior*, 1976, *7*, 331–348. (b)

Smith, P. B. 'Changes in relationships after sensitivity training'. *Small Group Behavior*, 1979, *10*, 414–430.

Smith, P. B. 'An attributional analysis of personal learning'. *Advances in Experiential Social Processes*, C. P. Alderfer and C. L. Cooper (eds.), 1980, *2*, 63–92. (a)

Smith, P. B. 'The T-group trainer – group facilitator or prisoner of circumstance?'. *Journal of Applied Behavioral Science*, 1980, *14*, 63–77. (b)

Smith, P. B. 'Changes in personal causality and sensitivity training experience'. *Small Group Behavior*, 1980, (at press). (c)

Smith, P. B. and Honour, T. F. 'The impact of Phase 1 managerial grid training'. *Journal of Management Studies*, 1969, *6*, 318–330.

Smith, P. B. and Linton, M. J. 'Group composition and change in self-actualisation in T-groups'. *Human Relations*, 1975, *28*, 811–823.

Smith, P. B. and Lubin, B. 'Emotional arousal during sensitivity training as a function of the length of the experience'. *Group and Organisation Studies*, 1980, *5*, 97–104.

Smith, P. B. and Willson, M. J. 'The use of group training methods in multiracial settings'. *New Community*, 1975, *4*, 1–14.

Snortum, J. R. and Ellenhorn, L. J. 'Predicting and measuring the psychological impact of non-verbal encounter techniques'. *International Journal of Group Psychotherapy*, 1974, *24*, 217–229.

Snortum, J. R. and Myers, H. F. 'Intensity of T-group relationships as a function of interaction'. *International Journal of Group Psychotherapy*, 1971, *21*, 190–201.

Solomon, L. N., Berzon, B., and Davis, D. 'A personal growth program for self-directed groups'. *Journal of Applied Behavioral Science*, 1970, *6*, 427–451.

Solomon, L. N., Berzon, B., and Weedman, C. W. 'The self-directed therapeutic group: a new rehabilitation resource'. *International Journal of Group Psychotherapy*, 1968, *18*, 199–219.

Sowder, W. F. and Brown, R. A. 'Experimentation in transactional analysis'. *Transactional Analysis Journal*, 1977, *7*, 279–285.

Stava, L. J. and Bednar, R. L. 'Process and outcome in encounter groups: the effects of group composition'. *Small Group Behavior*, 1979, *10*, 200–213.

Steele, F. I. 'Personality and the 'laboratory style' '. *Journal of Applied Behavioral Science*, 1968, *4*, 25–46.

Stock, D. and Thelen, H. A. *Emotional Dynamics and Group Culture*. Washington, D.C., National Training Laboratories, 1958.

Stone, W. N. and Tieger, M. E. 'Screening for T-groups: the myth of healthy candidates'. *American Journal of Psychiatry*, 1971, *127*, 1485–1490.

Storms, M. D. 'Videotape and the attribution process: reversing actors' and observers' points of view'. *Journal of Personality and Social Psychology*, 1973, *27*, 165–175.

Storms, M. D. and McCaul, K. D. 'Attribution processes and emotional exacerbation of dysfunctional behavior'. *New Directions in Attribution Research Volume I*,

J. H. Harvey, W. J. Ickes, and R. F. Kidd (eds.), Hillsdale, New Jersey, Erlbaum, 1976.

Strong, S. R. 'Causal attribution in counseling and psychotherapy'. *Journal of Counseling Psychology*, 1970, *17*, 388–399.

Sutherland, S. H. 'A study of the effects of a marathon and a traditional encounter group experience on self-esteem, defensive behavior and mood'. *Dissertation Abstracts International*, 1973, *33B*, 3963.

Tannenbaum, R., Weschler, I. R., and Massarik, F. *Leadership and Organization: A behavioral science approach*. New York, McGraw Hill, 1961.

Taylor, S. E. and Koivumaki, J. 'The perception of self and others: acquaintanceship, affect and actor-observer differences'. *Journal of Personality and Social Psychology*, 1976, *33*, 403–408.

Teahan, J. C. 'Role-playing and group experience to facilitate intragroup dialogue'. *Journal of Social Issues*, 1975, *31*, 35–45.

Terleski, D. R. 'The relationship between unstructured and structured sensitivity group experience and self-perceived changes of group members'. *Dissertation Abstracts International*, 1971, *31A*, 5139–5140.

Tesch, F. E., Lansky, L. M., and Lundgren, D. C. 'The one-way/two-way communication exercise: some ghosts laid to rest'. *Journal of Applied Behavioral Science*, 1972, *8*, 664–673.

Treppa, J. A. and Fricke, L. 'Effects of a marathon group experience'. *Journal of Counseling Psychology*, 1972, *19*, 466–467.

Trist, E. L. and Sofer, C. *Explorations in Group Relations*. Leicester, Leicester University Press, 1959.

Trueblood, R. W. and McHolland, J. D. 'Measures of change toward self-actualisation through the human potential group process'. Unpublished manuscript, cited by R. R. Knapp and E. L. Shostrom in 'POI outcomes in studies of growth groups: a selected review'. *Group and Organization Studies*, 1976, *1*, 203–222.

Tuckman, B. W. 'Developmental sequences in small groups'. *Psychological Bulletin*, 1965, *63*, 384–399.

Tuckman, B. W. and Jensen, M. A. C. 'Stages of small-group development revisited'. *Group and Organization Studies*, 1977, *2*, 419–427.

Turquet, P. M. 'Threats to identity in the large group'. *The Large Group: Therapy and dynamics*, L. Kreeger (ed.), London, Constable, 1975.

Uhes, M. J. 'Expression of hostility as a function of an encounter group experience'. *Psychological Reports*, 1971, *28*, 733–734.

Vail, J. P. 'The effect of encountertapes for personal growth on culturally disadvantaged negro girls'. *Dissertation Abstracts International*, 1971, *31A*, 5141.

Valins, S. and Misbett, R. E. *Attribution Processes in the Development and Treatment of Emotional Disorders*. Morristown, New Jersey, General Learning Press, 1971.

Valiquet, M. 'Individual change in a management development program'. *Journal of Applied Behavioral Science*, 1968, *4*, 313–325.

Vansina, L. 'Research concerning the influence of the T-group method on the formation of the participants' social values and opinions'. *Evaluation of Supervisory and Management Training Methods*, R. Meigniez (ed.), Paris, Organisation for

Economic Co-operation and Development, 1961.

Vicino, F. L., Russell, J., Bass, B. M., Deci, E. L., and Landy, D. A. 'The impact of PROCESS: self administered exercises for personal and interpersonal development'. *Journal of Applied Behavioral Science*, 1973, *9*, 737–756.

Vosen, L. 'The relation between self-disclosure and self-esteem'. *Dissertation Abstracts*, 1967, *27B*, 2882.

Vraa, C. W. 'Emotional climate as a function of group composition'. *Small Group Behavior*, 1974, *5*, 105–120.

Walker, D. N. 'A dyadic interaction model for non-verbal touching behavior in encounter groups'. *Small Group Behavior*, 1975, *6*, 308–324.

Walker, R. E., Shack, J. R., Egan, G., Sheridan, K., and Sheridan, E. P. 'Changes in self-judgments of self-disclosure after group experience'. *Journal of Applied Behavioral Science*, 1972, *8*, 248–251.

Walter, G. A. and Miles, R. E. 'Changing self-acceptance: task groups and videotape or sensitivity training?'. *Small Group Behavior*, 1974, *5*, 356–364.

Ware, J. R. and Barr, J. E. 'Effects of a nine-week structured and unstructured group experience on measures of self-concept and self-actualisation'. *Small Group Behavior*, 1977, *8*, 93–101.

Watzlawick, P., Weakland, J. H., and Fisch, R. *Change: Principles of problem formation and problem resolution*. New York, Norton, 1974.

Weick, K. 'Organizations in the laboratory'. *Methods of Organizational Research*, V. Vroom (ed.), Pittsburgh, University of Pittsburgh Press, 1967.

Weissman, H. N., Seldman, M., and Ritter, K. 'Changes in awareness of impact upon others as a function of encounter and marathon group experiences'. *Psychological Reports*, 1971, *28*, 651–661.

White, J. 'The human potential laboratory in the community college'. *Journal of College Student Personnel*, 1974, *15*, 96–100.

White, K. R. 'T-group revisited: self-concept change and the 'fishbowling' technique'. *Small Group Behavior*, 1974, *5*, 473–485.

Wicklund, R. A. 'Objective self-awareness'. *Advances in Experimental Social Psychology*, L. Berkowitz (ed.), *8*, 233–275, New York, Academic Press, 1975.

Winn, A. 'Social change in industry: from insight to implementation'. *Journal of Applied Behavioral Science*, 1966, *2*, 170–184.

Wright, F. 'The effects of style and sex of consultants and sex of members in self-study groups'. *Small Group Behavior*, 1976, *7*, 433–456.

Yalom, I. D. *The Theory and Practice of Group Psychotherapy* (2nd edition). New York, Basic Books, 1975.

Yalom, I. D. 'The impact of a weekend group experience on individual therapy'. *Archives of General Psychiatry*, 1977, *34*, 399–415.

Yalom, I. D. and Lieberman, M. A. 'A study of encounter group casualties'. *Archives of General Psychiatry*, 1971, *25*, 16–30.

Yalom, I. D., Tinklenberg, J., and Gilula, M. 'Curative factors in group therapy'. Unpublished study, 1967, cited by Yalom, 1975.

Young, J. R. 'The effects of laboratory training on self-concept, philosophies of human nature and perceptions of group behavior'. *Dissertation Abstracts International*, 1970, *31B*, 3696–3697.

Zand, D. E., Steele, F., and Zalkind, S. S. 'The impact of an organizational development program on perceptions of interpersonal, group and organization functioning'. *Journal of Applied Behavioral Science*, 1969, *5*, 393–410.

Zarle, T. H. and Willis, S. 'A pregroup training technique for encounter group stress'. *Journal of Counseling Psychology*, 1975, *22*, 49–53.

Zenger, J. H. 'The effect of a team human relations training laboratory on the productivity and perceptions of a selling group'. *Dissertation Abstracts*, 1968, *28A*, 4322.

Zullo, J. R. 'T-group laboratory learning and adolescent ego-development'. *Dissertation Abstracts International*, 1972, *33B*, 2799.

SUBJECT INDEX

Note: figures in italics refer to the tabular matter

leadership, 135
transferable change, 4, 167
see also personal change
transitions, 14
trust, 13, 18, 61–2, 97

universality, 56

VCIA role in group, 61–2
variation of activity, 110–11
Vocational Improvement Program, 154

volunteers *cf* non-volunteers, 32–3, 41, 121

war casualties, 125–6
welfare state, 156
Wilson-Patterson Measure of Conservatism, 41
women's movement, 163–4
work *vs* emotionality, 126–7
Wrightsman Philosophies of Human Nature Scale, 42

INDEX OF AUTHORS